GUEST OF ADOLF

GUEST OF ADOLF

The War of SSG Ernest V. Focht,
805th Tank Destroyer Battalion

MICHAEL H. ZANG

CASEMATE
Pennsylvania & Yorkshire

Published in the United States of America and Great Britain in 2024 by
CASEMATE PUBLISHERS
1950 Lawrence Road, Havertown, PA 19083, USA
and
47 Church Street, Barnsley, S70 2AS, UK

Copyright © 2024 Michael H. Zang

Hardcover Edition: 978-1-63624-455-6
Digital Edition: 978-1-63624-456-3

A CIP record for this book is available from the British Library

All rights reserved. No part of this book may be reproduced or transmitted in any form or by any means, electronic or mechanical including photocopying, recording or by any information storage and retrieval system, without permission from the publisher in writing.

Printed and bound in the United Kingdom by CPI Group (UK) Ltd, Croydon, CR0 4YY
Typeset in India by DiTech Publishing Services

For a complete list of Casemate titles, please contact:

CASEMATE PUBLISHERS (US)
Telephone (610) 853-9131
Fax (610) 853-9146
Email: casemate@casematepublishers.com
www.casematepublishers.com

CASEMATE PUBLISHERS (UK)
Telephone (0)1226 734350
Email: casemate@casemateuk.com
www.casemateuk.com

Front cover: Sergeant Ernest V. Focht's prisoner of war German identification card photograph with his German identification number, 111454. It was taken at Stalag VIIA, Moosburg an der Isar, on April 14, 1943. (Author's collection)

Maps throughout this book were created by Timothy M. Swartz using ArcGIS software by Esri. World Hillshade basemap was supplied by Esri using data courtesy of Esri, Airbus DS, USGS, NGA, NASA, CGIAR, N Robinson, NCEAS, NLS, OS, NMA, Geodatastyrelsen, Rijkswaterstaat, GSA, Geoland, FEMA, Intermap, and the GIS user community. ArcGIS® and ArcMap™ are the intellectual property of Esri and are used herein under license. Copyright © Esri. All rights reserved. For more information, please visit www.esri.com.

Contents

List of Maps	vii
List of Tables	viii
Foreword	ix
Preface	xiii

1	Growing Up	1
2	Military Training	21
3	Anti-Tank Force Development	39
4	North Africa 1942–43 (Operation *Torch*)	49
5	Sicily, Italy, and Moosburg, Germany	69
6	Stalag IIIB Fürstenberg	83
7	Stalag IIIA Luckenwalde	109
8	Liberation: The Way Home	123
9	Reunion and Asheville, North Carolina	135
10	Civilian Life	143

Appendix 1	*105th/805th Tank Destroyer Battalion History*	157
Appendix 2	*Ernest Focht's Lists*	175
Appendix 3	*Ernest Virgil Focht's Chronology*	187
Appendix 4	*Abbreviations and Acronyms*	197
Endnotes		199
Bibliography		205

List of Maps

Map 1	Early Years and Military Training, November 1914 to July 1941	24
Map 2	105th/805th Battalion Training Sites, August 1941 to July 1942	26
Map 3	Movement Overseas, August 1942	33
Map 4	Training in England and Movement to Algeria, August 1942 to January 1943	35
Map 5	805th TD Bn Movement to Tunisia, January to February 1943	55
Map 6	Company A, 805th TD Bn, Movement to the Front, February 1943	59
Map 7	Company A, 805th TD Bn, Area of Operations, February 15–17, 1943	61
Map 8	Prisoner of War Camps—Tunisia, Sicily, and Italy, February 17, 1943 to April 12, 1943	71
Map 9	Prisoner of War Camps—Capua PG 98 and Moosburg an der Isar Stalag VIIA, March 26 to May 4, 1943	76
Map 10	POW Camps in Germany, April 14, 1943 to May 6, 1945	112
Map 11	Stalag IIIA to Le Havre, May 6 to June 2, 1945	128
Map 12	Port of Debarkation to Army Discharge, June 11 to September 11, 1945	134
Map 13	805th TD Battalion in the Italian Campaign, November 1, 1943 to May 27, 1945	166

List of Tables

Table A	Personnel Authorizations by Table of Organization (1940–42)	30
Table B	Equipment Authorizations by Table of Organization (1940–42)	31
Table C	Reorganization of 28th Infantry Division Units Creating the 105th Infantry Battalion (Anti-Tank)	42
Table D	Authorized and Assigned Personnel Strength, 805th Tank Destroyer Battalion, February 1, 1943	58
Table E	Ernie's Clothing and Equipment When Captured on February 17, 1943	64
Table F	Team Roster for Screwballs Baseball Team, June 29, 1943	94
Table G	Clothing and Personal Articles in Ernie's Possession on November 10, 1943	97
Table H	Sergeant Focht's Clothing and Possessions on April 4, 1945	115
Table I	Personnel Authorizations by Table of Organization (1940–44)	173
Table J	Equipment Authorizations by Table of Organization (1940–44)	174

Foreword

February 25, 2003

My mother arrived as usual at the high school upon the conclusion of basketball practice to pick me up. At the time, I had my learner's permit, so she would typically allow me to drive home. However, this day was different. She was quiet, snippy, and for some reason in a hurry. Within 30 seconds of closing the door, she told me—matter of fact, mincing no words—that my grandfather had died. The remaining 15 minutes of the car ride home were spent in absolute silence, amongst tears and sniffles. I had just been with him two days prior in the assisted living facility. Ernest Virgil Focht, my grandfather, and my de facto second father, was no longer living on this earth.

I consider my grandfather to be the nicest, most decent human I have known in my life. This is not hyperbole or biased thinking. This is not meant as a slight to my father. This is not meant to diminish the impact and role of coaches, teachers, mentors, fellow brothers in arms, or members of the clergy. Even though my grandfather died when I was 16 years old, a sophomore in high school, his impact on my life was tremendous.

I grew up no more than 10 minutes from his house in Dillsburg, Pennsylvania. Countless nights were spent at his house. He always ensured candy corn and donut sticks were present in droves. He was the individual who was present when my father was away on military training or during drill weekends. He was the individual who would never miss an extracurricular activity of his grandkids. He was the individual who ensured my safety in my parents' basement during the one instance in which a tornado touched down in the vicinity of my childhood home.

He was the individual who came over at every holiday, and, contrary to what scientists will tell you concerning tryptophan in turkeys, it distinctly acted as a sleeping pill on my grandfather. Like clockwork, every Thanksgiving and Christmas, within two hours of the completion of the meal, my grandfather would be asleep, mouth open and snoring, on the love seat in my parents' family room while my father, brother, and I watched an old Western, war movie, or sporting event.

It was during one of these moments that my eyes were first opened. My father and I were watching the movie *Patton*, the acclaimed 1970 movie featuring George C. Scott as General George S. Patton in World War II. There is a scene in the movie in which American prisoners of war are standing idly within a circular barbed-wire-fence encampment in the middle of the North African desert, while German Field Marshal Erwin Rommel (the famed Desert Fox) is speaking to a member of his staff just prior to boarding a plane. At this exact moment, my grandfather woke up for just a fleeting moment, looked at the television screen, and, as if transported back to 1943, instantly became lucid and said the following words, "I was in one of those." As quickly as he uttered the words, he fell back asleep.

I was probably eleven or twelve when this happened. However, to this day, it is one of those seminal events in a young man's life that is unforgettable. My father, so long as I can remember, has been an avid reader of history. The bookshelves in my parents' house are littered with nonfiction works, many about the American Civil War and World War II. My paternal grandfather served in the 29th Infantry Division in World War II, landing on Omaha Beach on D-Day; surviving the Allied breakout from the beachhead that ultimately resulted in the taking of the city of St. Lo, France; and enduring the brutal cold and German onslaught in the Battle of the Bulge. Given his war experience, Thomas A. Zang was a strong, resolute man of few words. Unfortunately, he died of a brain tumor when I was nine years old.

Contrary to my paternal grandfather's war experience, my maternal grandfather—the voice behind this book—took part in active combat for, by our best research, no more than two to three days. His outfit was encircled and forced to surrender in large numbers during the German Africa Corps' westward attack, commonly referred to as the battle of

FOREWORD • xi

Kasserine Pass, in an attempt to destroy the American army before it capitalized on a link-up with the British Eighth Army under General Bernard Montgomery. The following 27 months were spent in a series of camps throughout North Africa, Sicily, Italy, and Germany. Given my proximity to him geographically, and his openness about his experiences, I always gravitated towards his story.

In May 2009 I was commissioned as an officer in the United States Army. The night prior to beginning my drive across the country for initial training, my father pulled a box out from underneath his bed. This was my first time being shown the contents of this box. In it, among other things, were pictures from World War II, newspaper clippings, Western Union telegrams (it is still virtually beyond comprehension that when my grandfather's name and hometown were read over the BBC announcing that he was missing in action or, later, a prisoner of war, families from sea to shining sea sent telegrams to my great-grandparents sending thoughts and prayers for my grandfather), and my grandfather's multivolume diary. I have always wondered why my father waited until then to show this historical and familial treasure trove to me. I was fascinated beyond belief and remain so to this day. Virtually all of the credit for this project belongs to my father, who spent countless hours transcribing the diaries, researching, collating information, scanning photographs, and talking to relatives.

This foreword is but my humble and, in all probability, insufficient attempt to memorialize my grandfather. He was a man who spent four years away from his home, while his sweetheart, my grandmother, waited patiently. A man who participated in the first American war effort of the European Theater and was abruptly sidelined, living day to day amongst American, Italian, British, and Russian prisoners, relying on his never-ceasing Christian faith to see him through dark times (his favorite biblical passage was Psalm 23).

This is not a book about politics, strategy, or featuring the movements of large and grand armies. It is a look at one man's journey from the hill country of north central Pennsylvania to England, to combat in North Africa, to years behind wire as a German guest.

I will always remember my grandfather's inability to speak ill of anyone. He never spoke ill of his captors, and he praised the Russians xii • GUEST OF ADOLF

for liberating him. I can still picture him on his vibrating recliner, Bible open on the coffee table next to him, *The Lawrence Welk Show* on his rabbit-ear television. Honestly, those were the best days of my life.

There is nothing glamorous or ritzy about this account. It is blunt, honest, and factual. It lacks pomp and circumstance, and that is just in accordance with how the Greatest Generation would have wanted it. When our nation called, they answered; they did not shirk their duty. Their efforts shaped the map and world in which we live today. I consider myself blessed to have been able to spend as much time with my grandfather as I did.

With love, respect, and admiration,
Patrick M. Zang

Preface

The men and women who lived through the Great Depression and World War II later became known as members of "The Greatest Generation." Staff Sergeant Ernest Virgil Focht is one of these men. This is his story; it is not unique but one that is similar to millions of others of this generation. He lived a quiet life growing up in a small town in rural Pennsylvania. His upbringing instilled a vigorous belief in God, a robust love for his country, and a sturdy work ethic. All three of these traits he embodied throughout his lifetime.

He was drafted into the U.S. Army in April 1941 and was discharged in September 1945. During his time in the Army, he spent 35 months overseas with 27 of those months as a German prisoner of war (POW). At the end of his military service, he focused on recapturing his life and moving forward. Ernie married his "Darling Fiancée LaRue," secured employment, raised a family, enjoyed playing with his grandchildren, and traveled. I became a member of his family upon marrying his only daughter, Karen, in 1973. Over the next 30 years, I listened to him speak numerous times of his youth and time as a POW and saw how he lived his strong faith each and every day. I write this saga for his children, grandchildren, great-grandchildren, and future descendants so that they may know what it was like to be a member of "The Greatest Generation." Ernie retained numerous mementos from his youth, his military service, his work, and his post-retirement travels.

I came into possession of this treasure trove of materials in the late 1990s. I spent a few minutes looking through the materials before storing them away for another day. This day arrived in early 2019 when I decided to preserve these items for the family before donating the collection to a museum. This decision led to scanning hundreds of documents, notes, and letters. In late December my youngest son, Patrick, and I photographed my father-in-law's three-volume POW diaries. The transcription of his diaries

xiv • GUEST OF ADOLF

required numerous hours over the next year. Sometimes a magnifying glass was required to read his writing and decipher the numerous abbreviations and misspelled words. While still working on transcribing the diaries I began to develop the story of his military service. As you can imagine, one thing led to another, requiring additional research resulting in a further expansion of the narrative. The end result is this book, which traces his ancestors, his youth, his military service, and his life after World War II.

In writing this book I used Ernie's words to provide the reader with a firsthand account of his thoughts, actions, and feelings. His words are interspersed throughout this biography as quotations without an accompanying citation. When asked what he did during the war, he replied, "I was a guest of Adolf." The sources for his words are either his three-volume POW diary; his letters to his parents and to his fiancée, LaRue Cassidy; and/or the oral history he completed in 1991. He recorded his meals, daily walks around the compound, books read, glee club practices and performances, and trips outside of the prison camps. He documented the names of more than one hundred fellow POWs, the contents of various types of personal and Red Cross parcels received, his hoard of clothing, the members of his gun crew and the baseball team he managed, and many poems and jokes written by his friends. I have included 25 of these entries either in the text or in Appendix 2 to provide the reader additional insights into his life as a POW. Unless otherwise noted, the information and photographs contained herein are from Staff Sergeant Ernest V. Focht's personal papers and mementoes that are in my possession.

I extend my deep gratitude to Timothy Swartz for creating the maps, and to Brigadier General (Retired) Hal Nelson, Lieutenant Colonel (Retired) James Simms, and my youngest son, Major Patrick Zang, for their review of the material and for their recommendations to strengthen the narrative. I would also like to recognize Ms. Lana Conrad, the assistant director of the Tyrone-Snyder Public Library, Tyrone, PA; Dr. Robert S. Cameron, historian, United States Armor School, Fort Moore, GA; Mr. Thomas Buffenbarger, library technician at the United States Army Heritage and Education Center, Carlisle, PA; and Mr. Charlie Oellig at the Pennsylvania National Guard Museum at Fort Indiantown Gap, PA, for their quick and thorough responses to my requests for historical records. Finally, I give a thank-you to my spouse, Karen, Ernest Virgil Focht's daughter, for her proofreading and support throughout this project.

CHAPTER I

Growing Up

On Monday, August 19, 1912, a young couple eloped to Hagerstown, Maryland. The reason for the elopement was that they had been raised in two different religions: Mary Helen was a Roman Catholic, and her groom, Gerald, was a Baptist. In order to be married in Mary Helen's church, Gerald would have had to convert to Roman Catholicism—an action that he was apparently not willing to do. Instead, they chose to be united in holy matrimony by Reverend G. L. Rider, pastor of the First United Brethren Church.[1]

Mary Helen had arrived in the United States some 14 years earlier. Her father, Martin G. Buranovsky, was born in the Czech Republic on July 25, 1863. His wife, Mary S. Wasilko, was also born in the Czech Republic on April 16, 1869. It is not known when they married, but by 1892, when Martin immigrated to the United States to find work, the couple had three daughters. He found his way to Ramey, Clearfield County, Pennsylvania, to live with relatives who were working in the local coal mines. Mary remained behind to care for their daughters while waiting for Martin to send word and money for them to book passage to the United States. In 1898 Mary and her three young daughters, Anna, Sue, and Mary Helen, immigrated to the United States. During the voyage Mary Helen, age seven, became separated from her family. After a frantic, multi-day search of the ship she was reunited with her mother. Eventually the ship landed at Ellis Island in New York Harbor. After being screened for diseases, completing the required paperwork, and being deemed acceptable to the Immigration Service, Mary and the girls were permitted to continue their journey to join Martin in Ramey,

Pennsylvania. Martin and Mary were reunited before the end of the year and continued their lives together, he as a coal miner and she as a homemaker. Their family grew in the next couple of years with the birth of two sons, Martin F. and John W. Martin passed on May 16, 1948, and Mary on August 11, 1951. They are both buried in Sacred Heart Cemetery in Brisbin, Clearfield County, Pennsylvania.[2] It is interesting to note that when she married, Mary Helen changed the spelling of her surname from Buranovsky to Bernosky.[3] This is the spelling she used for the remainder of her life.

The Focht family had come to Pennsylvania several centuries earlier. Ernest Focht's European ancestors resided in what is now the southern German state of Baden-Württemberg. This region borders the German state of Bavaria to its east with France to the west and Switzerland to the south. Throughout the 1600s and into the 1700s, the surname was spelled Vogt. After family members immigrated to the English American colony of Pennsylvania in the mid-1770s, the spelling was transformed to its current form, Focht. This modification in all probability was due to the German pronunciation of the letter v, which makes the sound for the English letter f.

Ernest Focht's earliest known ancestor is his seventh great-grandfather, Hans Dieterich Vogt. He was born in 1613 in the vicinity of Schwarzwald, Gotha, Thüringen, Germany, and died at the age of 56 on September 19, 1669, in Zuzenhausen, Rhein-Neckar-Kreis, Baden-Württemberg, Germany.[4] The family were still living in and around Zuzenhausen in the 18th century, when Ernie's third great-grandfather, Johann Georg Vogt (John George Focht), born in 1855, left for the New World. Exactly how and when the family immigrated to the British American colonies is uncertain, as two credible accounts exist. In one version Johann Georg was taken in 1761 as a six-year-old child by his father, Johann Petrus Vogt (born 1710), and his mother, Maria. In the second version, as related by his grandson David Henlein Focht, John George and his sister, Eve, traveled to Rotterdam, Netherlands, where they found passage on a ship to America in 1773. Upon arrival he was sold into servitude for four years to reimburse his patron since he could not produce a receipt for his passage. After serving his time and paying off his debt he lived near his married sister, Mrs. Horn, and his sister Eve.[5]

In 1778, at the age of 23, John George Focht was drafted into the Northampton County, Pennsylvania, militia for three two-month periods of service. At the conclusion of his time with Captain John Graves, he enlisted in the Continental Army for two years under Captain Abraham Wooding and Colonel Lettis Hooper Jr. serving in upstate New York as a teamster. He concluded his military service after again being drafted into the Northampton County militia for a fourth two-month period. This time he was stationed on the frontier near Wilkes-Barre, Pennsylvania, protecting the frontier from Native American incursions with Captain John Moritz.[6] In 1780 he married Barbara Beaver Planck and settled on land near Cedar Creek in Lehigh County for the next 16 to 18 years before moving to the Tamaqua area. The pair's oldest child, George John Focht, was born on January 30, 1783, in what is now Northampton County, Pennsylvania, while the family lived near Cedar Creek. At the time of his death on January 24, 1831, John George Focht was living with his son Adam in the Catawissa Valley in Union Township, Schuylkill County, Pennsylvania. He is buried in Saint Paul's Union Church Cemetery in Ringtown, Pennsylvania. Barbara Beaver Planck Focht survived her husband until 1834.[7]

In 1805 at the age of 22, George John Focht left the Tamaqua area and moved further west within the Commonwealth of Pennsylvania. He settled in the vicinity of Clover Creek in Huntington County (now Blair County), approximately eight miles south of Williamsburg, Pennsylvania. At the age of 24 he married Margaret Henlein on August 9, 1807. Within a year the first of their 10 children, Elizabeth, was born on May 25, 1808. Two years later their first son, Adam, Ernie's great-grandfather, was born on April 26, 1810, on the family farm in Clover Creek. There is some indication that George John Focht served in the United States Army as a private in the 1st Regiment (Weirick's) of the Pennsylvania Militia during the War of 1812 after the birth of his second daughter, Catherine, in June 1812. After George John completed his service, he and Margaret settled into life on the farm. Their family continued to grow with the birth of seven more children for a total of 10, six daughters and four sons. Surprisingly, nine of the 10 children lived to adulthood, with only their daughter Margaret living less than a year.[8]

4 • GUEST OF ADOLF

Adam was raised at his father's farm in Clover Creek, well educated in subscription schools and served as a teacher for many years. He learned cooperage and blacksmithing, two trades at which he occasionally worked. In 1840 he married Charlotte Dull (1819–91). Two years later the couple welcomed their first daughter, Catharine (1842–80). In the next seven years three more children were born: Margaret (1843–1913), Mary E. (1846–84), and Martin Luther (1849–1925). Between 1850 and 1852 Adam moved his family from Clover Creek approximately 14 miles east to the Shaffersville, Morris Township, Huntingdon County, Pennsylvania, area. The family continued to grow with the addition of three more children: Samuel D. (1853–1925), George M. (1856–1935), and Emma (1859–81). The family of nine lived and thrived on Adam's farm.[9]

Martin Luther Focht, Ernie's grandfather, was born on October 12, 1849, at the family farm in Clover Creek, Pennsylvania. On December 28, 1876, he was united in matrimony with Miss Henrietta Duffy (1856–1911) by the Reverend D. H. King, pastor of the Grace Baptist Church in Hollidaysburg, Pennsylvania. Henrietta was born on February 6, 1857, at Reservoir, Blair County, Pennsylvania. Together they had eight children, three of whom died as infants. The five children who survived to adulthood were John Harvey (1880–1959), Jesse (1883–1965), Eldora (1886–1964), Gerald Roy (1888–1976), and Lena Estelle (1890–1955). Martin raised his family on a farm for 25 years until 1901, when he and Henrietta moved to Tyrone, Pennsylvania. He resided in town working as a laborer until his death in 1925. Martin and Henrietta are buried together in Shaffersville Cemetery in Huntingdon County.[10]

Gerald Roy began to work for the Pennsylvania Railroad (PRR) in 1907 at the age of 19. His first job was as a fireman. He was the train crewman who shoveled coal into the furnace and tended the boiler on a steam locomotive. In some ways Gerald's role was more important than the engineer's, as it was he who ensured both that the train had the power necessary to negotiate hills and turns and that it didn't explode.

It was while he was working for the PRR out of Tyrone that he met Mary Helen Buranovsky. She was living and working at the Ward House on Pennsylvania Avenue directly across from the train station. The Ward House was the premier boarding hotel in Tyrone for many years. Mary Helen was living with Mr. and Mrs. C. M. Waple, either taking care of their youngest child, Katherine, or working as a servant for five years between 1907 and 1912.

After Gerald and Mary Helen's wedding, the pair left on an extensive tour through several eastern cities including Atlantic City; Washington, DC; Philadelphia; and New York.[11] They would then reside in a rented house at 1475 North Avenue, Tyrone, Pennsylvania, until 1931, when they rented another house at 607 West Fifteenth Street.

★★★

The Borough of Tyrone is nestled in the rolling hills of the Eastern Allegheny Mountains in Blair County, Pennsylvania, approximately 20 miles northeast of Altoona. It is situated at the junction of the Little Juniata River and Bald Eagle Creek and the junction of the old Bald Eagle and the Kittanning Paths. Initially, the Juniata Valley Native Americans extensively used these two paths as they traveled between their villages and those of their enemies. As the early white settlers moved into the region their presence in traditional hunting areas created conflict between the two groups. Naturally, this led to violence and the killing of men and women of both races. In 1768, a treaty was signed between the Native Americans and the Pennsylvania colony authorities in which the former agreed to move further west, abandoning their lands. This led to a few years of peace and tranquility for the settlers. However, during the American Revolution the English disturbed this state by encouraging the Native Americans to fight the settlers on the frontier, promising them a return of their traditional lands. These actions led to a general distrust of Native Americans and anyone who sided with the English during the war. Consequently, when independence came the Native Americans moved further west, ending any threat of violence between the two groups.

The result was an increase in the number of settlers coming to the area. The settlement was first called Eagleville, since the Little Bald Eagle Creek flowed through it; later it was called Shorbsville because the land originally belonged to Lyon, Shorb and Company. Then, in 1852, the community was called Tyrone City for County Tyrone in Ireland. This was shortened to "Tyrone" in 1857 when the settlement was incorporated as a borough. Its first public building was erected around the same time it was incorporated as a borough. The borough increased in size in 1893 by adding East Tyrone, and between 1910 and 1915 the Hillcrest section of Snyder Township was incorporated into the borough. This practice of incorporating sections of Snyder Township continued until 1959.

The town's fresh water supply came from two reservoirs, which provided clear mountain spring water using a series of wooden pipes. Indoor plumbing started to appear in 1900. Soon afterward the borough installed lines to dump the sewage into Bald Eagle Creek and the Juniata River. This practice continued until after World War II, when a sewage plant was constructed. Public transportation appeared in 1901 with the formation of the Tyrone Street Railway Company. It continued to operate until 1938, running a trolley through the streets of the town.

The population of Tyrone in 1860 was nearly 700. By 1880 it grew to 2,678, and in 1900 it more than doubled to slightly more than 5,800. The 1920 United States Census records a population of 9,084, which turned out to be the largest for the borough. One of the driving forces for this increased settlement was the abundant natural resources found in the region. Iron ore was plentiful, as were timber, limestone, and streams. These four resources combined made this the perfect place to develop an iron forge. Between 1797 and 1849 multiple forges and iron furnaces and a rolling mill were established around and in present-day Tyrone. These were in settlements named Ironville, Birmingham, Bald Eagle, and Warriors Mark, all of which exist today. None of this industry could exist without a market for its products and an excellent transportation network. The settlers were constructing wagon roads over the mountains between what is now Hollidaysburg and Pittsburgh. By 1819 a good road existed between Tyrone, Hollidaysburg, and Pittsburgh, which facilitated the shipping of iron products. In 1832 the Pennsylvania Canal opened, and two years later it was connected to the Portage Railroad. This connection created a direct route between Philadelphia and Pittsburgh.

While the cross-state canal was being constructed the steam locomotive began operations in eastern Pennsylvania. It was a few years before it was accepted as a means of transportation. In 1846 the Pennsylvania Railroad Company (PRR) received a charter to connect Harrisburg with Pittsburgh. The route selected followed the Juniata River and the existing Pennsylvania Canal westward to Petersburg. Here the line followed the Little Juniata River through Spruce Creek, Birmingham, Altoona, and Duncansville. The primary reason for the selection of this route was that these rivers already cut gaps through the mountains. However, due to the winding nature of the rivers, the PRR constructed more than 20 bridges between Petersburg and Tyrone.

Simultaneously with the construction of the railroad westward there was work on the line eastward from Pittsburgh to Johnstown. The Portage Railroad acted as the connector of these two lines for completing a cross-state railroad route. The line was completed to Duncansville in 1850 and to Pittsburgh in 1854. Several regional railroads were built to connect with Tyrone. These included the Bald Eagle Valley, Tyrone and Clearfield, Tyrone and Lock Haven, and Lewisburg and Tyrone railroads. These were leased to the PRR and provided a vital link for providing a market for the region's natural resources of timber, coal, and iron and the products manufactured in Tyrone.

In addition to the jobs associated with operating scores of trains daily, the PRR created rail yards and train shops to support its operations. The PRR also contributed to the social life of the town. In the early 1900s an athletic park was built with a well-maintained baseball field, a running track, a swimming pool, and a grandstand. Later the local Young Men's Christian Association (YMCA) drew much of its financial support from the PRR. However, by 1940 the number of daily trains passing through Tyrone was reduced by nearly 50 percent. Also, the PRR withdrew its support of the athletic park and YMCA.

The Tyrone Paper Mill was a large employer for the residents of this area. The enterprise began in 1878 by Morrison, Bare, and Cass and continued to operate under their supervision until 1899. In this year it consolidated with the West Virginia Pulp and Paper Company while continuing to operate as Morrison and Case Paper until 1910. The mill continued to grow, with the addition of the Bald Eagle Water Company, a bleach-making facility, and a carbon plant. The plant prospered until 1970, when the pulp mill ceased operations due to being noncompetitive with modern manufacturing processes.[12] Reliance Manufacturing Company of Michigan City, Indiana, opened their Tyrone factory in 1933. It produced

8 • GUEST OF ADOLF

the work shirt, "The Big Yank," considered the standard across the world. During World War II, the Keystone Plant in Tyrone produced many of the pants and shirts worn by navy personnel. The plant was an integral part of the Tyrone business community for many years. Unfortunately, in 1992 the company ceased their Tyrone operations.

There were numerous other businesses operating in Tyrone providing economic stability to the region in the 20th century, including the Wilson Chemical Company, Gardner's Candies, Chicago Rivet and Machine Company, Pittsburgh Plate Glass Industries, and Beyer and Company planing mill. Numerous small businesses also provided employment opportunities, including Acklin Jewelry Company; J. W. Fisher hardware; Bayer-Gillan & Company wholesale grocers; John Kienzle Bakery; and Templeton Company, a department store.

The residents of Tyrone did not have an all-work-and-no-play outlook on life. A few years prior to the community's incorporation as a borough the first volunteer fire company was established. Of course, its main purpose was to extinguish fires, but the accompanying camaraderie led to various social activities among its members. As the town grew in geographical size, population, and the number of buildings and homes, an increased need arose for additional fire companies. The third and final fire company incorporated itself in 1898.

While the fire companies were organizing, an increased interest in forming social groups developed among the men of the town. Beginning in 1871 the notion of belonging to a benevolent and fraternal organization spread throughout the community. In the next 20 years no fewer than a dozen groups were founded. These included The Free and Accepted Masons, Independent Order of Odd Fellows, Knights of Pythias, Benevolent Protective Order of Elks, Loyal Order of Moose, Knights of the Golden Eagle, and the Knights of Columbus. The common theme among the groups was their desire to develop friendships and participate in a variety of social events. Additionally, the groups all supported efforts to provide for distressed individuals in the community and provide relief to widows and orphans. Initially there were no social organizations for women to join. The first women's group, the Daughters of Rebekah, began in the late 1890s as an adjutant to the Odd Fellows. The Order of the Eastern Star established a chapter in 1919, and the Catholic Daughters

GROWING UP • 9

of America in 1920 provided the women a choice of three groups to join. These groups' focus was on the study of scripture and developing moral and intellectual improvement among their members. Over time they also adopted a variety of ways to support people in need similar to the men's organizations.

The youth were not forgotten as the men's and women's groups were formed in the 50-year period from 1870 to 1920. A group of leading citizens gathered at the Methodist church in 1870 to discuss creating a recreation center for the youth. The result was the creation of the Tyrone YMCA, which the townspeople and the PRR supported. Originally the group focused on prayer meetings, mission work, and visitations. The participation level in their activities increased so steadily that by 1900 a need existed for a larger building. The PRR was approached for a suitable lot on which to build this larger facility. The new building included dormitories, reading rooms, game rooms, a gymnasium, an auditorium, and a swimming pool. The YMCA expanded its reach into supporting organized athletics and a glee club for the youth. It also conducted classes in English for recent immigrants. In 1910, the PRR donated a parcel of 12 acres in East Tyrone on which the railroad constructed an athletic park. The resulting park was first class with a nine-hole golf course, a swimming pool, a baseball field with grandstands, clay tennis courts, and a running track. Naturally, this area was the epicenter for organized athletics. Unfortunately, beginning in 1920 the railroad closed its freight yards and repair shops and removed all its financial support for the town's recreational facilities. The town attempted to maintain the athletic park and was successful until the end of World War II. Today, there is hardly any evidence that this beautifully maintained recreational facility ever existed. Besides the variety of experiences and activities available through the YMCA, participation in the local Boy and Girl Scout troops provided additional youth activities.

The arts provided another outlet for the social life of Tyrone. There were a number of theaters and the Tyrone Opera House, which hosted locally produced theatrical plays and musical programs as well as nationally recognized performers. Besides these theatrical productions, local musicians performed in concerts along with the Tyrone High School band. There was a town-sponsored drum and bugle corps, the Boy Scout drum corps, and the Tyrone Sheridan band for individuals

10 • GUEST OF ADOLF

to display their musical talents. The most famous musician from Tyrone was Fred Waring. While a student at The Pennsylvania State University, he formed a quartet that played for local parties. The popularity of the group rose, and by the late 1920s they were performing across Europe and the United States. The popularity of his music continued into the 1950s.

Tyrone offered a diversified set of opportunities to its residents. Even though it was built on the success of the PRR and the paper mill, there were other employment options through the years. The social and fraternal organizations for adult men and women provided occasions to become engaged in supporting the community. A robust school system was created, supported, and expanded to ensure all children received an education. Scouting and the YMCA filled the social void for the youth with their myriad offerings. There was also a strong and fervent Christian faith shared by all members of Tyrone. This is the Tyrone in which Gerald, Ernie's father, was raised. It is also the Tyrone where Gerald and Mary Helen settled to raise their family in 1912.

★★★

Into their rented house at 1475 North Avenue, Tyrone, Mary Helen and Gerald would welcome each of their seven children—four boys and three girls. When their youngest was 14, on December 23, 1942, Gerald and Mary Helen finally bought their first house at 631 West Fifteenth Street. They lived in this house for the remainder of their lives.

Shortly after their marriage Gerald and Mary Helen officially joined the First United Brethren Church in Tyrone. The church was located at the northwest corner of Adams Avenue and Eighteenth Street only a short six- to eight-block walk from all three of their houses. The family attended church every Sunday morning and Wednesday evening. The children grew up in the United Brethren religious tradition. Gerald and Mary Helen's very devout Christian beliefs naturally transferred to all the children, who likewise developed a strong Christian faith. Gerald and Mary Helen raised their children in a very strict but loving environment. They were not permitted to attend movies or dances as these activities were considered gateways for developing an immoral and unchristian lifestyle. They also learned to obey their parents and elders without fail. As a consequence of this combination of home life and religious upbringing Ernie developed a strong belief in God and an unwavering moral compass. He abided by the lessons learned as a boy throughout his life.

Ernie's elder brother Mel was born January 1913, graduating from Tyrone High School in 1930. He was musical, playing the piano, flute, and violin in school and later in life. In 1936 he married Helen Goss, and they had four children. Mel received a dependents exemption from military service since he was married and had two children under the age of three. He worked as a driver and agent for the Railway Express Agency for 39 years before retiring in 1975.

Twenty-two months after Mel was born, Gerald and Mary Helen welcomed their second son, Ernest Virgil Focht, into their household on November 1, 1914. Their third child and first daughter, Madeline, followed along 13 months later in January 1916. She graduated from Tyrone High School in 1935. She married Scott Nearhoof in 1940 and had two children. Madeline was a self-employed piano teacher working from her home and local music stores in the towns where she and her husband resided.

Gerald and Mary Helen's second daughter, Josephine, lived only 22 months, dying from whooping cough and pneumonia in 1922.

Dean was the third son, born in 1920. In high school he was a member of the cheerleader squad, the glee club, and the baseball team, graduating in 1939. In 1941 he married Jean Nearhoof, and together they had three children. Dean enlisted in the United States Marine Corps in October 1943, serving until May 1946. He did not deploy to an overseas assignment but remained in the United States, being promoted to the rank of sergeant and serving as a drill instructor. After graduation he began working for the West Virginia Pulp and Paper Company in Tyrone, where he continued working until 1971 when the company drastically downsized operations. Afterwards he worked for another 12 years for Pittsburgh Plate Glass at their Tipton plant.

The youngest daughter, Vera, was born in 1926, graduating from Tyrone High School in 1944. For three years, 1945 to 1948, she attended Practical Bible Training School. Afterwards she served at a number of churches around Tyrone and in New York and New Jersey as a youth worker, pianist, organist, and secretary for the remainder of her life.

In addition she found employment as a bookkeeper in these locations. Vera returned to Tyrone in 1963 to care for her mother, who had fallen and fractured her pelvis. After returning to Tyrone she worked at the West Virginia Pulp and Paper Company for 24 years. Wayne, the youngest of the family, was born in 1928. He graduated high school in 1946 and then attended Northeastern Bible College, completing his work in 1953. He married Marilyn Fidje in 1955, and the pair had four children. Wayne was a minister who established two new churches, one in West Milford, New Jersey, in 1957 and one in Philipsburg, Pennsylvania, in 1974. For nearly 40 years, Wayne broadcast a faith-based inspirational program on a local Philipsburg radio station.

The children had a variety of chores to complete throughout the week besides washing and putting away the dishes after meals. The kitchen had a coal stove on which Mary Helen cooked the meals and baked bread and pies. In the morning one of the children was responsible for bringing in the kindling wood to start the fire in the stove and then feeding it with soft coal. In addition to making the stove ready for cooking this also heated up the kitchen and other parts of the house. The furnace required daily attention of adding coal and removing the ashes so they did not build up in it. Other chores included washing the cellar steps and the steps to the upper floor of the house, scrubbing the bathrooms, doing the laundry, and washing the dishes. These were just some of the chores Ernie and his siblings performed inside the house. Of course, they had the normal outside chores of maintaining the lawn, shrubbery, and garden and clearing the sidewalks of snow during the winter months. The children learned to do their chores as quietly as possible since railroad work made Gerald's schedule unpredictable. "When he was on freight," Ernie recalled, "you never knew when he was coming or going. We always had to be quiet, particularly if he'd come home in the morning or afternoons, he could get a proper rest." Unlike today where most children have their own bedrooms, the four boys slept in one room with two double beds and the two girls in another room. One could say that Gerald and Mary Helen ran a tight household, but Ernie always spoke of what loving parents they were to all the children.

In the fall of 1921 Ernie started school at the Adams Avenue School located on the northeast corner of Adams Avenue and Eighteenth Street adjacent to the First United Brethren Church. There were no school buses for the Focht children to ride, so they walked to and from school daily. While in Miss Helen Jones's second grade classroom Ernie was recognized in the *Tyrone Daily Herald* for perfect attendance during the months of November 1922 and February 1923. He continued in this school building until completing sixth grade in 1927. Ernie recalls a sad incident from his youth occurring in 1925 or 1926 when a cousin who lived in Idaho came to Tyrone to live and work. This cousin secured a job working for the Penn Central Light and Power Company. One day "they were clearing brush, and he got a thorn in his hand. And he got what they call tetanus—lockjaw I think it's called. It went in and healed on the outside, but not on the inside, it went up through his arm and went down and up the organs, and the stomach, and as a result it killed him."

The family was fortunate to own a piano, which enabled Ernie's two sisters, Madeline and Vera, and Mel to learn to play the piano. Their playing and singing naturally gave Ernie an appreciation for music. At the age of 12 in 1926, he joined the church's junior choir after he "went to the altar and accepted Christ as [his] savior." His participation in the choir further advanced his enjoyment of singing songs of all types. The choir would perform for their Sunday worship services and also travel to other churches in the surrounding area. At this same time Ernie began to participate in a youth program called the Junior Society of Christian Endeavor. The group met on Sunday evening, and a member was responsible for organizing the activities for the meeting under the supervision of an adult. A typical session consisted of music, scripture readings, discussion about the meaning of the readings, and recitation of Bible verses. The members also reported on the chapter of the Bible read during the week. Ernie's participation in this group led to his graduating to the men's brotherhood by the time he was in high school. Ernie's love of singing led him to join the Otterbein Glee Club of his church, the First United Brethren. This club would perform a program of religious and semi-classical music at churches in the Tyrone region. In August 1934 they performed at Lakemont Church of God in Altoona, Pennsylvania, and in December 1939 there was a performance at Otterbein United Brethren Church, also in Altoona.

In August 1928 the economy of the United States began to slow, and unemployment started to increase, leading to the stock market

14 • GUEST OF ADOLF

crash of 1929. This ushered in a period that became known as the Great Depression. The economic downturn continued until June 1938, although unemployment remained over 10 percent until 1941. The effects on Gerald and Mary Helen's family were minimal since Gerald remained employed as a fireman by the PRR throughout this time. In fact, to lessen the impact on his fellow railroad workers threatened with the possibility of being laid off, Gerald and others with more seniority would take one or two days off a week. This enabled the more junior employees to stay employed for at least two days a week.

Growing up during the Depression era, Ernie never complained about not having enough food to eat or clothes to wear. His mother, Mary Helen, was an excellent cook. She baked her own bread and made pies for the family. The family grew a variety of vegetables in their garden and canned much of their harvest. The children would also go to local areas where huckleberries, strawberries, and raspberries grew wild to pick buckets full, and these were canned as well. When Gerald was away for work with the PRR, Mary Helen assumed full control of the household. Ernie often referred to her as the assistant boss when speaking of the times his father was out of town. His parents always ensured that the children received small gifts at Christmas. Mary Helen would begin her shopping the week before Christmas to find small items for each of her six children. Ernie recalls receiving a pocketknife as a present one year. He was extremely thrilled with the gift as it was something he very much wanted, and he carried it with him for the remainder of his life. Typically, the gifts were clothes, stockings, knickers, or shoes.

The family always had a tree at Christmas, although in those days there were no strings of electric lights. The tree would go up on Christmas Eve, and Santa would decorate it during his nighttime visit. Ernie's parents never used candles to illuminate the tree, but his Buranovsky grandparents in Ramey would illuminate their tree with them. "They had a clip, set the candle into it and put it on the tree," he recalled. "But you had to put it on so that it wouldn't catch the tree on fire. They always had candles on their trees at Christmastime, and it was always a joy." Ernie remembers traveling to these grandparents for Christmas. Since Gerald and Mary Helen did not own an automobile, the family would take the train from Tyrone. However, it was necessary to change trains twice—once at Osceola and then at Houtzdale—to arrive at Ramey. They would leave in the morning and arrive in the late afternoon in time for dinner. One of the highlights of his grandmother's Christmas dinner in Ernie's estimation was "what they called bundricke pies, much like our pizzas today. It was made of bread dough with mashed potatoes kneaded in the middle of it and rolled out in a nice roll like the pizzas are today, and baked in the oven, and they take it out and butter it and put salt and pepper on it. But they were good." Naturally he enjoyed his mother's Christmas dinner, which usually consisted of either roast chicken or turkey, mashed potatoes, corn and other vegetables, and for dessert a nice piece of hot mincemeat pie.

Gerald eventually rose through the ranks, becoming a train engineer, while Mary Helen maintained the household. Gerald mainly worked on what was referred to as the Main Line of the PRR between Altoona and Harrisburg as the engineer on passenger trains. The daily nonstop passenger train run was only two hours and 20 minutes without stops one-way. However, once in Harrisburg he would have a two- to three-hour layover waiting for the westbound train. So, in an eight-plus hour day it was only possible to make one round trip. As he moved up in seniority Gerald began to pass on weekend jobs so he could be home with his family and attend church on Sundays.

A benefit of Gerald working for the PRR was that the family was permitted to travel on the railroad for free. The family took full advantage of this benefit to travel throughout the United States. As a family they traveled to Portland, Oregon, in 1921. On two other occasions the family went to Gooding, Idaho, to visit relatives who previously lived in Tyrone. In 1931 Ernie and his brother Mel secured rail passes to ride the rails to Gooding, Idaho, for six weeks. They traveled in a passenger car, taking three days and nights to reach their destination. During this time, they worked on their relatives' cattle and dairy ranch having a marvelous time. One very hot day Ernie was assisting his cousin caponizing the roosters. "It was a very tedious job to do," he recalled, "and they were fainting on us, but we didn't realize that, so as they'd faint, we'd knock their heads off." After doing this to a half-dozen, they realized the roosters were fainting and not dying. The end result was that they ate a lot of chicken that night for supper. On another occasion Ernie was assisting with the harvesting of alfalfa. After unloading the wagon, he jumped up in the driver's seat and grabbed the horses' reins. To Ernie's surprise, the horses immediately began to pull the wagon. He initially struggled to control the horses but finally got them to walk in a circle. The horses had minds of their own, however, and seeing the corral open, they headed for it. At this point Ernie tried to get the horses and the wagon to stop, but he was successful only with the latter; the horses kept going. Consequently, he destroyed a nice pair of harnesses. His cousin merely stood by laughing throughout the entire incident. In addition to bringing in the alfalfa, he and his brother worked the hay fields, loading the bales onto a flat wagon. During this experience they discovered many snakes underneath the bales. He developed a proficiency in milking cows and many other farm-related tasks while visiting his Idaho relatives. Ernie often traveled the rails with a group of fellows while in high school. Every member of the group received a free pass since their fathers worked for the railroad. He also traveled to Portland, Oregon; St. Louis, Missouri; Norfolk, Virginia; Buffalo, New York; and Philadelphia, Pennsylvania.[13] Gerald concluded his 51-year career with the Pennsylvania Railroad as an engineer making his last trip between Altoona and Harrisburg, Pennsylvania on May 28, 1958. His youngest son, Wayne, had the privilege of riding in the diesel engine with his father on this last run.

In the fall of 1927, Ernie began attending Tyrone High School, located on Lincoln Avenue, starting as a seventh-grade student. His parents' home was seven blocks from the school, so he walked there every day. When he matriculated to ninth grade, he selected the commercial course of study. The school did not have a cafeteria, so the students went home for lunch. When Ernie spoke about this time he explained, "I had approximately, roughly, close to a mile to walk to school each time, so, with an hour off for lunch you didn't dare fool around too much." Those students who lived farther away would either drive home or bring their lunch with them. Occasionally, Ernie and some of his friends got to goofing around on these walks home for lunch. This was especially true when there was snow on the ground and they would "throw snowballs and things like that"—never trying to hurt anybody, "just fun." Of course, this reduced the amount of time for eating their lunches before it was time to head back to the high school. In Ernie's case this presented a slight problem since before returning to school for the afternoon he needed to make sure the dishes were washed and put away.

So, daily Ernie made two round trips to and from school. This he did regardless of the weather, and in the wintertime he often had what he referred to as the walker's hack. Regarding his time in school, he indicated that there wasn't anything that he didn't like. He enjoyed the whole experience and tried to get as much out of the courses as he could. Among his extracurricular activities were Biology and Science Clubs, track, and the Hi-Y Club. This last club was affiliated with the Tyrone Young Men's Christian Association, and its purpose was "to create, maintain and extend high standards of Christian character" in its members. As part of the club's activities Ernie attended the weekly Bible study sessions. In the 1933 issue of the Tyrone High School yearbook, *The Falcon*, Ernie is described as follows: "Earnest as Ernest his name. He is a serious and sincere student." He did try out for the football team once, but he stopped going to practices before the season started. The lateness of coming home, eating by himself, and keeping up with his chores and schoolwork were all too much for Ernie. Playing sports with his many friends, including Bill Engelman and Ken Eschbach, was an integral part of his youth. He enjoyed all sports: football, basketball, baseball, swimming in the local swimming hole, riding horses, sledding, and tobogganing in winter.

In the wintertime a group would frequently get together to go sledding after school or on weekends on Hag's Hill, which had a stream at the bottom of it. After finishing up one round of sledding and before downing their evening meal, Ernie and company would "go home and get tubs and things" to do what they called "icing the hill." They'd "get the water and pour it on the snow" to make an iced path for faster sledding. After supper they headed back to the hill for hours of bobsledding under the light of the moon. The next day the snow was still covered with ice, and their rides down the hill were very fast. They would post a guard at the road crossing to watch out for on-coming cars and to stop them to permit the sleds to pass by without collision. There was an occasion where one of the toboggans was hit by a car and some of the riders were injured. They also went ice-skating on a nearby lake when conditions were not suitable for sledding. Before the YMCA opened their pool, Ernie would often go to a nearby stream to swim. The stream was not far from his parents' house, and the local reservoir emptied into it. Ernie and his pals put in some labor to make an area deep and large enough to swim in. "A gang of us would get together, get all the burlap sacks, and go up and fill the sacks with dirt, put it on the breast" of the reservoir, he recalled. "We had a nice swimming hole there."

The United States was in the midst of the Great Depression in 1933 when Ernie's class of 115 graduated from high school. The Reverend Dr. Joseph A. Speer at United Brethren Church gave his baccalaureate sermon on Sunday afternoon, May 28, 1933. This was followed the next day by the senior banquet at the Water Street Inn. Ernie's graduation ceremony was on Friday, June 2, 1933, at the Tyrone YMCA auditorium.[14] As a high school graduate, Ernie was expected to go to work. "It was the tail-end of the Depression, you might say, and work was scarce, and you were lucky if you could get a job. So I started working at service stations pumping gas" for 17 cents a gallon. He left this job after a few months for a better paying job at Fine Foods, a coffee concern in Tyrone where different brands of coffee (Samoan, Bogota) were produced. He was a packer of roasted coffee in one-pound bags and was "able to pack approximately a thousand pounds an hour." Occasionally, he would drive a truck to Baltimore, Maryland, to pick up green coffee in the Beltsworth warehouse that was on the waterfront. He worked in the coffee packinghouse until 1936, when he took a more regular hourly job with the West Virginia Pulp and Paper Company.

The types of jobs he performed in the paper mill were very different from any he had performed for his previous employers. Ernie did not have a permanent assignment, so his daily tasks were in whatever area a person was needed for the day. One of the assignments he often described was his working in the area he called "wood ranks." This was where the logs that were harvested from the forests surrounding the Tyrone region were delivered to the paper mill. They arrived either by railcars or tractor trailers coming from upwards of 60 miles away. He assisted in the classification of the logs into the different types of soft- and hardwoods as the various types of wood were used to produce different kinds of paper. The logs were sorted, cut into lengths between 10 and 12 feet, and stored in 15-foot-high groups. On other occasions in the "wood ranks," he loaded small railcars that moved the logs to the chipper area, where they were fed into the big chippers with blades "eight, ten foot in diameter" to be cut into small pieces. He also described how he often worked in this area picking up wood scraps that were discarded during this process or anything that cluttered the area. The majority of the wood scraps consisted of the bark from the logs. "They used a lot of these chips and stuff for some reason, and they would glue them together and put it out in four-by-eight sheets. It would be smooth on one side and maybe just sort of rough on the other side and be good enough for walls." One of the ingredients used in making paper is starch. Ernie would sometimes be assigned the task of delivering the large bags of starch from the warehouse to the production line or asked to act as a guard when the mill was not operating. In this last role, he walked around the mill every hour with a time clock checking specific areas where he was to make note of the time and situation. Regardless of the type of assignments he performed while working at the paper mill, he considered himself fortunate to have a job even if it only paid 49 cents an hour.

When Ernie met Elizabeth LaRue Cassidy, she was still attending Tyrone High School as either a sophomore or a junior. LaRue's parents were Clayton Samuel Cassidy (1896–1978) and Rhoda Rebecca James (1898–2000). Clayton was born to William Jacob Cassidy (1867–1933) and Mary Emma "Emaline" Gates (1868–1919) in 1896 in Birmingham, Blair County, Pennsylvania, a small community on the outskirts of Tyrone. By the age of four his parents had moved into the town of Tyrone. Rhoda was born on July 1, 1898, in Cold Stream, Centre County, Pennsylvania. She was the fourth of nine children of Thomas and Elizabeth Harwood James. Clayton and Rhoda married in 1918 and resided in Tyrone. Less than two years later, in February 1920, their daughter Elizabeth LaRue Cassidy was born. Their house was at 415 Park Avenue in Tyrone, approximately one and one-half miles from the Focht residence on West Fifteenth Street. LaRue attended Tyrone's third elementary school, the Washington School. This school was located within five blocks of the Cassidy residence. While in seventh grade in 1933, LaRue was a member of the performing cast of the Minuet in G at the Washington School in Tyrone. While attending high school, LaRue was in the academic course of instruction and was active in many organizations. She participated in Glee Club, Operetta, French Club, and the Tri-Hi-Y. Her 1938 Tyrone High School yearbook portrayed her as invariably cheerful: "Laughing, talking, never blue, can anything annoy LaRue?" Upon graduation in 1938, she enrolled in the Zeth Business School of Altoona, completing this course in 1940.

Ernie and LaRue met casually in 1936. He had seen her multiple times before he approached her and introduced himself as she and a group of friends were walking home from town. Ernie asked if he could walk her home that evening, which he did before going home himself. Their initial dates consisted of Ernie attending their Methodist worship services with LaRue and her parents. He also attended the Epworth League, a Methodist young adult association, with her after worship concluded. These activities constituted their initial dating ritual on Sundays. Eventually, Ernie was permitted to take LaRue for a walk with her dog; then they were allowed to go out together with a group of friends. In the winter they would go sledding in the afternoon before changing and going back to LaRue's church. These initial Sunday evening dates included going out for a couple hours together afterwards.

Some of their other dating activities included going for a walk in the woods, visiting friends, taking a ride in Ernie's 1923 Studebaker, playing tennis, singing while someone played the piano, and horseback riding. Another favorite date was going to a local restaurant with a group of friends for a hamburger and a drink for 40 cents. They saw a lot of each other during the week with dates on Wednesday, Friday, and Saturday nights. Ernie and LaRue particularly enjoyed the company of Gilbert Summers and Gertrude "Gertie," who later married. They would often be in either LaRue's or Gertie's home for the evening singing. One evening someone said, "Well, let's make a freezer of ice cream." Ernie remembered tucking into some of the homemade confection. "I said to them, 'Boy, it tastes like, this tastes like Epsom salts in this stuff.' And sure enough there was Epson salts in it. Those girls had doctored our ice cream up."

Ernie, his father, and brother Dean attended a banquet recognizing the Otterbein Glee Club of which LaRue was a member in 1940.

CHAPTER 2

Military Training

In December 1940, the Altoona Draft Board sent Ernie his draft notice. He received this notice since a number of men in the first call-up had not passed the physical examination and so were excused from military service. This notice did not require him to report immediately; he was to wait for further instructions.

In the 1930s the Army acknowledged that its small active-duty force was incapable of providing the basic protection for the United States in any future conflict. Consequently, the Army developed the Protective Mobilization Plan that would enable it to quickly expand in a time of national emergency. Germany's invasion of Poland on September 1, 1939, shocked the world and resulted in President Franklin D. Roosevelt declaring a state of limited national emergency. General George C. Marshall, Army Chief of Staff, remembered his experience as a member of the American Expeditionary Forces in World War I, where he witnessed the Army's unpreparedness for battle. He was determined that if the United States entered another world war the Army would be much better prepared than in 1917. He immediately set out restructuring the Army's fighting formations, strengthening its readiness, and updating doctrine. These actions and the continued expansion of hostilities in Europe and North Africa led to the president approving the implementation of the Protective Mobilization Plan by September 1940. This plan specified the mobilization of various National Guard divisions for a period of one year beginning in September 1940. Simultaneously, Congress approved the Selective Service Act, which required all men aged 21 to 45 to register for the first peacetime draft in the nation's history. The War Department implementation instructions specified that all National Guard and regular army selectees were to be accessed gradually to prevent existing facilities from being overwhelmed.[1] These actions expanded the Army eightfold to 33 divisions and resulted in the units being manned to their authorized National Guard strengths through the draft.[2]

The 28th Infantry Division (ID) of the Pennsylvania National Guard reported for mobilization training on February 1, 1941. As an organic unit to the 28th ID, the 105th Infantry Battalion (Anti-Tank) simultaneously reported for duty at their respective armories. The initial rosters for the battalion, dated February 3, 1941, confirm 26 officers and 274 enlisted soldiers reporting for duty. This was an excess of six officers and understrength of 10 enlisted soldiers when compared to the Pennsylvania National Guard authorized strength figures. Among the officers reporting for duty was the battalion commander, Lieutenant Colonel Charles L. Supplee, who had received his promotion to lieutenant colonel the previous day. Upon the battalion's mobilization, however, it immediately was subject to the full requirements of the Active Army Table of Organization 7–115, dated November 1, 1940. The authorized and required strength more than doubled to 710: 30 officers and 680 enlisted soldiers. Consequently, the battalion was severely understrength by four officers and 406 enlisted soldiers.

Under these developing national and world circumstances, Ernie registered for the draft in the last quarter of 1940. In February 1941, Ernie received a postcard from the Selective Service Board of Blair County, Pennsylvania, to report to a doctor in Tyrone, Pennsylvania, for a physical examination. A few days later he was classified 1-A, meaning he was physically acceptable for military service, with an order number of 571. Ernie accepted his impending military service as one of the obligations of a good citizen. At this time, his length of service was expected to be only one year since the United States was not involved in the war raging in Europe.

A few weeks later he received orders to report to the military in mid-April along with his closest friend, Bill Engelman, and two other men from Tyrone. He was to report to the Howard Avenue Armory in

Altoona, Pennsylvania, on April 15, 1941, to verify his physical status and, if found acceptable, be inducted into the U.S. Army. Shortly after receiving this news, he proposed marriage to LaRue on April 5, 1941. LaRue recalled that he gave her a beautiful diamond ring. LaRue would remain faithful to Ernie throughout his military service and his time as a prisoner of war. A prolific letter writer, she posted a letter to him almost daily.

At the conclusion of the induction ceremony, Ernie traveled to the New Cumberland, Pennsylvania, reception center along with a group of other men. Over the next three days, Ernie came to appreciate the meaning of "hurry up and wait" as he completed his military in-processing. The first order of business was the completion of a thorough physical examination to validate his fitness for military service. After successfully passing this examination, he received a variety of inoculations and vaccinations. Next was the completion of numerous military forms on which he listed his personnel and family information, signed up for a government insurance policy, listed his interests and hobbies, and provided detailed information on his civilian occupations and skills. Finally, he received his initial issue of military clothing, participated in basic drill and ceremony exercises, and received his military assignment to the 105th Infantry Battalion (AT).[3] The morning of April 19, 1941, Private Ernest V. Focht shipped out to Fort Meade, Maryland (Map 1). Upon arriving, he and Bill Engelman were assigned to Company A, 105th Infantry Battalion (AT). They were two of the many draft selectees assigned to the battalion to slowly bring the unit up to table of organization (T/O) authorized strength of 30 officers and 680 enlisted soldiers.

Ernie immediately started his 13-week basic and specialty training programs directed by a cadre of officers and non-commissioned officers (NCO) from the battalion. It involved six weeks of basic training, which included physical conditioning, instruction in fundamental military knowledge, drill and ceremony, weapons qualification, and an introduction to the rudiments of discipline and army life. Other topics were map reading, sanitation, vehicle maintenance, and first aid. The specialty phase of his training consisted of learning his military service specialty as a heavy truck driver.[4] Upon graduation from the

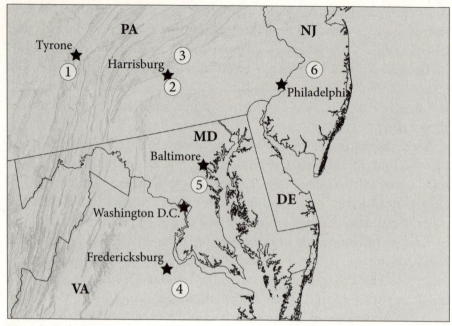

Map 1: Early Years and Military Training, November 1914 to July 1941. 1. Altoona, PA; 2. New Cumberland, PA; 3. Indiantown Gap Military Reservation, PA; 4. Camp A. P. Hill, VA; 5. Fort Meade, MD; 6. Fort Dix, NJ. (Timothy M. Swartz. World Hillshade copyright © Esri)

six weeks of basic training, Ernie received a permanent pass. This gave him the opportunity to leave Fort Meade for the weekend whenever he did not have duty. He and his friends would pile into someone's car and travel the four hours to Tyrone to see their girls. Consequently, LaRue and Ernie spent almost every weekend together from mid-May to the end of July 1941. On the few occasions Ernie did not make it home to Tyrone, LaRue and either her mother or Ernie's mother made the trip to Baltimore so they could be together. During these visits Ernie and LaRue spent time in Annapolis and at Tolchester Beach, Maryland.

In August 1941 the 105th Infantry Battalion (AT) left Fort Meade and traveled to Camp A. P. Hill, Virginia, for training in preparation for participating in an Army-wide exercise beginning in September. This exercise was the second of two Army-wide maneuvers conducted in 1941. General Marshall's training model for providing a significantly better prepared Army for a future war included maneuvers that provided small units experience in teamwork and combined arms. The culmination of this prewar mobilization period was the general headquarters (GHQ) maneuvers during which entire armies engaged in simulated combat. There were two GHQ maneuvers conducted in 1941. The first occurred in northern and west central Louisiana during August and September 1941 involving the forces of Second and Third Armies. In the aftermath of the maneuvers there were many removals and reassignments of officers of all ranks along with a reassessment of force structure and tactical doctrine. The second GHQ maneuvers occurred in southern North Carolina and northern South Carolina during October and November 1941 and involved the forces of First Army and IV Corps (Reinforced). The participating units began arriving in the maneuver area throughout September and October, conducting various training exercises in preparation for these GHQ maneuvers. These began on November 16, 1941, and ended at the conclusion of Phase 2 on November 29, 1941.[5] Ernie's unit, the 105th Infantry Battalion (AT), participated as a member of the 28th Infantry Division and First Army (Blue Forces) throughout the second phase of maneuvers, commonly referred to as the Carolina Maneuvers.

The 105th Infantry Battalion (AT) assembly area was in the southern pines area of North Carolina near the town of Hoffman, approximately 50 miles west of Fort Bragg, North Carolina (Map 2), through early December 1941. Ernie enjoyed being away from a military base and out in the woods. At this time, he was a heavy cargo truck driver and was promoted to the rank of private first class with an increase in his base pay from 31 to 40 dollars a month. In this capacity, he hauled supplies and equipment from Fort Meade, Maryland, to and around the exercise area. The Army's growth in manpower exceeded its capability of equipping individual soldiers with weapons and gear and in providing all of the heavy equipment and artillery pieces for a unit. Ernie's unit trained with wooden replicas of their rifles and crudely made metal pipes as mockups of their 37-millimeter anti-tank guns instead of the actual military equipment. The gun crews would sneak up on their opponents and throw bags of flour at the opposing force. When an umpire noticed a gun, a vehicle, a piece of equipment, or a soldier dusted with flour, the equipment and soldier were removed from the exercise for the remainder of the day. Ernie recalled that they typically began their attack early in the morning with a reconnaissance vehicle in the lead searching for the enemy. The other soldiers would be moving slowly through the woods ready to respond when the enemy was located. "A lot of times we would pull an early attack, maybe we would get up earlier and the other guys would just be getting out of bed and you would run into their bivouac area and catch the reds. They weren't prepared for the day." At that point an exercise referee who traveled with the group made the determination as to whom and what equipment were knocked out of action for the day.

Although the mess section prepared three hot meals a day, the soldiers often complained about the food. Therefore, Ernie's company commander, Captain John C. Forney, would often provide extra food for his soldiers by going into town and purchasing it. "I'll never forget

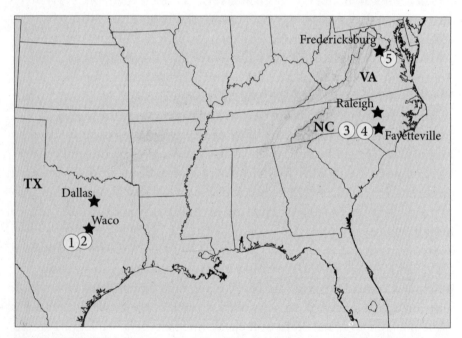

Map 2: 105th/805th Battalion Training Sites, August 1941 to July 1942. 1. Copperas Cove, Texas; 2. Camp Hood, Texas; 3. Charlotte, North Carolina; 4. Hoffman, North Carolina; 5. Camp A. P. Hill, Virginia. (Timothy M. Swartz. World Hillshade copyright © Esri)

MILITARY TRAINING • 27

one funny thing one time a fellow put a can of beans, we usually had fires going around the place, and we'd clear it out that it wouldn't spread or anything like that, and a fellow set a can of beans over that, and it exploded went all over our company commander. He didn't punch a hole in it, so it exploded." The soldiers were permitted to go to town when off duty. One of the most popular reasons for going to town was to locate a hot shower; the alternative was a portable shower using cold stream water. Ernie writes of a group of four going to town to buy bread and lunch meat to make sandwiches and sitting on a curb enjoying themselves. "We really wanted a bath, so we got up our nerve and went up to a house there and said, 'Could we possibly take a shower? We'll be glad to repay you for it.' Well, imagine, there was four of us, complete strangers going to a strange home, and they let us take a shower there. We had a marvelous time."

In addition to going into the nearest town, the soldiers were permitted to travel to other locations within North Carolina. Ernie availed himself of this freedom by attending two college football games, the first on October 11, 1941, at Duke Stadium in Chapel Hill, North Carolina, for the Fordham–North Carolina game. The other game was a week later at Kenan Stadium in Durham, North Carolina, where Duke played Colgate. He writes of attending a third game at Shenandoah University, Winchester, Virginia, with LaRue. Ernie continued to attend religious services whenever possible. Among his artifacts is the Sunday bulletin from the First Methodist Church in Charlotte, North Carolina, dated November 9, 1941. Although the unit was still on maneuvers during the Thanksgiving holiday, the company commander made sure his soldiers ate a traditional Thanksgiving meal. The cooks prepared the turkeys over a fire pit on a spit. On the unit's return trip to Fort Meade, Maryland, on December 7, while they were overnighting at Camp A. P. Hill near Bowling Green, Virginia, the men heard of the Japanese bombing Pearl Harbor. "Just one of the fellows had a battery type radio that he just picked it up. We thought it was a play on T.V. or, on the radio. But it wasn't, it was the real McCoy." Although the country was now officially at war, Ernie was permitted to go home for Christmas before returning to Fort Meade a couple of days after the holiday.

While the 105th Infantry Battalion (AT) was preparing to travel back to Fort Meade after concluding their participation in the Carolina Maneuvers, the Army published two orders that would have a significant impact upon the unit. A War Department letter of November 27, 1941 officially ordered the activation on or about December 1, 1941 of a Tank Destroyer Tactical and Firing Center at Fort Meade.[6] This established a specific command element to oversee the formulation, development, and training of the Army's anti-tank forces. On December 15, 1941, the eight existing provisional AT battalions were all redesignated as tank destroyer (TD) battalions. The 105th Infantry Battalion (AT)'s new designation was the 805th Tank Destroyer Battalion. Furthermore, it was reassigned from the 28th Infantry Division to Army General Headquarters. The directive also created an additional 44 tank destroyer battalions from other existing Army assets. This new T/O 18–25, dated December 24, 1941, effective April 1942, added a reconnaissance company consisting of five officers and 127 enlisted to the battalion structure while simultaneously reducing the number of enlisted soldiers assigned to each of the three tank destroyer companies. The revised authorized strength of the battalion now was 842 personnel: 35 officers and 807 enlisted soldiers.

In late January 1942 numerous additional personnel were assigned to the unit from Camp Croft, a United States Army training facility outside of Spartanburg, South Carolina. Their arrival altered the hometown composition and atmosphere of the battalion and gave it a nationwide complexion. Even with these additional soldiers the battalion was still below its authorized strength. In the meantime, Ernie continued to be assigned to Company A. Although the unit now had a different designation, new positions, and a new organizational structure, it still did not have the proper equipment. Therefore, the training was still not very realistic and concentrated more on individual skills rather than building platoon or company technical and tactical proficiency. Ernie and his friends continued to take advantage of the permanent pass, making many weekend trips to Tyrone to visit their girls.

In early February 1942 the unit received its new individual equipment, new vehicles, and new artillery pieces. The biggest difference was that instead of towing all their artillery pieces using wheeled trucks,

MILITARY TRAINING • 29

each company was issued a few of the new M3 Gun Motor Carriage (75-mm) half-tracks. Now that the soldiers had some of their authorized equipment, the training program underwent a dramatic transformation. The Tank Destroyer Tactical and Firing Center distributed the training notes, procedures, and experiences of the 93d/893d TD Battalion from its experiences in the recently completed GHQ maneuvers to all TD units and directed that they form the basis of their training program. This revised training program from January 15 to May 15, 1941, emphasized the development of effective leadership in both the officer and non-commissioned officer ranks, the massing of fires of all weapons on specific targets both from a stationary position and during maneuvers, and the cross-training of soldiers to develop a pool of experienced drivers capable of stepping into leadership roles if necessary. In order to accomplish these objectives, first the soldiers needed to demonstrate proficiency in map and aerial photograph reading, both motorized and dismounted reconnaissance, operation and maintenance of motor vehicles, and maintaining proper intervals and formations during convoy operations, among other individual soldier skills. The next phase of this comprehensive training program focused on building confidence in their ability to destroy tanks, developing the principles of both offensive and defensive operations against tanks, identification of friend and foe equipment, conducting tactical road marches, the firing of both the 50- and 30-caliber machine guns, and engaging targets with their 37-mm and 75-mm guns against both stationary and moving targets.[7] Ernie was assigned as the driver of one of these half-tracks. In late February 1942, Ernie was promoted to technician fifth class. This rank is the equivalent of a corporal without the authority or duties associated with that rank. The unit spent a considerable amount of time in the woods conducting field problems. During these exercises the majority of the time was devoted to improving driver confidence—including driving under blackout conditions—and the map-reading skills of every soldier.

A typical exercise involved the company first establishing a defensive position. Once done, it moved to the offensive with part of the unit maneuvering to an alternate position while the remainder of the unit provided cover for this element. These drills were based on the pre-publication of *Tank Destroyer Field Manual* in early March 1942. This pattern was continually repeated throughout the months of March and April 1942. In mid-March Ernie was able to visit with LaRue and his family, showing off his new rank and sitting for a formal portrait in his uniform. In early April, the unit experienced another significant influx of new selectees to fill the positions in the reconnaissance company. These newest arrivals, lacking their initial 13 weeks of basic training, were trained by an experienced group of officers and noncommissioned officers from their company.[8] While these latest arrivals participated in their initial training, the remainder of the battalion continued to improve their skills. The training emphasis for May 1942 included tactical exercises and convoy operations; continued training on crew-served and individual weapons; and attendance at battalion-operated schools on radio communications, motor maintenance, or intelligence gathering. It was not all-work-and-no-play as each company fielded basketball and baseball teams to compete in leagues sponsored by Fort Meade. Additionally, there were weekly Wednesday afternoon trips to Griffith Field in Washington, DC, to enjoy a Washington Senators baseball game.[9]

As the end of May approached the battalion received orders to report to Camp Hood, Texas. This directive interrupted the initial basic training for the majority of the soldiers assigned to the reconnaissance company after only

Table A: Personnel Authorizations by Table of Organization (1940–42)

	105th Bn	105th Bn	805th Bn	805th Bn
T/O Date	4/12/1940	11/1/1940	12/24/1941	6/8/1942
T/O Number	PANG GO	7–115	18–25	18–25
Officers	20	30	35	38
Enlisted	284	680	807	860
Aggregate	304	710	842	898

Table A shows the authorized strength figures of the 105th Infantry Bn (AT) and its successor, the 805th TD Bn, from April 1940 through June 1942. (Sources: 22nd Cavalry Division Disbanded, *The Pennsylvania Guardsman*, December 1940, Table of Organization 7–115 for the 105th and Table of Organization 18–25 for the 805th TD Bn) (Note: PANG GO stands for Pennsylvania Army National Guard General Order.)

five weeks. The battalion departed Fort Meade, Maryland, for Camp Hood, Texas (Map 2), to continue training at the newly created Tank Destroyer Forces School before the end of the month. The first week of June the unit underwent its fourth change to its personnel and equipment authorizations since the unit stood up in September 1940. This change increased the officer ranks by three to 38 and the enlisted to 860 with an overall strength of 898 soldiers, up from 842. The only significant changes to the equipment were the loss of the 18 self-propelled anti-aircraft vehicles and an increase in the number of 30- and 50-caliber machine guns (Tables A and B).

The Tank Destroyer Tactical and Firing Center and Tank Destroyer Forces School were transferred to Camp Hood in January and March 1942, respectively. When Ernie's unit arrived at Camp Hood there were no barracks, support, or training facilities in existence since the construction

Table B: Equipment Authorizations by Table of Organization (1940–42)

	105th Bn	805th Bn	805th Bn
T/O Date	11/1/1940	12/24/1941	6/8/1942
T/O Number	7–115	18–25	18–25
.30 Carbine	340	504	633
M1 Rifle	51	0	177
.45 Pistol	325	314	62
50-caliber MG	0	36	60
30-caliber MG	0	15	32
Rocket Launcher	0	0	0
81-mm Mortar	0	0	0
37-mm AA	0	18	0
37-mm AT, SP	36 (towed)	12	12
3-inch AT Gun	0	24★	24★
76-mm SP, M18	0	0	0

★The 75-mm self-propelled (SP) M3 gun was substituted for the 3-inch AT gun. Table B illustrates the equipment authorization for the 105th Infantry Bn (AT) and its successor, the 805th TD Bn, from November 1940 through June 1942. (Sources: Table of Organization 7–115 for the 105th and Table of Organization 18–25 for the 805th TD Bn) (Note: AA stands for Anti-Aircraft.)

32 • GUEST OF ADOLF

of these facilities was just beginning.[10] Therefore, upon arrival the unit was directed to an area off Camp Hood, just outside the town of Copperas Cove. "We had to clear the area of weeds and things like that. As a result, there was a lot of ticks and things and mosquitos in there." After completing this task, the unit established a bivouac site, erecting tents and constructing some fixed facilities. This became the area where everyone worked, ate, and slept, four or five to a tent. In addition to the austere environment, everyone had to contend daily with ticks, chiggers, rattlesnakes, copperheads, spiders, scorpions, armadillos, and other such critters. The armadillos typically created a ruckus in the early evening when they ventured out of their hiding places. The boys from the East enjoyed participating in daily armadillo chases, attempting to capture one out of curiosity. Fortunately for the animals not many of these chases resulted in their capture.[11] These antics provided a bit of comic relief for all of the soldiers relieving the tension of the day's training activities. The prescribed training program emphasized technical training the first month and tactical training during the second month. This is where the real training on the new equipment began.

During the next two months, Ernie became proficient in driving and maintaining his half-track. The battalion and its companies participated in numerous exercises to hone their unit-level tactics. Throughout this time, the soldiers had plenty of opportunities to visit the areas around Copperas Cove as most weekends were non-training days. Ernie's fiancée, LaRue, visited him for three days during the last week of July 1942. "I had a place for her in Coper's [Copperas] Cove" with a local family, Mr. and Mrs. Byron Gilmore, who worked for the post office. "And I was able to go in the evenings to spend the evening with her." On July 30, 1942, the 805th TD Battalion departed Camp Hood with all its equipment and personnel by rail for Indiantown Gap Military Reservation (IGMR), outside of Annville, Pennsylvania (Map 3), arriving there on August 2, 1942. The following two days were a flurry of activity as all personnel made final preparations for deployment to England. It was during these two days that Lieutenant Colonel Supplee was found to be gravely ill. He was suffering from an infection complicated by an existing heart condition. The battalion surgeon first confined him to the base hospital and later transferred him to Walter Reed General Hospital in Washington, DC. Thus, as the battalion completed its preparations for overseas duty it was without its commander.[12] On the morning of August 5, LaRue traveled from Harrisburg to IGMR to visit with Ernie one last time to say her goodbyes and to see her sweetheart off. The unit then departed and began its journey to Brooklyn, New York, where all the soldiers boarded troop transport ships that departed New York Harbor on August 6, 1942. The unit embarked upon its transport at approximately 72 percent of its personnel strength, with only 650 soldiers out of the 898 authorized.

The troop transport ship departed Brooklyn, New York, and made course for Halifax, Nova Scotia, arriving off the coast on Saturday, August 8, 1942. The ship waited off the coast for a day while other ships of various types continued arriving. Once all the ships assembled, they formed Convoy AT-18, the largest troop convoy yet assembled. It consisted of 12 troopships and 19 escort cruisers and destroyers.[13] The ports of debarkation for the troopships included Liverpool and

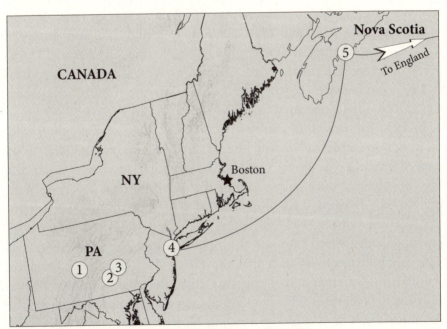

Map 3: Movement Overseas, August 1942. 1. Tyrone, PA; 2. Harrisburg, PA; 3. Indiantown Gap Military Reservation, PA; 4. Brooklyn, NY; 5. Halifax, Nova Scotia. (Timothy M. Swartz. World Hillshade copyright © Esri)

34 • GUEST OF ADOLF

Bristol in England; the Firth of Clyde in Scotland; Swansea, Wales; and Iceland. The weather during the passage varied: there were six days of calm seas, while the other five days brought high winds, rain, fog, and choppy seas. On August 14 the USS *Brooklyn*, a light cruiser and one of the convoy escort vessels, received an advisory message that a German submarine was operating approximately 70 miles east of its position. In the early morning hours of August 15, a United States merchant vessel was reported as being sunk less than 45 miles from the convoy.[14] The sinking of this vessel resulted in Axis Sally reporting that Ernie's ship had been sunk in the North Atlantic by a German submarine. Ernie and the rest of the fellows on the ship enjoyed a good laugh at this pronouncement, "a bunch of ghosts running around." The person known as Axis Sally was Mildred Gillars, who was an American citizen and a middle-aged former showgirl from Ohio. She made daily radio broadcasts for Nazi Germany beginning in 1934, and after 1941 her broadcasts were an attempt to break the morale of Allied troops. She was captured on March 15, 1946, spending the next two and a half years in Allied prison camps before returning to the United States to await trial on a charge of treason. She was found guilty in March 1949 after a three-month trial and sentenced to 10 to 30 years imprisonment with a $10,000 fine. She served 12 years at the Alderson Reformatory for Women in West Virginia, was paroled in 1961, and became a teacher at a Roman Catholic convent school near Columbus, Ohio. She died in 1988.[15]

In 1951 the troopship manifest records were intentionally destroyed, so it is impossible to identify the exact vessels Ernie and the 805th were on for the voyage to Scotland. It is possible to narrow down the ship possibilities since only three of the 12 troopships departing from the Brooklyn Naval Yard used Firth of Clyde berths as their port of debarkation. These were *Argentina*, *Monterey*, and *Wakefield*. In all probability the 805th transited the Atlantic using two of these vessels. This is based upon the fact that the 894th Tank Destroyer Battalion transited in the same convoy on two ships, the *Andes* and the *Thomas H. Barry*. Furthermore, Ernie mentioned in his oral history crossing the Atlantic Ocean on *Monarch of Bermuda*. However, this is incorrect, since this vessel was not one of the 12 troopships in his convoy. However, its sister ship, *Queen of Bermuda*, was part of this convoy, but it traveled to Iceland and not Scotland (Map 4).

While in England the unit was initially stationed at Tidworth Barracks, where Ernie lived in a tent. During this period Ernie received a promotion to corporal in September 1942, becoming a noncommissioned officer. His basic pay at this time was $66.00 plus a 20 percent Foreign Service bonus of $13.20. Ernie paid $6.90 for his $10,000 serviceman's life insurance premium and made a Class E allotment of $45.00 to be paid to his parents in Tyrone, Pennsylvania. This left him with only $26.30 a month to spend on things for himself. In early October he moved to Shrivenham and lived on an air base in married men's quarters. The airbase drew the attention of one German reconnaissance plane that flew over the base every evening. It was a tri-motor plane that made a very distinctive sound. The soldiers referred to him as "Bed-Check Charlie."

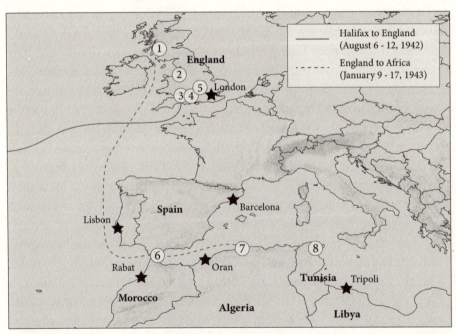

Map 4: Training in England and Movement to Algeria, August 1942 to January 1943. 1. Firth of Clyde, Scotland; 2. Liverpool, England; 3. Bristol, England; 4. Oxford, England; 6. Rock of Gibraltar, United Kingdom; 7. Algiers, Algeria; 8. Tunis, Tunisia. (Timothy M. Swartz. World Hillshade copyright © Esri)

A few hours later, the air raid sirens would begin their wailing to warn of an impending German bombardment. "You would see these big spotlights of light up in the air. They really pick a plane out pretty well."

A few weeks after arriving in England, LTC Allen H. Foreman was assigned as the new battalion commander. Throughout the unit's time in England, it continued to train and prepare for combat operations. The individual soldier training was patterned after British Commando training and was conducted by a British cadre. It consisted primarily of physical training, hand-to-hand combat skills, knife training, night patrolling, and survival techniques.[16] Ernie tells of doing a lot of walking the first couple of weeks in England because the unit's equipment had not arrived. "Believe me, that was awful, after being on the water for twelve days, not very much walking. It was very tiring exhausting. We'd start out on a march and, with no vehicles, and it would be nice. Then a rain would come up, so you would stop, put your rain coat on, and as soon as you would get your rain coat on, it would stop and you would have to walk to the next break before you could take it off." Naturally, he was very happy when the vehicles arrived and he was able to drive his vehicle around the countryside during the training exercises. The equipment's arrival was both a joyous occasion and a disappointment. Once the Ordnance Department had completed its inspection "to make sure everything was all right with the trucks and vehicles and things," Ernie explained, "they just issued them out to the first activities that was alerted to go on to the east coast of England, Bristol in that area." Consequently, the 805th TD Battalion received very little of their own vehicles and equipment since they did not participate in the initial landings for Operation *Torch* on the North African coast in November 1942.[17] Their maneuver training and artillery practice occurred at Newquay, Penhale, and Torquay on the coast of the Cornwall region.

Near the end of November 1942, Company A, 805th TD Battalion posed for a photograph at Shrivenham Barracks. This is one of the many photographs Ernie kept in a scrapbook of his military experiences. In mid-December, Ernie was hospitalized with pneumonia and was discharged from the Oxford Hospital on December 22, 1942, with only a few days to spare before the unit was to leave England. Though there was no official word as to when they were to ship out, the residents

MILITARY TRAINING • 37

around their base started to tell the soldiers they were leaving soon. Naturally, the residents' information was accurate, and the unit soon made preparations to deploy. In anticipation of departing England in a few days, Ernie writes to his parents on January 3:

> Very glad you are well, the same goes for me. Hope these few lines find you the same. ... Say that was swell Dean & Scott both getting nice bucks. Gosh some venison would certainly taste good. ... Mel and Helen's box came as well as LaRue's box on the 27 of Dec. Boy did things taste good. Of all I received have nothing left, just a bunch of chowhounds. Everything was in fine shape, but don't worry I am a perfect thirty-eight. ... Now take things easy and don't be worrying too hard. ... God be with you till you hear from me & meet again. Your prayers ever needed. No church today. Bill & Greg are OK.

On January 5, 1943, the 805th TD Battalion officially ended their training in England when they departed Shrivenham for the coast of Scotland. Once there the soldiers boarded the vessel *Monarch of Bermuda* for the voyage to North Africa and to participate in its liberation from the Germans and Italians.

CHAPTER 3

Anti-Tank Force Development

During World War I, the British employed tanks for the first time at the battle of the Somme in 1916. The French and Americans soon followed suit, using tanks as an offensive weapon in a limited capacity. Meanwhile, the Germans manufactured less than two-dozen combat-worthy tanks and employed about the same number of captured British and French tanks. The Germans countered the Allied use of tanks by utilizing their existing 77-mm field guns as an anti-tank (AT) weapon. Additionally, they formed mobile groups of these field guns to counter the use of tanks anywhere along their lines. The limited use of tanks by the Germans and the use of field artillery guns to counter their use led the Allies to conclude there was no need to develop a specific anti-tank capability. The United States Army adopted the philosophy of using existing artillery resources positioned in-depth and including some mobile gun sections as its defense against the use of tanks by an enemy.

During the interwar years, the British and Germans both improved upon their tank doctrine. In Germany, Adolf Hitler's rearmament program resulted in the creation of the first panzer army led by Heinz Guderian. This was truly a combined arms approach to warfare built around the aggressive use of tanks. Meanwhile in Great Britain, the theorists F. C. Fuller and B. H. Liddell Hart explored the use of large-scale mechanized forces. In the United States very little was being done in the advancement of an anti-tank doctrine.

The U.S. Army began to formulate an AT doctrine in the early 1930s in response to the emerging theory on employing tanks on the battlefield. During this time "officers were instructed in the tactics of an 'anti-tank box' which was a static defense-in-depth with the anti-tank guns placed in the four corners of a rectangular 'killing ground.'"[1] Tanks were considered invincible, sweeping aside any force in their path. This impression created a "tank terror" at all levels of the Army. In 1936 the Army's initial tank doctrine suggested that each division be assigned an AT battalion and each regiment possess an AT company. A year later, the 2nd Infantry Division conducted field tests exploring the concept of integrating AT weapons into its authorized structure. The exercise recommendations included changing the division structure to a triangular organization composed of three infantry regiments with an eight-gun anti-tank company as an organic asset. The next significant event was the publication in 1939 of a manual by the Command and General Staff College titled "Antitank Defense (Tentative)." This publication espoused that the regimental AT assets be employed to protect the front-line soldiers while an AT battalion be established as a division asset. These assets espoused the principle of a massed AT reserve held out of action and ready to respond to a tank threat anywhere, be it at the front, flank, or rear areas. Interestingly, it was Brigadier General Leslie J. McNair, who was the director of the Army field tests in 1937 and in 1942 was the Army ground force commander, who was intimately involved in both AT doctrinal advancements.

When the war in Europe erupted with Germany's invasion of Poland in September 1939, the United States began the process of rearmament. General George C. Marshall, Army Chief of Staff, implemented the triangular division as recommended in 1937 with all its anti-tank guns under the control of the artillery. This decision led to confusion between the infantry and artillery branches as to who was responsible for the development of AT doctrine and capabilities. Very few of the artillerymen responsible for AT defense had ever seen a tank in action, and even fewer had ever fired their weapons at a moving tank. Furthermore, the prevailing belief among artillery officers was that these AT weapons were for their own defense and not for the defense of the entire division. The uncertainty of who provided AT defense for the division was partially addressed with the implementation of another recommendation from the 2nd Infantry Division 1937 field exercises for the creation of

AT battalions as a division asset. Consequently, eight provisional anti-tank battalions were authorized on January 1, 1940. The first of these units to stand up was the 94th Infantry Battalion, Anti-Tank, at Fort Benning, Georgia, by the end of June 1940. It had the distinction of being the first Army-wide unit with the mission of destroying enemy tanks. Two additional active-duty infantry battalions (AT) were created the following month, the 93d at Fort Meade, Maryland, and the 99th at Fort Lewis, Washington. These three battalions were formed through the reassignment and conversion of existing Army artillery batteries. By the end of September 1940 five additional anti-tank battalions (101st, 102d, 103d, 104th, and 105th) were established. These battalions were formed from existing Army National Guard units with the 101st and 102nd in the New York Guard, the 103d in the Washington Guard, the 104th in the New Mexico Guard, and the 105th in the Pennsylvania Guard. These five National Guard units were to be organized under Table of Organization 7–115, Infantry Battalion (AT) with an effective date of April 12, 1940.

When the Pennsylvania National Guard published its general order directing the reorganization of existing units to form the 105th Infantry Battalion (AT) effective on September 22, 1940, it did so at much lower strength levels. This order provided for an authorized strength of only 20 officers and 284 enlisted soldiers. The reorganization of units is illustrated in Table C. In October 1940 the newly formed 105th Infantry Battalion (AT) began its reorganization and training during its monthly drill period for a mission that was still being defined by the Army. Compounding their organizational difficulties was the lack of an approved anti-tank doctrine, lack of an anti-tank weapon, and a lack of authorized vehicles and weapons. These deficiencies were further exacerbated in November 1940 when the War Department published revisions to the tables of organization for all the infantry battalions (AT). This new authorization document radically increased the authorized strength from 304 to 710 soldiers. The officer ranks increased by 10 to 30 and the enlisted ranks swelled from 284 to 680. Now, the unit was not only struggling to train without the proper equipment but also was severely understrength, which required the undertaking of a massive recruiting campaign to fill its ranks.

Table C: Reorganization of 28th Infantry Division Units Creating the 105th Infantry Battalion (Anti-Tank)

New Designation	T/O	T/O Date	Station	Old Designation
Headquarters	7–115	4/12/1940	Harrisburg, PA	Hq, 122 QM Squadron
Hq Co less Svc Platoon	7–116	4/12/1940	Harrisburg, PA	Hq Det, 22d Cav Div & Hq Det, 122 QM Sq
Svc Platoon Headquarters	7–116	4/12/1940	Fleetwood, PA	Troop C, 122 Med Sq
Company A	7–117	4/12/1940	Bloomsburg, PA	Hq Troop, 22 Cav Div
Company B	7–117	4/12/1940	Tamaqua, PA	Troop B & C, 122 QM Sq
Company C	7–117	4/12/1940	Oil City, PA	Anti-tank Platoon, Hq Co 112th Infantry
Medical Department Detachment	7–115	4/12/1940	Philadelphia, PA	Hq, Service Detachment & Troop B 122d Medical Squadron

This table illustrates the reorganization of existing 28th Infantry Division units within the Pennsylvania Army National Guard to form the newly authorized 105th Infantry Battalion (AT). (Source: 22nd Cavalry Division Disbanded, *The Pennsylvania Guardsman*, December 1940) (Note: Hq = Headquarters, QM = Quartermaster, Co = Company, Svc = Service, Det = Detachment, Cav Div = Cavalry Division, Sq = Squadron, and Med = Medical)

The five provisional National Guard AT battalions continued to train as best they could under the circumstances. One of the significant training handicaps was that the soldiers likely had never seen a tank and they possessed no weapons with which to engage and hopefully defeat a tank. Despite the turmoil and lack of specific guidance from the Army, the 105th Infantry Battalion (AT) continued to prepare its soldiers. Around this time, the Army's Ordnance Department made a unilateral decision on an anti-tank weapon. It adopted a weapon very similar to the German Pak 36, a 37-mm AT weapon, and rushed it into production. It was not until the beginning of 1942 that any of these AT guns were available for the unit to conduct training.

While these eight provisional AT units were organizing and initiating training programs, the confusion over anti-tank assets was further compounded with Germany's invasion of France and the Low Countries in May 1940 and the defeat of the Allies (French, British, Belgian, and Dutch) with its quick striking panzer divisions. In response, the concept of a static AT defense-in-depth began to evolve into one of stopping tanks through offensive action with AT weapons. In early 1941, Brigadier General Harry Twaddle, chief of the Operations and Training Division (G3) of the War Department General Staff, conducted a conference for the purpose of establishing AT responsibilities. In attendance were representatives of the Infantry, Field Artillery, Armored Force, Calvary, Coast Artillery, GHQ, and the War Department. Unfortunately, the conference ended without a consensus among its participants with each stating their case as to why they should be the AT proponent. "In the end, the G3 recommended to the Army Chief of Staff, General Marshall, that Infantry exercise jurisdiction over anti-tank matters until such a time as an official armored arm was established, whereupon armor would assume responsibility, presumably whether armor wanted it or not."[2]

The combination of these factors led General Marshall to instruct the G3 to form a planning branch led by Lieutenant Colonel Andrew D. Bruce in May 1941. The purpose of this group was to study the unsolved problems with anti-tank warfare. One of the first actions of this group was to conduct its own smaller AT conference. The result was the confirmation that each division should have its own internal AT battalion to complement its AT companies. These were formed from existing divisional anti-tank assets, mainly from the divisional artillery AT assets. Consequently, their employment was that of a traditional artillery battalion; that is, the AT guns were to be set up in a fixed position. However, this concept of employment was short-lived as General Marshall issued a directive stating that "prompt consideration be given to the creation of highly mobile anti-tank/anti-aircraft units as Corps and Army troops for use in meeting mechanized units."[3]

Ahead of the GHQ Second Army versus Third Army maneuvers in Louisiana and Texas (Louisiana Maneuvers), in September 1941 the Third Army formed three anti-tank regimental size groups. These were formed from existing 37-mm anti-tank battalions and 75-mm battalions from various artillery units. This would be the first field exercise to demonstrate the United States's emerging anti-tank strategy. During the maneuvers these mobile anti-tank units successfully thwarted the armored thrust of Second Army. However, an analysis of the exercise rules of engagement clearly demonstrated that the anti-tank units were provided an advantage over the armor units. Specifically, the effectiveness of anti-tank weapons was exaggerated, and tanks could only destroy an anti-tank weapon by overrunning it. These maneuvers also demonstrated a need for the Armor Force to reconsider how it employed its assets on the battlefield.

The second GHQ Red Army (IV Corps) versus Blue Army (First Army) maneuvers occurred in November 1941 in North and South Carolina (Carolina Maneuvers) (Map 2). In preparation, both the Armor Force and the anti-tank component adjusted the employment of their assets. The Blue Army received three GHQ anti-tank groups and organized three tank attacker groups on its own. It also had the advantage of being assigned the provisional 93d Anti-Tank Battalion with its experimental self-propelled 75-mm guns. These maneuvers were the testing ground for moving into an offensive mindset regarding destroying an enemy's tanks. All these anti-tank assets provided the Blue Army a decisive advantage over the armored units of the Red Army. Among these AT assets was the 105th Infantry Battalion (AT). The high concentration of AT assets combined with favorable rules of engagement led to the Blue Army repeatedly being successful against the Red Army. Exercise observers commented on this success by stating: "It is believed success of AT units due to piecemeal [armored] attacks … rather than to AT units' effectiveness" and "the lack of sufficient infantry in armored units was a principal factor behind the high tank losses."[4]

While the Blue and Red Army forces were moving into their respective Carolina Maneuver exercise areas during October 1941, a meeting occurred between General Marshall and Colonel Bruce on the future of the Army's anti-tank program. Its outcome was the approval for every division to have four organic anti-tank battalions and a renaming of the anti-tank battalions to tank destroyer (TD) battalions. These decisions were acted upon by the War Department on November 27, 1941, with the issuance of a letter ordering the activation of 53 tank destroyer battalions under the direct control of GHQ and the creation of the Tank Destroyer Tactical and Firing Center to be temporarily located at Fort Meade, Maryland, with Colonel Bruce as its commanding officer. This new organization was tasked with formulating recommendations on tank destroyer tactical and training doctrine. It was further responsible for developing the tables of organization of personnel and equipment for TD units, both light and heavy, and for selecting a permanent site for the TD school.

In a letter published on December 3, 1941, the War Department specified the organization of tank destroyer battalions. It is this letter that officially created the tank destroyer units. The provisions of the letter specified its effective date of December 15, 1941. It is this letter that authorized the redesignation of some units, the inactivation of others, and the creation of the tank destroyer forces. In all, 52 TD battalions were stood up from existing Army assets. The eight provisional AT battalions were redesignated as heavy self-propelled TD battalions, all with the prefix of "8." Twenty-eight TD battalions were formed from the Army's existing AT batteries and troops in the infantry divisions and cavalry units and given the numeral "6" as their prefix. An additional 12 were given the prefix "7," being created from resources in the five armored divisions and from artillery brigades. Four more TD battalions with the "8" prefix came from field artillery assets assigned to GHQ. Thus the 105 Infantry Battalion (AT) became the 805th TD Battalion (Heavy) and was transferred from the 28th Infantry Division to Army General Headquarters. It was reassigned to First Army by the War Department letter of January 30, 1942.

The Tank Destroyer Tactical and Firing Center was very busy during its first four months of existence. As previously mentioned, it was responsible for everything remotely connected to TDs. This included developing the field and technical manuals to guide the existing TD battalions in their training, securing all types of supplies and equipment, and making

46 • GUEST OF ADOLF

recommendations as to the type of weapon system and vehicles necessary for a tank destroyer battalion to accomplish its mission. Fortunately for Colonel Bruce's organization, the provisional 93d Infantry Battalion (AT) that participated in both the Louisiana and Carolina maneuvers was transferred to his fledgling organization on December 13, 1941, and redesignated the 893d TD Battalion. The experiences of this battalion during the maneuvers and its utilization of the experimental equipment became the basis for both the tables of organization and equipment as well as the initial training program for the other TD battalions. In early January 1942, the 893d TD Battalion was assigned as the Tank Destroyer Tactical and Firing Center School Troops. A few months later they were joined by the 753d TD Battalion to expand the number of soldiers assigned as school troops.

Since the initial debates on developing an anti-tank force, the problem of where it would be located was part of the conversation. There were potential sites in four states: Kentucky, North Carolina, Tennessee, and Texas. A site near Killeen, Texas, was selected in January 1942. The name Camp Hood was selected in honor of the Confederate General John Bell Hood. Immediately, a small cell from both the Tactical Firing Center and School and the 893d were dispatched to Temple, Texas, to begin the process of opening this new camp. However, first they needed to overcome several obstacles, the least of which were improving the road network, acquiring the land and moving its inhabitants off of it, contracting for the construction of the cantonment area, and preparing temporary camps for the two battalions of school troops and for the first group of TD battalions.

The Tank Destroyer School organized itself into a headquarters and five academic departments. These were tactics, communication, pioneer, automotive, and weapons. It was also active in surveying Camp Hood to identify bivouac sites, tactical firing ranges, and sites to locate its forward headquarters. Additionally, it was vigorously finalizing the Army's first official publication on the employment of tank destroyer battalions—FM 18–5, *Tank Destroyer Field Manual: Organization and Tactics of Tank Destroyer Units*—and the many other manuals on the tactical employment of TD units and the maintenance of equipment. These manuals were officially published and distributed in mid-June 1942. The training period for the TD battalions was either two or three months, depending on its technical and tactical proficiency level at the end of the first month. The training program emphasized technical training during the first month and tactical training during the second month. The training emphasized that the battalion was the smallest unit to be engaged separately according to paragraph 39 of FM 18–5. This paragraph further stated: "Employment of smaller tank destroyer units as independent defensive elements and their distribution with a view to covering every possible avenue of tank approach or to affording immediate protection to all echelons of the forces leads to uncoordinated action and dispersion with consequent loss of effectiveness."[5]

The first group of TD battalions arrived the first week of June 1942 with some of these units departing for their port of embarkation by the end of July 1942. The training time afforded to these first units was shortened by Army Ground Forces to as little as seven weeks in order for them to be available for the upcoming invasion of North Africa. The 805th TD Battalion was in this first group to process through the newly established Tank Destroyer Command at Camp Hood, Texas, departing on July 30, 1942, for its port of embarkation. This was more than two weeks prior to the establishment of the Tank Destroyer Center on August 17, 1942, and six weeks before the formal opening ceremony for the center. Regardless of the timing, Camp Hood was fully operational, conducting training exercises to validate existing tank destroyer units, training newly formed units, conducting an officer candidate school, and conducting the tank destroyer replacement-training center. However, these first units faced "the unpleasant fact they were joining an Army that was largely ignorant of tank destroyer doctrine."[6]

CHAPTER 4

North Africa 1942–43
(Operation *Torch*)

Benito Mussolini had visions of grandeur, visions of recreating the glory of ancient Rome under Caesar. Unlike Germany of the 1920s—dispossessed of national pride due to the terms of the Treaty of Versailles, thereby serving as a rallying cry, coupled with the "stab in the back," mystique to fuel German nationalism—Italy had fought on the side of the victors in the Great War. As such, while Germany swallowed the Sudetenland, exercised the *Anschluss*, and defeated and subsequently bifurcated Poland with the Soviet Union, the Italian economy and military lagged. As Hitler's armies ravaged across the Low Countries and France at break-neck speed, Mussolini remained indecisive. It was not until the German army was at the doorsteps of Paris that Mussolini finally held up his end of the Pact of Steel and declared war on France, subsequently invading along the Riviera and capturing inconsequential land and settlements.[1] Italy's declaration of war against Great Britain precipitated the gathering of armies to fight a seesaw war across the North African deserts.

After Marshal Philippe Pétain of the Vichy French government settled terms with Italy on June 24, 1940, Mussolini, emboldened by numerical superiority on land and apparent parity in naval capital vessels in the Mediterranean Sea, decided that attacking the British in Africa was a means to acquire land and impress Hitler.[2] On July 4, 1940, elements of the Italian garrison in Ethiopia attacked British frontier guards in what is now the South Sudan and Kenya. The fact that Italy maintained a garrison of more than two hundred thousand men in Libya, along Egypt's western border, prevented the British from checking the Italian offensive in the south.[3] On September 13, 1940, Italian forces crossed the Egyptian border and set the wheels in motion that would directly contribute towards SGT Ernest Focht being captured in February 1943.[4]

Given the topography of the North African desert, bordered to the north by the Mediterranean Sea and to the south by the Qattara Depression, mounted maneuver was limited to the area immediately contiguous to the coast road. After initial success following the invasion of Egypt, the Italian army under Marshal Rodolfo Graziani stalled after 60 miles to establish a logistics base for future operations. On December 9, 1940, the British Western Desert Force under General Richard O'Connor launched a counteroffensive, driving the Italians four hundred miles west. Finally, on February 7, 1941, the British army achieved success when an element conducting a "hook"—south and west into the depression and to the rear of the Italians—cut off the Italian retreat.[5]

Instead of this moment achieving decisive results, two events tipped the scales. First, Churchill ordered a significant portion of the Britain's Western Desert Force to Greece in the wake of the German invasion, and second, Hitler sent General Erwin Rommel, soon to be Field Marshal Rommel, along with the 5th Light and 15th Panzer Divisions to Africa to bolster Italian operations. Within nine days of beginning his offensive on March 24, 1941, Rommel had driven the British back to their original starting positions from December 1940.[6] Given the German invasion of the Soviet Union on June 22, 1941, resupply and replacements were minimal. Despite these limitations, Rommel continued to attempt to break through the British defenses to capture Alexandria and Cairo.

The British *Crusader* winter offensive of 1941 achieved success and lifted the siege of Tobruk on December 10, causing the Germans to retreat to the lines from which Rommel began his operation in March 1941.[7] However, the exigencies of war intervened and forced the British to divert troops to the Far East after the fall of Singapore.[8] As the British chased Rommel westward across the desert, they became overextended and provided Rommel with an opportunity to catch his breath, regroup, and prepare for future offensive operations.

A major factor in the war in North Africa was the resupply difficulties stemming from the scarcity of suitable seaports and the British navy.

Ernest Focht's parents, Gerald and Mary Helen Focht, on their 50th wedding anniversary, August 1962. (Author's collection)

The house of Gerald and Mary Helen Focht at 631 West Fifteenth Street in Tyrone, Pennsylvania, purchased in December 1942. (Author's collection)

LaRue Cassidy's parents, Clayton and Rhoda James Cassidy, in 1964. (Author's collection)

LaRue Cassidy in 1937. (Author's collection)

Ernest Focht and LaRue Cassidy, April 18, 1937. (Author's collection)

Ernest Focht, February 23, 1941. (Author's collection)

LaRue Cassidy, February 23, 1941. (Author's collection)

Ernest Focht's notification to report for his military physical on February 26, 1941. (Author's collection)

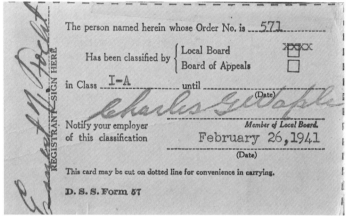

Ernest Focht's military draft card, February 26, 1941. (Author's collection)

Ernie Focht and LaRue Cassidy sitting on a bench outside her parents' house on April 14, 1941, the day before Ernie reported for military training. (Author's collection)

Private Ernest Focht and his buddy from Tyrone, Private Bill Engelman, at Fort Meade, Maryland, April 19, 1941. (Author's collection)

Privates William Heffron and James Young in Ernie's truck, Fort Meade, Maryland, June 1941. (Author's collection)

Ernie and friends by his truck at Fort Meade, Maryland, June 1941. Standing (L to R): Ernie, Heffron, and Andrew Robel. Front row (L to R): James Young and Albert Gearlack. (Author's collection)

Private Ernest Focht at his home on 607 West Fifteenth Street in Tyrone, Pennsylvania, September 1941. (Author's collection)

Company A, 105th Infantry Battalion (AT)'s mess tent, Carolina Maneuvers, fall 1941. (Author's collection)

Ernie (standing far left) and others in the woods outside Hoffman, North Carolina, during the Carolina Maneuvers, November 2, 1941. (Author's collection)

Ernie's truck parked among the trees during the Carolina Maneuvers, September to December 1941. (Author's collection)

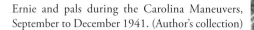

Ernie and pals during the Carolina Maneuvers, September to December 1941. (Author's collection)

LaRue greeting Technician 5th Class Ernest Focht outside her parents' home in Tyrone, Pennsylvania, in March 1942. (Author's collection)

805th Tank Destroyer Battalion bivouac site outside Copperas Cove, Texas, during their Camp Hood training in June and July 1942. (Author's collection)

Company A, 805th Tank Destroyer Battalion chow house, Copperas Cove, Texas, June and July 1942. (Author's collection)

Company A, 805th Tank Destroyer Battalion in England, December 1942, weeks before departing for Algiers, Algeria, on January 6, 1943. (Author's collection)

Ernest Focht's Tank Destroyer Forces patch. (Author's collection)

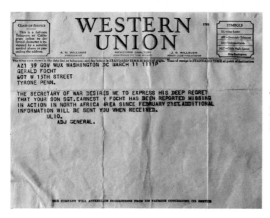

Telegram notifying Ernie's parents that he is missing in action in North Africa, March 11, 1943. (Author's collection)

Sergeant Ernest Focht's prisoner of war registration card, Stalag VIIA, Moosburg, Germany, April 14, 1943. (Author's collection)

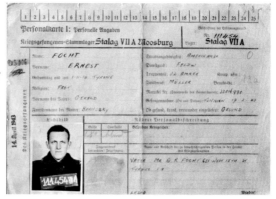

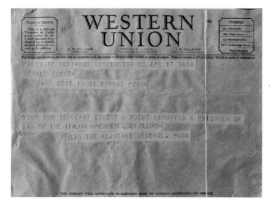

Telegram to Ernie's parents informing them of his prisoner of war status, April 17, 1943. (Author's collection)

Postcard received by Mr. and Mrs. Gerald Focht notifying them of Ernie's prisoner of war status from a shortwave radio operator listening to a German radio broadcast, April 24, 1943. (Author's collection)

On May 27, 1941, Rommel pre-empted a British offensive near Gazala and drove the British back deep into Egypt, leaving a South African division to garrison Tobruk to prevent the Germans from capturing the city and using it as a port of debarkation for supplies.[9] However, on June 21, 1941, Tobruk surrendered and General Claude Auchinleck retired towards El Alamein, near the Nile River.[10] On August 15, 1941, on a visit to Egypt, British Prime Minister Winston Churchill decided a change in leadership was necessary. Auchinleck was replaced with General Harold Alexander and General Bernard Law Montgomery was promoted to command the British 8th Army (formerly known as the Western Desert Force).[11]

Rather than attempt the same strategy of outmaneuvering the Germans that his predecessor attempted, Montgomery sought a set-piece battle that would cripple the German army in Africa. On October 23, 1941, Montgomery began the battle of El Alamein, conveniently while Rommel was back in Germany recovering from exhaustion. By November 2, the Germans were forced to commit the last of their reserves, and after *Ultra* intelligence intercepts confirmed that there were no more German reserve forces available, Montgomery reinforced the southern sector while Rommel committed his last units to the northern sector. The crushing defeat and subsequent chase by the British would drive Rommel from the gates of Cairo almost two thousand miles across the North African desert to the defensive Mareth Line in southern Tunisia.[12]

While Rommel was being chased across Libya, the Japanese attacked Pearl Harbor, thereby dragging the United States into World War II formally. Shortly after the attack on Pearl Harbor, Germany upheld its treaty obligations with the Japanese Empire and declared war on the United States. Given that the United States was attacked by Japan, it is difficult to understand how the United States adopted a "Europe first" strategy. Its origins lie in Admiral Harold R. Stark's "Memorandum on National Policy," published on November 12, 1940. As the chief of naval operations, Admiral Stark postulated, "If Britain wins decisively against Germany we could win everywhere; but if she loses...while we might not lose everywhere, we might, possibly, not win anywhere." Subsequent war planning efforts moved along these lines, and at the Arcadia Conference

(December 22, 1941, to January 14, 1942) President Roosevelt and Prime Minister Churchill formally decided upon the "Europe first" strategy.[13]

In the wake of the American naval victory at Midway in June 1942, the imminent invasion by the 1st Marine Division on the island of Guadalcanal to secure the vital shipping lanes to Australia and New Zealand, and the pressure on the Soviet Union, the need for a second front in Europe was formally ordered by President Roosevelt on July 30, 1942. The president notified his military commanders that the invasion of North Africa to "bloody" American forces while not directly invading Europe was to occur in 1942.[14]

French North Africa was under the political control of Marshal Henri Philippe Pétain's Vichy French government. The British in early July 1940 attacked and destroyed much of the French navy at the port of Mers-el-Kébir near Oran, Algeria. This action stiffened the resolve of the Pétain government to oppose any British military action in the region and to move into a collaborative arrangement with Nazi Germany. A disagreement existed among the Combined Chiefs as to how the Anglo-American armies would be received. Would they be welcomed with little to no resistance, or would the French colonial forces strongly resist the invasion? This led to the decision that the American military would assume the leading role in the invasion. It was hoped that the Pétain government would not strongly oppose an American landing force.

As the Germans were retreating across North Africa, Operation *Torch* landed in three separate elements stretching from the French Moroccan coast on the Atlantic Ocean to Algiers. The Western Army Task Force led by Major General George S. Patton landed in French Morocco at Safi, Fedala, and Mehdia, with thirty-four thousand soldiers and the city of Casablanca as its final objective. These soldiers were from the United States 3d and 9th Infantry Divisions and two battalions from the 2nd Armored Division. The task force sailed from Hampton Roads, Virginia, on October 24, 1942, on its 4,500-mile journey to the coast of French Morocco. The Center Task Force led by Major General Lloyd Fredendall had as its objective the seizure of Oran, Algeria. His force of 18,500 soldiers included the United States 1st Infantry Division, the 1st Armored Division, and 2nd Battalion of the 509th Infantry Regiment.

The Eastern Task Force led by British Lieutenant General Kenneth Anderson consisted of the United States 34th Infantry Division, a brigade of the British 78th Division, and two British Commando units. The objective of this force of twenty thousand soldiers was Algiers, Algeria. These last two task forces sailed from the British Isles on October 26, 1942. United States Lieutenant General Dwight D. Eisenhower was the overall commander in chief for this operation.

The landing of personnel from the three task forces began on November 8, 1942. The French resistance was very strong in Morocco and in Oran, but the Eastern Task Force experienced almost no resistance. However, three days later, an agreement between General Eisenhower and Admiral François Darlan, commander of all French forces in North Africa, ended hostilities. Small pockets of resistance continued throughout the region until the middle of November. Originally, the plan specified that the Anglo-American forces were to quickly move eastward into Tunisia to capture the port city of Tunis, denying the Germans and Italians access to its seaport and airfields. However, with its forces spread out over 750 miles, with thousands of soldiers assigned to a variety of garrison and guard duties and an uncertainty of the loyalty of the French forces to their new allies, the movement into Tunisia did not occur. At the end of November, a small force consisting of one division moved into Tunisia. In early December another three divisions and a parachute brigade were sent as reinforcements. However, during the delay the Germans and Italians moved five new divisions into Tunisia through Tunis. As a result, the Allied advance stalled, resulting in a stalemate between opposing forces. Simultaneously with the reinforcement of German forces in the north, Rommel's Africa Corps moved into Tunisia from the east in response to the British Eighth Army's pursuit across Libya.

The intent was to catch Rommel between the hammer and anvil of American, British, and French forces driving east towards Tunis and Bizerte, with Montgomery pushing Rommel across Libya. The objective of Axis forces was to enable Rommel to utilize the coastal plain along Tunisia's eastern border with the sea. To achieve this, Axis forces would need to secure four passes in the eastern Dorsal mountains: Pichon and Fondouk in the north and Faid and Rebaou in the south. The Pichon pass

54 • GUEST OF ADOLF

was captured in December 1942, and, as Rommel moved into southern Tunisia, the desire to secure the remaining three passes precipitated what is referred to as the battle of Kasserine Pass.[15]

Among the additional American and British military units arriving in North Africa in early January 1943 was Technician Fifth Class Ernest Focht's 805th Tank Destroyer Battalion. It was organized in compliance with Table of Organization (T/O) 18–25 dated June 8, 1942, and commanded by LTC Allen Foreman. The battalion consisted of a headquarters and headquarters company with 14 officers and 155 enlisted soldiers, three tank destroyer companies (heavy) of five officers and 181 enlisted soldiers each, a reconnaissance company of six officers and 139 enlisted soldiers, and a medical detachment of three officers and 23 enlisted soldiers. The aggregate number of soldiers authorized in the battalion was 898, comprised of 38 officers and 860 enlisted soldiers. The individual soldier's weapon was a .30-caliber carbine, a .30-caliber rifle, or a .45-caliber pistol. The three tank destroyer companies were equipped with four self-propelled 75-mm anti-tank guns mounted on the M3 half-track, eight three-inch self-propelled anti-tank guns, six .30-caliber light machine guns, six self-propelled anti-aircraft guns mounted on the M3 half-track, and nine .50-caliber heavy barrel machine guns. The battalion departed England at less than full strength in both personnel and equipment.

On January 5, 1943, the 805th TD Battalion departed their assembly area in Shrivenham, England, moving toward the coast of Scotland where the entire battalion boarded the vessel *Monarch of Bermuda* along with 3,354 other soldiers. It was deploying with 39 officers and 662 enlisted soldiers or at only 74 percent of its authorized strength of 898 soldiers. The ship hoisted anchor on January 9, 1943, to join 18 other vessels comprising Convoy KMF.7 for the eight-day trip to Algeria. At first the convoy of 12 merchant/troopships and seven escort vessels[16] headed further into the North Atlantic to avoid the German U-boats before changing its course towards Gibraltar and the Mediterranean Sea. The convoy did experience "very stormy, rough seas. We listed very badly at times. Sometimes we were told that if we listed two more degrees, we would have capsized out in the North Atlantic. But we made it." Ernie was not a water person as he was repeatedly seasick on this voyage. During the voyage, he was promoted to sergeant, increased his allotment to his parents to $70.00, viewed the Rock of Gibraltar, and witnessed a formal sea burial of a member of the ship's crew (Map 4).

The *Monarch of Bermuda* docked in Algiers, Algeria, on January 17, 1943, and the 805th TD Battalion immediately moved into staging areas in the vicinity of El Biar and El Achour, which are approximately four miles west of Algiers, staying in an abandoned brickyard and schoolhouse where Ernie "had plenty of dates, tangerines, and also figs" to eat. The soldiers' first task, after settling into their quarters, was to restore their sidearms and equipment to proper working order due to some components exhibiting signs of corrosion. This occurred because equipment was not properly prepared for the journey. "In fact, a lot of it, the rust and stuff would get in the carburetors and rust the little floats. Which were brass. And as a result, the vehicle would start, and then as you go along a little bit, it would fill up with gasoline. In other words, it would settle down, shut off the flow, and as a result your vehicle would stop." By January 24, 1943, the equipment was ready and the armored and tracked vehicles were loaded

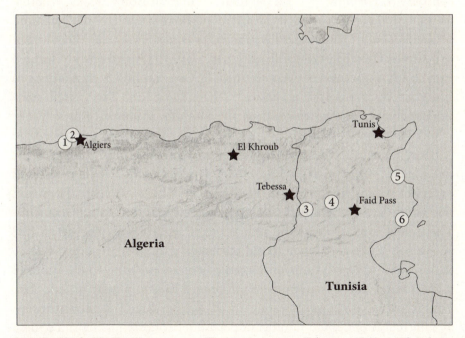

Map 5: 805th TD Bn Movement to Tunisia, January to February 1943. 1. El Achour, Algeria; 2. El Biar, Algeria; 3. Bou Chebka, Tunisia; 4. Sbeitla, Tunisia, 5. Sousse, Tunisia, and 6. Sfax, Tunisia. (Timothy M. Swartz. World Hillshade copyright © Esri)

on railcars for the journey to the front lines. Prior to leaving this area, Ernie "visited Algiers on an evening pass to take in a Red Cross program."

The next day the train departed for El Khroub, 252 miles east of Algiers, with Ernie among the unit's personnel riding with the equipment (Map 5). He was surprised by the climate and terrain as the train traveled across northern Algeria. "I always figured that there was a nice warm climate when you said you were in Africa, and it was all desert. But it wasn't. There were quite a few mountains in that area, believe me." Once the train arrived at its destination, the equipment was off-loaded and organized for a 147-mile road march to its bivouac site near Bou Chebka, Tunisia. This was completed between February 2 and February 6. On February 5 the convoy stopped for the night near Tebessa, sleeping in a wooded area. Upon waking up Ernie was surprised that the ground was covered in snow. "So, don't let anybody tell you that it doesn't snow in Africa. It wasn't much, but just enough, the ground was covered. It melted and was really messy until noon." In the early afternoon of February 6, the convoy drove the final 26 miles to Bou Chebka, where it set up its bivouac site to await the arrival of the remainder of the battalion.

Six days after Ernie began his journey to Tunisia, General Hans-Jürgen von Arnim launched the battle on January 30, 1943, and quickly secured Faid and Rebaou passes.[17] Always wary of German military intentions to attack the Allies in northern Tunisia to secure Bizerte and Tunis, intelligence led Eisenhower to shift forces from the southern mountain passes.[18]

On February 1, 1943, the advance party of the 805th departed for Tebessa, Algeria, for the purpose of preparing the battalion's next bivouac site. Finally, on February 7, 1943, the remainder of the battalion received orders to report for duty with II Corps at Tebessa, Algeria. However, this same day, 236 enlisted soldiers reported for duty as replacements. These new men brought the unit up to its authorized strength of 898 personnel (Table D). Their arrival presented a movement problem since the unit did not have sufficient organic vehicles on hand to transport all its personnel due to the previous shipment of equipment by rail. The issue was resolved by authorizing additional personnel to move forward by rail. It also presented significant personnel cohesion issues since these new soldiers represented 28 percent of the battalion's strength. They and the existing soldiers were personally unfamiliar with one another and

NORTH AFRICA 1942–43 (OPERATION *TORCH*) • 57

had not trained together. This unfamiliarity with one another could potentially lead to a serious breakdown during combat operations, particularly as the unit was moving to the front lines. The entire battalion was settled into their bivouac site near Bou Chebka by early evening on February 9. Within four hours Company B and a platoon of the reconnaissance company were ordered to report to Colonel Frederic Butler, the commanding officer of Allied Task Force Gafsa, Tunisia. This company assumed responsibility for protecting the Zannouch Station located approximately 20 miles east of Gafsa.

As the battalion arrived in Fériana, Tunisia, Ernie wrote these words to his parents on February 10, 1943, only a few days before entering combat and a week before he was captured.

> Dearest Mother & Father,
>
> Just a few lines to let you know I am fine & hope these lines find you all the same.
>
> I hope you are taking things easy & enjoying the new home. Think of you often & pray each night for you. Tell Vera & Wayne hello. I hope school is going OK & they are being good as well as—hello to all the rest.
>
> The picture of the Barnwells is swell. They are some boys. Tell them Uncle Ernie said hello & to be good boys.
>
> Have had swell weather in the day but plenty cold at night. Had a light snow last night but is all gone now.
>
> I haven't heard from you for about two weeks but pray God you are well.
>
> Received yesterday a couple Dec Heralds & the Dec issue of the Readers Digest which LaRue subscribed for me.
>
> Don't worry & remember me in your prayers. God be with you till we meet again.
>
> So Long
> Ernie

His parents received these encouraging and hopeful words after Ernie was a prisoner since the Army postal service did not postmark the letter until February 16, 1943.

These would be the last words Ernie's parents would hear from their son until April 1943.

That same day the remainder of the battalion moved to the vicinity of Fériana and was attached to the 26th Regimental Combat Team (RCT) of

58 • GUEST OF ADOLF

the 1st Infantry Division (ID) Division under Colonel Alexander N. Stark Jr. (Map 6). For the next three days elements of the 805th TD Battalion conducted numerous reconnaissance patrols along the Fériana–Gafsa and Gafsa–Sidi Bou Zid roads.[19] At this time Allied forces were in defensive positions along the eastern side of the Dorsal mountain range and were expecting a German attack. The defensive line extended from south to north beginning at the salt marshes below El Guettar, Meknassy, Faid, Pont du Fahs, Medjez el Bab, to Cap Serrat on the Mediterranean Sea. There were two German armies—General von Arnim's Fifth Army and Field Marshal Rommel's Africa Corps—preparing to launch another attack. The Africa Corps attacked from Gabes towards Gafsa, while the Fifth Army's offensive was aimed at Sidi Bou Zid and Sbeitla beginning on February 13, 1943.

Table D: Authorized and Assigned Personnel Strength, 805th Tank Destroyer Battalion, February 1, 1943★

	HQ	HQ Co	Co A	Co B	Co C	RCN	Med	Total
Officer Authorized	6	8	5	5	5	6	3	38
Officer Assigned	6	10	5	5	5	6	2	39
Enlisted Authorized	0	155	181	181	181	139	23	860
Enlisted Assigned	0	127	117	126	117	120	16	623

★This table illustrates the actual strength of the 805th TD Bn on February 1, 1943. The unit had a full complement of officers but was short 237 enlisted soldiers. (Note: RCN = Reconnaissance) (Sources: 805th TD Bn by name roster dated February 1, 1943, and Table of Organization 18–25 dated June 8, 1942)

This played directly into Germany's hands, and on February 14, 1943, amid a raging sandstorm, the Germans launched a major attack through Faid Pass to encircle the American 3d Battalion, 168th Infantry on Djebel Ksaira under Colonel Thomas D. Drake and Combat Command C under Colonel Robert I. Stack in the vicinity of Sbeitla and Sidi Bou Zid. During the German onslaught, Allied reactions were delayed and piecemeal. Lieutenant Colonel Louis Hightower, commanding 51 tanks, 12 tank destroyers, and two artillery battalions of the American 1st Armored Division, initiated a counterattack on February 14 to relieve pressure on Colonel Drake's forces on Djebel Ksaira and Lieutenant Colonel John K. Waters's elements of the 1st Armored Division on Djebel Lessouda (nine hundred troops, 15 tanks, a reconnaissance section, a tank-destroyer platoon, and a battery of 105-mm howitzers). Hightower's counterattack cost him all but seven of his tanks, and the continued German attack on Drake's forces resulted in the capture of an entire American reconnaissance company. At this point in the battle, all semblance of command and control disintegrated as German aircraft relentlessly attacked American positions and communications lines were cut.[20]

In response to the attack, more Allied forces moved to the immediate front lines along both axes of the German attack. On February 14, 1943, Company A and the Third Platoon of the reconnaissance company from the 805th TD Battalion were detached from the battalion and

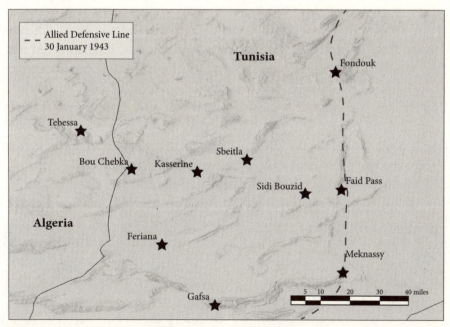

Map 6: Company A, 805th TD Bn, Movement to the Front, February 1943. (Timothy M. Swartz. World Hillshade copyright © Esri)

attached to the 1st Armored Division's Combat Command A (CCA) at Sbeitla under the command of Brigadier General Raymond McQuillin. Upon arriving the company received orders to immediately deploy to Djebel Hamra (Hill 673) with the 1st Battalion 6th Armored Infantry under the command of Colonel William Kern. This area later came to be known as "Kerns Crossroads" on the Sbeitla–Faid road. Colonel Kern then detached two platoons to support Colonel Drake and his 168th Infantry Regiment (-) command at Djebel Ksaira (Hill 560) and Garet Hadid (Hill 620), six miles south of the town of Faid (Map 7). Ernie's platoon was one of the two that reported to Colonel Drake.[21] The two positions were eight kilometers apart and not mutually supportive of each other, making them two isolated outposts. This situation was the result of the II Corps commander and his staff not understanding the area's terrain and their dictating the positioning of the units without consulting the commander of Combat Command Alpha.

Consequently, Ernie with his M3 half-track with a mounted 75-mm gun and 10-man crew was positioned on the extreme southern portion of the American front lines. As a sergeant he was the noncommissioned officer in charge of this 10-person gun crew. The crew consisted of an assistant non-commissioned officer in Corporal Thomas Banfield; two drivers, Roy Ringler and John Carter; two gunners, Richard Hild and Paul J. Mizwa; two assistant gunners, Bechingham and Freeze (Ernie's misspelling of the latter's real name, Cecil Freese); and two loaders, Everett and Miller. This weapon system was the Army's first attempt at an anti-tank weapon. They "moved closer to the front, took over from the 701st TD" and later in the day they experienced their first bombings. German "Stukas visits and first casualties of Co. [Company], 2LT Joseph Behm, PFC Stephen Pascavitch, and Metafe," Ernie recorded. The majority of the action on Monday, February 15, occurred as the Americans executed a counterattack on the German fortified position in Faid Pass. "We sent in fifty tanks and forty-five were knocked out," Ernie recalled. "We could see the Germans tanks shifting back and forth as artillery was going over our heads." During the next two days his platoon engaged German tanks as they began to execute a pincer movement to surround his position. By 3:30 p.m. on February 16, 1943, the units under Colonel Drake's command were the American front-line troops engaging the Germans, and they "withdrew to sand dunes to alternate positions." At 5:30 p.m. on February 16 all the American forces received orders to escape the encirclement and make their way to Djebel Hamra (Hill 673) eight kilometers away at Kerns Crossroads to rejoin American forces. During this movement, at "6:50 P.M. LT Corey [first name William, Platoon Leader, Company A, 805th TD Bn] gave the order to abandon equipment after passing through a terrible crossfire" and fall back westward eight to 10 miles in hopes of joining up with other American forces. The men then made their way down the slopes of the hill across ploughed fields and onto the open plain towards their destination taking with them "a few rations and personal belongings." After walking westward for most of the night through shifting sand Ernie and other members of his platoon bedded down for a few hours of rest in a cactus patch short of Kern's Crossroads and Djebel Hamara. During the night he could hear German voices in the distance and bombings. On the morning of February 17, it was "very bad for us, still very deep in German territory, saw our own equipment but in German hands."[22]

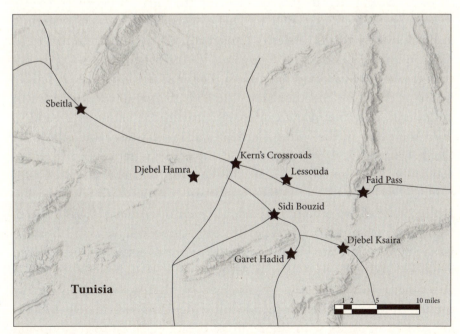

Map 7: Company A, 805th TD Bn, Area of Operations, February 15–17, 1943. (Timothy M. Swartz. World Hillshade copyright © Esri)

62 • GUEST OF ADOLF

Upon waking up, they realized they were right up against a German unit that responded quickly and captured the group of 45 American soldiers.[23] After taking these prisoners, "they went over there with their tanks and just riddled the place. Fired to make sure there was nobody hiding in there."[24]

Rather than press home their advantage, the Germans chose to wait for the inevitable American counterattack rather than conduct Blitzkrieg-style operations that had served them so well in France in the face of a demoralized opponent. Conversely, the Allied high command chose to have the preponderance of its forces continue its retreat westward towards the vital mountain passes in the western Dorsal passes while simultaneously rushing forces forward from Algeria and initiating limited counterattacks to keep the Germans off-balance. One such attack was led by Lieutenant Colonel James D. Alger's tank battalion of the 1st Armored Division to relieve pressure on the beleaguered defenders of Djebel Ksaira and Djebel Lessouda. Alger's attack resulted in him being captured, along with 313 other members of his command, and 50 of his tanks being destroyed.[25] During the night of February 15–16, orders were issued for the men on Djebel Ksaira and Lessouda to attempt to break out westward to Kern's Crossroads. Of the nine hundred or so men on Djebel Lessouda, roughly one-third reached Kern's Crossroads with the balance captured or missing. The men under Drake on Djebel Ksaira received the breakout order late and attempted such an endeavor in daylight, resulting in the capture of virtually the entire command.[26]

At this point in the battle, German–Italian relations came to a head. On February 16, 1943, Rommel completed his retreat across Libya and arrived at the Mareth Line. When the German Africa Corps deployed to Libya to soothe the embarrassment Mussolini felt in having Hitler come to his rescue, a nebulous chain of command was created. General Albert Kesselring was deployed to Rome to serve as the German liaison there, while the Italian Comando Supremo served as the ultimate decision-making body.[27] While American forces were being battered in southern Tunisia, instead of pushing towards Tebessa and potentially routing American forces, Comando Supremo demurred, thereby providing American forces with the requisite breathing space to regroup and prepare for Germany's inevitable continued advance westward.

At 7:00 a.m. on February 17, 1943, SGT Ernest V. Focht became a German POW along with 26 other soldiers from his and the reconnaissance platoon. This included Banfield, Everett, Hild, Mizwa, and Ringler from his gun crew. Before Ernie started his journey to a POW holding area, the Germans relieved him of his Thompson submachine gun and ammunition. Ernie retained his field bag, which made him "very happy" since it contained his "Bible, shaving kit, socks, underwear, [and] rations. "Was questioned by a German Officer," he wrote, "were treated swell." He was also permitted to retain his C-rations, D-bars, combat pants and jacket, field jacket, extra underwear, denims, hat, and shoes. The fact that he retained the Bible he received in 1926 at the age of 12 in Sunday school and LaRue's personal hygiene kit with its comb, medicine drops, ear cleaner, styptic pencil, and head brush really pleased him. Ernie compiled a more detailed accounting of these and additional items in his diary in April 1943. These are listed in Table E.

After being searched, he began to walk with his fellow POWs towards Faid Pass, Tunisia, where they "joined 1,000 more Yanks prisoners marching 15 miles until 8 PM halting for the night." In the morning they continued marching eastward towards the town of Sfax, which lies on the Mediterranean Sea. As empty German resupply vehicles passed by the column of marching POWs, they stopped to pick up a few of the prisoners. On February 19, Ernie reached Sfax, where he stayed in the area around an old school building for a couple of days. "And then they got us in groups and took us down to the train shed. We were given these luxurious, 40–8 Pullman cars" for a two-day trip traveling through Sousse and onward to the city of Tunis. He described the car as being crowded, with little room to sit down and a five-gallon bucket at the door to relieve oneself.

These cars received their names because they could carry 40 men or eight horses, as was clearly painted on each boxcar. During World War II, the "forty-and-eight" boxcars transported supplies and troops to the front, but they also returned to Germany with new cargoes. Many Allied prisoners of war rode to German POW camps in these boxcars—sometimes with as many as 90 men forced into each boxcar. Many POWs endured harsh conditions during their trips to POW camps, which sometimes included attacks from Allied aircraft.[28]

64 • GUEST OF ADOLF

Table E: Ernie's Clothing and Equipment When Captured on February 17, 1943

Combat pants	Combat jacket	Field jacket
One-piece denims	Wool undershirt	Two pairs of shorts
Hat	Two pairs of socks	Shoes
Scarf	Leggings	Razor
Blades	Comb	File
Head brush	Medicine drops	Ear cleaner
Cuticle shears	Mirror	Styptic pencil
Blade sharpener	Odor on a case [possibly roll-on deodorant]	Shaving brush
Case	Towel	Tray and soap
Toothbrushes	Tooth powder	Handkerchiefs
Sewing kit—Dean	Two spools thread	Salve

During this time, Ernie's fervent belief in a supreme being comforted him, and he comforted others. Each railcar only had two small windows high up on its sides through which passengers could look out at the countryside. The train made several stops during its journey northward, but the POWs were not permitted to exit the boxcars. The train arrived in Tunis the morning on Monday, February 22. After exiting the boxcars, the POWs were marched out of the city to an old racetrack, where Ernie slept in one of its abandoned horse stalls. Ernie was appreciative of the food he received: "While we were there we had some very delicious food. We got the meat right in with the beans and things." He was also thankful that he was able to attend a couple of church services conducted by the POWs. His stay in this holding area ended after eight days on the morning of March 2, 1943. He marched to the airport where, after the POWs unloaded a German Ju 52 trimotor transport aircraft, they boarded it for the flight to Capua, Italy, for internment in an Italian POW camp.

While Company A was engaged around Sidi Bou Zid, Company B reverted to battalion control near Fériana. The company assumed responsibility for conducting patrols in the area bounded by the Fériana–Gafsa and the Fériana–Sidi Bou Zid roads for the next two days. Company C was employed setting up defensive positions in the pass leading into the town of Fériana. When the battalion received the order to withdraw from the commander of the 26th RCT to Kasserine and report to the commander of the 19th Engineer Regiment, Company C failed to receive this order. This placed the company in an isolated position in front of the Allied lines. Consequently, the company was nearly surrounded and had to fight their way back to Kasserine. During this engagement, on February 17, the company ceased to be an effective fighting force, losing 75 soldiers and all 12 of its anti-tank guns.

By nightfall the battalion was collecting the remaining soldiers of A and C Companies into its assigned area west of Kasserine Pass astride the south fork of the road entering the pass. The Germans continued their attack, exploiting their initial success by driving towards the town of Kasserine. During February 18 through 22 the attack was pressed through Kasserine Pass and Fériana with the town of Tebessa being their objective. Meanwhile the 805th was defending its portion of the pass and initially stopped a German tank battalion attack. On February 20, it was ordered to report to the commander of the 26th Armored Brigade at Thala. During its withdrawal the battalion suffered the loss of additional personnel, guns, and equipment. The battalion's remnants remained in Thala for three days. The German advance ended two days later with their withdrawing to their original lines of departure beginning on February 23. At this time what was left of the 805th TD Battalion was removed from the line and sent 158 kilometers to the rear at Aïn Beïda, Algeria, for reorganization and rehabilitation. The battalion's effectiveness was destroyed during the seven-day period of February 12 through 19. In this period, it lost 224 soldiers (11 killed in action, 45 wounded in action, and 168 captured),[29] the majority of its vehicles, and all but four of its 44 anti-tank guns.

On February 18, Rommel was granted permission to attempt a lightning dash; however, von Arnim's forces were not to participate in concert. While the Axis was suffering from indecision and division within the command, the Allied command found its backbone, and General Harold Alexander, visiting the front lines, assumed command two days ahead of schedule and resolved to develop strong defensive positions within the western Dorsal mountains; the withdrawal would go no further. When German reconnaissance elements probed the western Dorsal passes on February 18, they were met in strength by elements of Combat Command A of the American 1st Armored Division, remnants of a French division, the British Derbyshire Yeomanry, and remnants of an American infantry battalion, an American ranger battalion, and parts of Combat Command B of the American 1st Armored Division. When the Germans sent in panzer grenadiers, British and American reinforcements drove them back. Rommel's ensuing reconnaissance left him impressed with Allied strength, forcing him to look for another avenue.[30]

On February 20 Rommel, becoming increasingly unnerved because General Montgomery had that day attacked his defensive positions on the Mareth Line in southern Tunisia, sought a decisive, lightning-quick victory. Due to lack of coordination with von Arnim, battle-weary Africa Corps elements, ineptitude of the Italian Centauro division, and the defensive resolve of British and American defenders, Rommel was forced to accept the inevitability of events, and on February 22 Rommel called off his planned attack due to his assessment that victory was not possible before Montgomery attacked the Mareth Line in strength. It was not for another 48 hours that Allied forces truly recognized that the Germans had withdrawn.[31]

While at Aïn Beïda some of the battalion's equipment loses were addressed, and 206 replacements—seven officers and 199 enlisted soldiers—joined the unit between March 2 and 10. On March 17, the battalion again moved forward, first to Fériana, then to Sbeitla, Gafsa, and El Guettar. Its assignments were to provide secondary defense against an attack at various headquarters and road junctions, establish roadblocks, and conduct mine removal operations. This pattern continued for the remainder of the North African campaign with the battalion moving between Sened Station, Gafsa, Sbeitla, Bou Chebka, Sidi Bou Zid, and finally five miles south of Faid. On April 3, another officer and 45 enlisted replacements reported for duty with the battalion. Beginning on April 12, 1943, the battalion moved back to Bou Chebka and then moved an additional three times before ending up in the vicinity of Bizerte on May 29, 1943. During this two-and-a-half-month period the battalion reported to eight different senior headquarters—1st TD Group, 894 TD Bn, Commanding General (CG), II Corps Artillery, 1st Armored Division, Force Commander II Corps, Commander 1st Ranger Battalion, and CG CCA 1st Armored Division—before being assigned to the 34th Infantry Division on May 18, 1943. The Allies concluded the North African campaign on May 13, 1943, with the surrender of several hundred thousand German and Italian soldiers.

CHAPTER 5

Sicily, Italy, and Moosburg, Germany

Ernie and the other POWs aboard the German Ju 52 transport plane settled in for the flight to Naples, Italy. However, the flight altered its course due to the Allied bombing of cities on the west coast of Italy. Instead, the plane landed at Palermo, Sicily, "at 11:15 A.M. and the POW Camp at 5:00 P.M." on March 2, 1943. Once on the ground, the prisoners were taken to an Italian *prigioniero di guerra* (prisoner of war) camp, PG 98 San Giuseppe Jato.[1] The camp was located outside of the village of San Giuseppe Jato in the hilly region approximately 19 miles southwest of Palermo (Map 8). It was a transitional camp with the prisoners staying no longer than 40 days before being moved to another Italian POW camp. It had no permanent buildings or facilities in which to house or feed the prisoners. Ernie arrived at this camp, after being searched, having 1,300 francs taken by a guard, and having "the pleasure of standing out stark naked to get [his] clothes deloused." He recalled: "It was pleasant to get, if we had any, any unfriendly guests in our clothing, to get rid of them." Later that evening he was able to write the following postcard to LaRue:

> Darling,
> Am well and safe. God is with me. Don't worry. Send box, 5lbs, via Red Cross. Ever in my thoughts. Say Hello to all. Hope you are well. Pray for me. Always, Ernie

Through these brief words Ernie expresses his positive attitude and optimism concerning his first fifteen days of captivity through the Red Cross. This short note was the first of what was to be hundreds he would write

70 • GUEST OF ADOLF

during the next 27 months. He habitually wrote to his parents and his fiancée, LaRue, while in England, North Africa, and as a prisoner of war in Italy and Germany. He recorded every letter he mailed and every letter he received in his diaries. Unfortunately, those to whom he wrote kept only eight of his letters while he saved nearly 70 of the letters he received. Most of these saved letters were from LaRue.

Ernie and the other POWs lived in tents and often slept outside under the stars. The Italians provided each prisoner with a large blanket for warmth. However, in Ernie's case, "if you covered up your feet, your head was stickin' out, and if you covered up your head, your feet was stickin' out." So, he slept in his clothes and used the blanket for extra warmth. The Italians had a heavy contingent of guards always watching the POWs. The guards would sing periodically throughout the night, which kept many of the POWs from getting a good night's rest. During the day, they were expected to work on the construction of a road into the camp. Ernie participated in this task by "carrying stones and waded [*sic*, wadded] mud" down from the mountain to the new roadbed. Although he worked most of the day on this project, he ate better in this camp than he had eaten since being captured. Still, he complained of not having enough to eat. His rations consisted of bread, some cheese, and a hearty soup. For his first experience in a regular POW camp, Ernie expressed his belief that he was treated well.

On Sundays the Italians permitted the prisoners to conduct church services and have a relaxing day. A number of the prisoners had relatives living in the area and somehow, they were able to make contact with them. This led to an interesting experience where the relatives appeared at the camp for a visit bringing additional food for a regular Sunday feast. It was through these visits that information was passed along to the prisoners concerning the conduct of the North African campaign. Ernie was pleased when the Red Cross came to the camp to register the POWs. A Red Cross representative spoke to each prisoner, recording his personal information to include name, hometown, nationality, branch of service, and unit. Once registered, Ernie emitted a huge sigh of relief, for now the fact that he was a POW would become known to the United States military and to his parents back home in Tyrone, Pennsylvania.

He believed because of what he knew of the Geneva Convention that neither the Italians nor the Germans would be able to simply kill him or make him disappear on a farm or in a factory.

On his 22nd day, March 23, 1943, at the San Giuseppe Jato camp, Ernie and a large group of POWs boarded a regular railroad passenger car for the trip to Messina, on the eastern coast of Sicily, arriving around 2:00 p.m. the next day. While waiting for a ferry transport across the Strait of Messina to Villa San Giovanni (Saint John's) in the province of Reggio di Calabria, Italy, he experienced multiple Allied air raids. These raids left parts of the rail yard and surrounding area in flames. One air raid siren wailed when a ferry transporting gasoline and other supplies had just pulled into the port and tied up at the dock. Ernie and the other POWs were standing near the dock waiting to board the ferry. They all scurried for shelter among the dock piers and piles of rubble

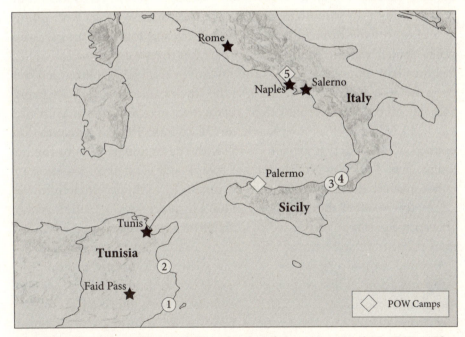

Map 8: POW Camps—Tunisia, Sicily, and Italy, February 17 to April 12, 1943. 1. Sfax, Tunisia; 2. Sousse, Tunisia; 3: Messina, Sicily; 4. St. Johns (Villa San Giovanni), Italy; 5. Capua, Italy. (Timothy M. Swartz. World Hillshade copyright © Esri)

72 • GUEST OF ADOLF

while "the Yanks visited, presented us with bombs, us in the middle of affair, nobody hurt" beyond a few bruises and cuts from taking cover. Eventually, the ferry was unloaded, and Ernie boarded it with the other POWs for the trip across the strait by 5:00 p.m.

Upon Ernie's arrival in Saint John's an hour later, the air raid sirens sounded again. This time there was a large culvert that served as the POWs' air raid shelter. Ernie remained in the shelter through multiple air raids until 11:00 p.m. on March 25. The POWs were gathered and marched to the rail yard, where a passenger train was waiting for the group to board. Ernie was pleased that he was not in another forty-and-eight boxcar but in a regular passenger train with separate compartments. "It was a beautiful car, railroad coach with compartment for six men and two guards for each compartment." When the guards fell asleep that night the prisoners disassembled their guns, removing and discarding the firing pins. The train hugged the western coast of Italy for most of the trip, passing Pompeii and Mount Vesuvius. "It was really beautiful going through the mountainous areas there, repeatedly, as we were going in and out of the tunnel. You could sit there and look out and see the water, which was the Mediterranean Sea, on the west. We had to really feel they had something nice." When the train reached Naples, it left the coast for 30 kilometers (19 miles) to the town of Capua (Map 8). Ernie and the other POWs exited their railcar and marched the mile to the Italian POW camp PG 66 at Capua on March 26, 1943. The camp was opened in 1941 as a transient camp, with the prisoners staying for no longer than 30 days with 20 men per tent. It was located on a section of raised ground along a bend in the Volturno River approximately three kilometers west of the town of Capua. However, when Ernie's group arrived at the camp it consisted of both barracks and tents in which more than 6,200 men were housed.

British Commonwealth prisoners were the predominant group in the camp and were "a fine bunch of chaps." They had established order and routines in the camp, which the Americans were expected to follow. The normal issue of camp rations consisted of a small piece of bread accompanied by a soup, which was mostly water with some rice added. Fortunately, Ernie received his first Red Cross parcel (RCP), a British parcel, on March 26 to supplement his camp rations. One of the parcel items was a pudding or cake, which was a very rich food. He "had to be very cautious, after not having rich food for a long period of time. In fact, we became ill over it." Ernie's love of sweets initially resulted in some minor health concerns until he learned to eat this pudding in moderation. Not long after arriving at the camp, he was able to get his first good warm bath since being captured over a month previously.

Near the end of March 1943, a Roman Catholic priest presented Ernie with a small 1943 monthly devotional book published by the Vatican Polyglot Press. It contained a message to the prisoners of war from Pope Pius XII, monthly calendars and spiritual messages, numerous hymns, and blank pages. It is on these pages that he began to record his daily activities, the weather, and comments on his health beginning on January 5, 1943. Ernie continued to make daily notes until the day he arrived back in Tyrone, Pennsylvania, on June 15, 1945. Over time he expanded what he recorded to include the names of his POW pals, the contents of RCPs, his daily schedule, his belongings and equipment, and poems composed by fellow POWs. An assortment of these items is included in Appendix 2.

On March 28 Ernie was able to send a telegram via the Vatican to his parents notifying them that he was a POW and in Italy. In a letter to LaRue on March 31, 1943, he writes:

> Darling,
> It is now mid afternoon of a fair day. The weather has been fair. I hope these few lines find you in the best of health. As for myself I am well & O.K. The time seems to be flying around quite fast. Stiner & a lot of the other boys are here. I don't know where Bill & Gregg are they weren't with me when captured. Have received several Red Cross Boxes & what a treat. Just like Christmas morning. One per week. You may send a ten-pound package via Red Cross. Inquire about the same. This happens to be bro Dean's birthday. Don't worry. You are ever in my thoughts & prayers. I miss you very much. Love, Ernie

In spite of being a POW for over six weeks, working on constructing a road near Palermo, Sicily, and surviving multiple Allied bombings before and after crossing the Strait of Messina, Ernie maintained a positive attitude, which came through in his written words. His request that LaRue send him additional foodstuffs via the Red Cross indicates that he fully expected to remain at the Capua POW camp.

74 • GUEST OF ADOLF

Ernie's method for dealing with his emotions was through his participation in various camp-sponsored activities and reading and rereading LaRue's letters. He also focused on his love of and trust in God through daily devotions, attending Sunday church services, and attending a weeknight prayer service. The choir was another activity that diverted his mind from the daily drudgery of POW life. In addition to singing at Sunday services, the choir performed concerts and was an integral part of the many camp shows performed by the POWs. However, despite these diversions, Ernie most cherished the receipt of mail and the ability to write a letter to his parents or to LaRue Cassidy. The Italians and the Germans limited the prisoners' opportunity to write home to one day a week. This was normally on a Sunday and only if there were not any problems or issues in the POW camp during the week. Ernie commented on not receiving paper to write a letter: "Again for 2nd week get no forms to write home due to an incident in camp. Very unhappy about it too." He received either a 3.75-by-5-inch postcard or a 5.5-by-10-inch letter template with 23 lines on one side on which the prisoners could write a letter to someone. Ernie always took advantage of these opportunities, principally writing to LaRue. His first postcard to LaRue was written from the Italian POW camp near Palermo, Sicily, during the first two weeks of March 1943. On March 31, 1943, he wrote his first letter to her from the Italian POW camp at Capua, Italy. LaRue did not receive either of these notes until August 1943, five months into his captivity. As she was reading his words, the Allies had concluded the invasion of Sicily.

The harbor at Naples was a frequent Allied bombing target since German and Italian ships were continuously loading and off-loading supplies. The bombings continued daily, with the Americans making the runs during daylight and the British conducting the evening bombing runs. "Of course we were really enthused, which was a terrible thing in a way too, when our bombers would come over at night and bomb the places, particularly around Naples." Ernie remained aware of the bombing damage of the Naples harbor due to firsthand reports from the POWs returning from daily work details to repair bomb damage. It is here that he began using the word "termites" to designate Allied bombing raids. He assumed the Allies were aware of the camp's location and were cautious not to bomb near it. His daily routine consisted of prayer and devotions along with writing in his diary and attending Sunday church services. His last Sunday service in Italy on April 11 continued throughout the "afternoon and evening with group singing old fashioned hymns." The routine at PG 66 Capua abruptly ended after 16 days on April 12, 1943, when Ernie started on another journey, one that would take him into Germany.

In anticipation of the impending transfer to another location, Ernie and other American POWs were issued RCPs and loaded into forty-and-eight boxcars modified with benches for seating. As they boarded the railcar, "there was always a crowd of people around for some reason. And they would flash you the 'V' for victory sign," bidding the POWs farewell and sending good wishes. This amazed Ernie in that although he was the enemy here, the Italians were in their own way cheering the POWs. These cars had only a small window at one end, and it was covered with barbed wire. The POWs were aware that their next destination was a camp near Munich, Germany. Throughout the next three days the train passed the Italian cities of Itri, Rome, and Bologna, continuing through northern Italy and Innsbruck, Austria. While on the train Ernie would occasionally be able to look through the open window at the countryside. "Things were really beautiful as far as I was concerned. You tried to observe anything you could around you, because this was one trip in a lifetime." He noticed that the POW cars were mixed in as part of a much larger freight train. This gave him pause to wonder if the cars were well marked as carrying POWs so the Allied aircraft would not attack the train. In addition to the RCP, he "had some German bread, some fresh and 1938 bread and corn willy" to eat during the trip. "1938 bread" refers to the fact that the bread was from 1938, and thus was five years old, but it was well preserved and had a protective covering. When the train arrived in Innsbruck, Austria, at 6:00 a.m. the POWs were permitted to exit their boxcar for 30 minutes to an hour to stretch and relieve themselves. Afterwards as the ride continued, Ernie saw "snow tip mountains on all sides, witnessed many beautiful sights, saw ski jumps and much farm lands." In the late afternoon of April 14 the train briefly stopped in Munich, Germany, to reorganize the railcars, separating the freight and the POW cars. During this period, Ernie was able to see the previous night's bombing raid destruction with buildings still smoldering throughout the city. The last leg of this journey was to the town of Moosburg an der Isar, 60 kilometers (36 miles) northeast of Munich. After exiting the boxcars at 5:30 p.m., they were marched the last mile to the main gate of Stalag VIIA (Map 9).

This POW camp was constructed in September 1939 and welcomed its original group of ten thousand prisoners the following month. It was located north of the town of Moosburg between the Isar and Amper Rivers on an 85-acre flat plain. Until the summer of 1940 the majority of prisoners were housed in tents until wooden barracks were constructed. The camp was divided into three main compounds: north, south, and main. The Nordlager (north compound) was the reception area for all incoming POWs. They stayed here for 48 hours being searched, deloused, and undergoing a medical exam before being sent to one of the two remaining compounds. The Südlager

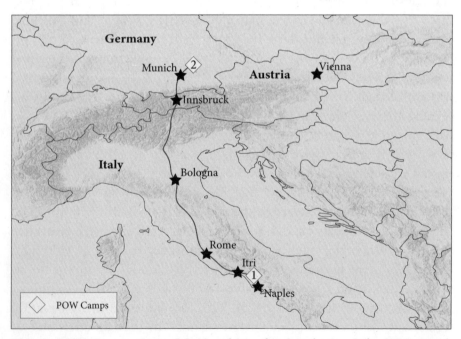

Map 9: POW Camps—Capua PG 98 and Moosburg an der Isar Stalag VIIA, March 26 to May 4, 1943. 1. Capua, Italy (arrived March 26, 1943); 2. Moosburg an der Isar (arrived April 14, 1943). (Timothy M. Swartz. World Hillshade copyright © Esri)

(south compound) housed the Russian prisoners, while the Hauptlager (main compound) lodged prisoners from all the other nations at war with Germany. These included France, Britain, Belgium, Poland, southeast Europe, British Commonwealth countries, and the United States. The Hauptlager was divided so that each of these different nationalities was confined to a separate area. The wooden barracks were designed to hold 180 prisoners in two sections divided by a central room used for washing and eating. However, as the number of POWs increased to more than ten thousand, a third bunk was added to the existing bunk beds. Eventually, four hundred prisoners were housed in each barracks. The Geneva Convention permitted belligerents to assign prisoners to work details in agriculture and industries producing non-war material. The Germans took advantage of this provision, and at Stalag VIIA there were 83 work detachments between Munich, Augsburg, and Landschut.

Since Stalag VIIA was both a transient and a permanent camp, Ernie's group was immediately assigned to the Nordlager compound for initial in-processing. His processing into the German POW system included undergoing another search, being fingerprinted, having his picture taken, and being issued an identification number. In addition to being registered by the Germans, he also registered again with the Red Cross. This was an important step, for now there existed an official non-German record of his being a POW and of his current location. This action made it difficult for the Germans to disavow his POW status and his current location. After completing his in-processing he was assigned to Barracks 3 in the Hauptlager compound along with two hundred others. The next morning, on April 15, 1943, Ernie celebrated two years of Army service. "Up at 6:45 A.M. Issued first American Red Cross Parcel, sure swell. Shaving kits issued razor, cream, brush, soap, tray, toothbrush, paste, sewing kit, comb case (a real Christmas). Thought plenty about home and what happened 2 years ago."

The RCPs were to become a main food source for him and the other POWs during the remainder of their captivity. Some of the items included were Prem (canned meat similar to Spam), liver paste, corn beef, biscuits, Velveeta cheese, a soluble coffee, dried soup powder, salmon, jam, peanut butter, and three to five packs of cigarettes. Occasionally, the parcel would contain a dried soup powder, which he would mix with

78 • GUEST OF ADOLF

hot water or heat up using one of the POWs' homemade stoves to create a liquid soup, which he found to be very nutritional. Some parcels also contained concentrated milk. He "could either mix it up as a drink or mix it up with some sugar and then some chocolate and call it an icing or make it and call it a milkshake or however you wanted to do it." He used the icing as a topping for either the biscuits or cakes contained in the parcels. He received another RCP the next day and commented: "Plenty to eat now, stomach sore getting stretched, hunger for sweets, getting satisfied, cheese and potatoes for breakfast. Letter to Ma-Pa, Still have the Faith, Jim Cunningham eating with me."

Ernie did not smoke, but he faithfully hoarded the cigarettes he received with every RCP throughout his time as a POW. He quickly learned that "they were used as money in Germany. You could trade them off for extra bread, potatoes, onions" from guards, locals, and prisoners of all nationalities. For example, he was able to purchase a loaf of bread and extra potatoes and onions for a couple of cigarettes. As the number of cigarettes available for trading increased, the price for all items increased proportionally. Initially a loaf of bread could be purchased from a German guard for three cigarettes, but the price quickly rose to a full pack of cigarettes, which was 10, 12, or 16 depending on which numbered RCP the soldier received. The Germans preferred American cigarettes to their own brand because they contained much more tobacco and lasted longer.

Ernie found this camp to be well organized, and the POWs were able to participate in many organized activities. There was a band with instruments provided by the Young Men's Christian Association (YMCA), baseball and soccer teams, and a glee club. Early on he was able to send cards home to his parents and to LaRue Cassidy. Before Ernie's parents received his postcard, they learned of his whereabouts through numerous notes, letters, and postcards sent from scores of shortwave radio listeners (SWL). The Germans broadcast many notes from prisoners, and one of these was Ernie's postcard to his parents. Ham radio operators and SWLs throughout the United States heard these German broadcasts. They meticulously copied the messages and sent his parents either a postcard or a letter with his message. Ernie's parents received more than 45 postcards and letters from all over the United States with his message from April 24, 1943, from Stalag VIIA. A Mrs. H. B. Loomis of Texarkana, Arkansas, sent the following message to Ernie's parents on April 25, 1943.[2]

> Dear People,
>   I heard the following message relayed to you over shortwave from Berlin Saturday night. "Dearest All, I have arrived safely from Italy, am now in Bavaria. The scenery is beautiful. Say hello to Paul and Louise. Love, Ernest"
>   Ernest was one of a trainload of Americans captured in Tunisia and taken to Germany. Perhaps you know all of this, but I hope this card gives you added assurance of Ernest's safety.
>   Yours truly,
>   Mrs. Loomis

Throughout his time at Stalag VIIA Ernie regularly received a hot shower and was frequently deloused. He attended religious services every Sunday conducted by an English chaplain. Ernie was surprised that he was selected to attend a concert in Munich on April 17. He did receive an issue of clothing, including long johns, a British overcoat, a shirt, socks, handkerchiefs, and a pair of wooden shoes. Ernie and the other prisoners were responsible for doing laundry and preparing their own food. The Germans provided chicory coffee and maybe a biscuit for breakfast. "[For dinner] we'd usually have a soup which was mostly broth, which consisted of some rutabagas. You never got enough of it. It was mostly broth and it wasn't long until you were hungry again."

For supper Ernie received three small potatoes, sometimes a piece of meat, and two or three slices of bread with maybe some sugar, syrup, or a little butter on the bread. Occasionally on a Sunday the supper meal might include a piece of cheese, usually full of maggots the POWs tried to pick out before either eating the remaining cheese or throwing it away. Ernie considered these rations to be totally unsatisfactory since he was always hungry. Ernie was especially happy whenever he had an RCP since this provided most of his daily food ration. On Easter Sunday, April 25, 1943, he writes: "Communion Service 10:00 A.M., very fine crowd, English Chaplin, St. Luke Chap 24 (letter to LaRue), Sure would like to be home but the Lord is very near today. Supper fish, potato, bread, butter, salt, pudding, lemon drink. 2:30 P.M. church service by Englishman, fine songs, soccer game by French & Czechs." The majority of this meal consisted of items from an RCP and not what the Germans provided to the POWs. A few days later his meals consisted of "milk and biscuit soup also coffee for breakfast ... corn and potato soup for lunch ... potatoes, bacon, coffee for dinner." His diary entries continue to feature his meals and daily routine and include various listings of his equipment, poems he copied, and prison pals. Ernie included the following Stalag VIIA daily POW schedule in his diary.

Prisoner of War's Day

6:00 a.m.	Get up
6:15 a.m.	Issued Coffee
7:00 a.m.	Count—Roll Call
9:00 a.m.	Calenthics [Calisthenics]
9:45 a.m.	Free Time
10:00 a.m.	Exercise
10:45 a.m.	Free Time
11:30 a.m.	Dinner
12:00–3:00 p.m.	Free Time
3:00 p.m.	Games
5:00 p.m.	Supper
6:30 p.m.	Count—Roll Call
10:00 p.m.	Lights Out

Stalag VIIA had numerous compounds where prisoners from different nationalities were housed separately. One day the guards sent a dog into the Indian compound. However, the dog never returned. Ernie figured that it must have been good eating. This was the last time a dog was sent into this compound. The men were responsible for providing their own personal security and accomplished this by banding together in small groups with one or two men performing the night watch duties. Ernie's time at his camp came to an end the morning of May 4, 1943, when the POWs were organized into groups of one hundred. He gathered his belongings, underwent another search, was issued a ration of bread, and then was loaded into the good old forty-and-eight railcar for the journey to another stalag (Map 10).

During this trip the train stopped often because it did not have the signal to proceed or at a Red Cross station where he was given "hot pea soup or something to warm you up a little bit." As the train continued its journey, Ernie and many of the other POWs expressed their concerns that the Allies might bomb it. The tops of the railcars were to have had a red cross painted on them. However, Ernie never saw a single painted red cross. The train passed through Gaschwitz, Leipzig, and Reisa as it proceeded east. When the train finally reached its destination on May 6 after a 435-mile trip Ernie learned he was now at Stalag IIIB, Fürstenberg, Germany, where the Oder River and Oder Canal came together at the German–Polish border. In 1950 Fürstenberg was renamed after Joseph Stalin as Stalinstadt and later in 1961 during the Soviet Union de-Stalinization period it became Eisenhüttenstadt.

CHAPTER 6

Stalag IIIB Fürstenburg

At 6 a.m. on the morning of May 6, 1943, Ernie walked out of the forty-and-eight railroad car and marched the two miles through Fürstenberg to Stalag IIIB. The camp was 870 yards square with the fences topped by triple-strand barbed wire with separate compounds for American, French, Italian, Serbian, Croatian, and Russian prisoners. The dimensions of the American compound were 100 by 670 yards. It initially consisted of six barracks of 300 POWs each but eventually increased to 12 barracks of 450 men. Each barracks consisted of two sleeping areas separated by a communal lavatory and a small room that was used as a kitchen.[1] The Oder–Spree Canal formed the rear boundary of the camp, which made the camp constantly damp. In the winter the canal frequently froze over, making the air around the camp even colder and damper. The number of Italians in the camp increased significantly after Italy surrendered to the Allies on September 9, 1943. The Italian military was given a choice to continue fighting for the Germans or to become POWs. Ninety-four thousand elected to fight for the Germans while between 650,000 and 710,000 became POWs. In 1944 these POWs were reclassified as military internees, enabling the Germans to use these men as forced laborers in the armament industries.[2] On September 12, 1943, more than seven thousand Italian POWs and civilians arrived at Stalag IIIB. This stalag served as a transient camp for the Italians. Shortly after their arrival they were sent out to various work sites.

After walking through the main gate, Ernie went through the typical in-processing: "deloused, shower, typhus shot, vaccinated and as usual

84 • GUEST OF ADOLF

searched losing First Aid packet, clipped hair and billeted in groups of 200." Initially assigned to Barracks 12 for a week, he moved to Barracks 10 for the second week before finally moving into Barracks 15 on May 22. He remained in this barracks for the remainder of his time at Stalag IIIB except for 12 days while in the hospital and four days living in Barracks 9. The barracks were "nothing more than a concrete floor laid and a very cheap building put up, with just a shell of brick on the outside and a small furring strip and fiberboard on the inside." They were also poorly heated since the Germans provided "a few measly lumps of coal a day" for the barrack's stoves. "The only heat within the building was what came off of each man." On his second day, Ernie wrote: "Still trusting God. Run across old pals who left Tunis right before us. Also, Potter and J. Lewis" from the unit. On the morning of May 16 there was "a visitor, everybody dressed for morning count, 4:30 conducted church service with silent meditation for the boys who finished the African Campaign."

Ernie was elected a barracks leader or confidence man for the 245 men in Barracks 15 in July 1943. In this position he met with the camp's American leadership to discuss conditions in the camp. "You tried to have some type of organization so you could get together and talk about things and problems." He was also responsible for the accountability of all POWs assigned to the barracks, creating and enforcing duty rosters, and maintaining order. Any German guard entering the barracks would speak to Ernie through an interpreter, announcing that showers were available for the barracks or giving instructions for the POWs to fall out for roll call or vacate the barracks so the Germans could conduct a search for contraband. When another POW assumed this position in September 1943, Ernie was thrilled with handing over these responsibilities: "No more billet leader, great relief. Just one of them now." In October 1943 the Germans were pressing the noncommissioned officers, especially the sergeants, to volunteer as commandos. This is an Americanized word for the German *Arbeitskommandos* or working detachments. The Geneva Convention permitted POWs below the rank of sergeant to be employed in a variety of nonmilitary tasks. These included coal mining, agricultural work, quarrying, factory work, road repair, manufacturing, and vineyard work. Tens of thousands of POWs were sent to various work sites throughout the region around every POW camp.[3]

At one of these special commando recruitment formations in mid–September 1943 he commented, "Formation to get Commandos out. Still trying to force NCOs out which according to the Geneva Convention is not permitted … News good, Ger [Germans] succeeded in forcing them out after dinner." His awareness that this tactic was a violation of the Geneva Convention led him to go to the camp leadership and complain of this German practice. It wasn't long after this complaint that the Germans discontinued their efforts to get the NCOs to volunteer as commandos. He also reported to the German guard, Unteroffizer (Corporal) Schmidt, assigned to his barracks, with whom he had a good relationship. He and the guard conversed most days through an interpreter. At Christmastime 1943, Ernie took up a collection from the POWs in his barracks for Unteroffizer Schmidt.

The daily life of a POW can be a lonely and monotonous one that often leads to a feeling of abandonment and then to depression. One of Ernie's earliest recorded expressions of loneliness appears in his diary after only five months as a POW. He writes: "Oh! <u>Darling</u> you seem so near if we could only be together. Life at times seems so unfair. I pray this is over soon." He expresses these feelings again on a day in December 1943 when he received a number of letters from home: "Sure glad to receive them. Been in such a____humor and I don't mean maybe. Why I don't know? I do know I long for you Darling. At this date almost 1 year-half is a long time to be separated from the one you 'Love'—Loved ones. I pray God for help. It is so hard." As 1943 came to an end he again wrote of his loneliness: "Almost 11 mos P.O.W. As a whole I can't say much for the year. The Lord has cared for me but how discusted [sic] I've been. I wonder how many more days I'll spend as P.O.W. Some time it is no wonder a fellow would lose faith???" Later in April 1944 he again expressed his loneliness and despair: "Heart aching longing for home. Has been terrible past week as if can't stand it. Times certainly trying, seem deserted. Wonder at Life, because to me this life. It____. At least nothing to be proud of. No matter how hard one tries one can stand so much. After that____?"

86 • GUEST OF ADOLF

The POWs kept up with news from the outside through a clandestine radio that was hidden underneath the floor of Ernie's barracks. "A hole was knocked through the concrete floor, the sand ... thank God it was sand and not heavy dirt ... was dug out during the night and carried outside and scattered over the other sand within the compound." The men carried it out on their evening strolls and mixed it into the compound sand as they walked. They listened to British Broadcasting Corporation (BBC) nightly to keep current with the war's progress. "It really worked very, very well. You could always pick up on the latest news and just knew where we were, where the invasion was, all that stuff. It was really ideal." Unfortunately, several of the POWs talked about the radio and its location, and the Germans overheard their loose talk. The Germans evacuated the barracks for a couple of days while they cemented the hole shut. However, there was a second radio in the camp that continued to provide information. This one was a roving radio. The POWs established a watch system that would send out an alert any time a German entered the compound and the radio "was moved from building to building." In this manner the radio remained concealed from the Germans for the remainder of Ernie's time at this stalag. Another way the POWs received news was through the German newspapers that were provided daily. There were many fellows who were fluent in the German language. They interpreted the newspapers, providing a daily synopsis. Of course, according to the German papers, they were not losing but making "strategic withdrawals."

Since Stalag IIIB was considered a permanent camp, the POWs turned it into a miniature American town. Over time they constructed a theater and a chapel with materials supplied by the Germans, salvaged from the RCP shipments, or purchased using cigarettes from the guards. In October 1943 Ernie wrote: "[The theater] has progressed. Just got our stage curtin [sic], lights, painting up. Really is nice now. Takes a long time to get anything done here. Everything on permission from Germans." The theater included a revolving stage that could be turned around to reveal another set of performers. The bearings for the stage were greased using margarine from the RCPs. Ernie assisted with building the Chapel and decorating it for special occasions and holidays.

Regarding a Sunday service in September 1943 he observed: "Church looked very nice, newly painted pictures, fresh flowers and the presence of the Lord." Early on he joined the glee club that rehearsed two or three times each week. He often commented on the rehearsals and how the singing of a particular number was progressing. In early November 1943 they began to practice the "Hallelujah" chorus. His initial remarks were: "a stiff number but beautiful" and "coming along nicely so far." The glee club typically presented a special musical number, cantata, or oratorio at Sunday service. Ernie rarely missed attending these rehearsals and Sunday services even though "all service censored & Germans present. But the Lord is just the same." Occasionally, he participated in conducting the service to include singing a duet with Sergeant Dick Gray of "Take Up Thy Cross and Follow Me" on November 7, 1943. Sergeant Gray, a fellow Company A, 805th TD Battalion member, was one of two POWs who assumed the role of lay Protestant minister for the camp. Ernie recorded in his diary when he assisted with the serving of Communion. He also related his providing Sergeant Russ Boettcher, the second lay minister, with the outline for a sermon he delivered at the Palermo camp titled "Life of Solomon."

In his diaries, Ernie recorded many of the songs the glee club sang. These included "Ode to Peace," "Hallelujah" chorus, various Christmas carols, "Maccabeus," "Sanctus," "Lead Kindly Light," "Behold God the Lord," "Camptown Races," and "American Suite." On Christmas Eve the glee club visited each billet and the guard post singing a variety of Christmas carols to their fellow POWs. In addition to Sunday services, Ernie participated in regular Bible discussions, Thursday evening prayer meetings, and daily devotions. His standard message concerning these activities ran as follows: "Still have trust in God that this will end soon and let me return home to be with you Alwa–ys Dear."

The glee club afforded Ernie the opportunity to leave the camp on four occasions to perform for POWs held in German work camps. These POWs were referred to as commandos. Ernie writes that in August 1943, 2,700 American POWs were working in various commando camps supported by Stalag IIIB. The Geneva Convention permitted the holding belligerent to employ soldiers below the rank of sergeant to work in nonmilitary related areas. These commando camps were located throughout Germany. Ernie made these trips in conjunction with the band or orchestra and the American POW leaders who monitored the condition of these POWs. Two of these trips were to two separate commando camps near Fürstenberg on August 29, 1943, and October 3, 1943. Ernie wrote about the first trip, saying: "12:30 Glee Club-Orchestra went out to Furstenberg Commandos. Saw a lot of old friends. Searched on going out of camp and coming back. Had a fine time on visit, fellows enjoyed program which lasted about 1½ hrs. Fed us bread, coffee, mashed potatoes, cucumbers, and corn willie. Lodging conditions very good, fellows seem satisfied. Brought back civilian bread, potatoes by means of musical cases. Some was taken." In commenting on the October trip, he noted: "All along the road people waved at us, We are hard on German moral [morale]. With R.C. Parcels many things they cannot get & we have it. Got a loaf of civilian bread for package of butts." Ernie's words describe what a great time he had on both trips outside of the confines of the stalag. In particular the quality of the food was better than in the camp and both provided an opportunity to acquire additional foodstuffs for himself and his small eating group of pals. On September 19, 1943, the glee club at "8 A.M. got ready to go Trattendorf. After counting, recounting, checking, taking some fellows off of acct [account] insufficient room finally left 10 A.M. via truck. Took us 4 hrs. ... Saw Jack Lewis first in six months. As well as other boys from outfit. Glee Club—Orchestra put on program for nearly two hrs. The camp isn't near as nice as Furstenberg Com [commando] Camp. Boys have a different feeling." It is apparent from these comments that the living conditions and food were not as good as in the Fürstenberg commando camp.

There were a few other occasions when Ernie was able to leave the confines of the POW camp. On August 20, 1943, he and two others were selected to go to Frankfurt an der Oder by train. This was a trip of 30 kilometers north of the camp. "Left camp at 6:30 for station to board train for Frankfurt (Oder). Bennet, Hansen, & myself went to sit in on trial of boy on Commando. Private convicted of hitting civilian given 9 mos sentence. Visited city & several churches one a portion built 1200, the remainder 1520. Really beautiful. Fellow played Pipe Organ for us. Really swell to be out. The Lord is really caring for me. Had some cakes & soft drinks bought by English speaking German von Fricken." On October 8, 1943, Ernie and 20 others (barracks chiefs, librarian, glee club director) walked 10 kilometers south of Stalag IIIB to the town of Neuzelle. The group "was in a beautiful catherial [cathedral] which was very old, 1200. Had been destroyed & rebuilt several times. Got picture of interior of same ... Russell Hare played organ. Oh! was swell. He is our Glee Club Director. Was also on hill above town and saw same view as picture. The guard took our pictures several times and is going to try to get us some extras made." The other occasions when Ernie left the confines of the stalag were to take an item to the repair shop under guard, to attend sick call, and to go to the railhead on a work detail to unload RCPs from railroad cars. On a two-day work detail in July 1943, he assisted in the unloading of more than 10,800 RCPs from five railcars. "We went to the R.R. station. Sure a relief to get outside for the very first since coming here. Everything was so different. Cherry's [sic], pears, apples on the trees and the garden growing nice. The flowers were really beautiful." His comments certainly indicate how much he enjoyed being outside of the camp's barbed-wire fences at least for the day. Ernie recorded what happened when he was walking around the compound with MacGowan the evening of December 21, 1943: "Pete Foster asked us to help him with R.C.P. Also helped carry parcels down to Reviere [sic, German for a defined area] for the sick fellows. Saw sp [special] Christmas parcel displayed. Keeping secret to surprise fellows. Rec 12,000 R.C.P. today these Christmas Parcel being among them." His last trip outside of the camp occurred on January 22, 1945, to the town of Guben, 30 kilometers south of the camp: "1:30 went to Guben unloaded 3 wagons R.C.P. 6,200. Thank Dear Lord. No sup [supper] prem sandwich. 9:30 finished. Truck trouble arr (arrived) camp 1–2 A.M."

Ernie eagerly anticipated receiving mail and personal parcels. He recorded when he received a letter, when it was mailed, and who sent it. His diary entry for June 6, 1944, contains this example: "Then I received four letters which I really needed to boast [boost] my moral [morale]. From Jan 22–Home, Jim, Mary–Mar 8 and two lovely letters from you

Honey, Feb 1–Mar 1." Another entry from two months later shows his excitement in receiving mail: "Rec letters Home, Apr 20, You Sweetie Pie, Mar 29, Apr 14–20. How my moral [morale] jumped." Likewise receiving a personal parcel was equally important to him. These provided much-needed clothing and foodstuffs. A few of the items received were sweaters, socks, a tie, T-shirts, soap, rinse, chewing gum, hard candy, tea, sugar, nuts, and vitamin tablets. While a POW he received six personal parcels. Upon receiving the sixth personal parcel from his sweetheart, he remarked, "Gosh was swell. Those vitamin tablets, the tee [tea] badly needed. All food swell." The first letters arrived six months into his captivity on August 27, 1943, at Stalag IIIB. They were from his darling fiancée LaRue and Pearl Cowher. The letters were mailed on June 16 and June 21, respectively. A week later he received a second letter from LaRue in which she enclosed her photograph. He commented, "That picture is beautiful. It thrilled me to look at it. I have always prayed you would be happy the picture shows it. Ever in my thoughts, prayers. Also, the letter thrilled me and gave me new encouragement."

LaRue wrote Ernie at least five times a week from mid-1943 through May 8, 1945, when she learned he was safe and doing well in Hildesheim, Germany. In her letters she frequently comments on her weekend trips to her parents' home in Tyrone, Pennsylvania, and the many girlfriends she has at her job and those she met through her apartment roommate in Harrisburg. In her first letter of 1945 she describes her New Year's visitors: "We had a swell time over the weekend. I hate to say that but I know you want me to have as good a time as possible. Alice, Sylvia, and Dottie come up for the weekend. Saturday night we went to the movies and then came home and talked to 4:00 in the morning."[4] Often LaRue mentions how she has grown up and changed since he left for England in August 1942. She goes on to say, "I hope you are still the same Ernie that went away, so tolerant in such a swell personality."[5] A frequent comment is how long it has been since she received any letter or postcard from Ernie. In a September 1944 letter she states that it has been seven weeks since she last heard from her beloved Ernie, and she wishes she would receive a letter from him soon. LaRue finally received a letter from Ernie that was written on May 28, 1944, on September 14, 1944, after not hearing from him for nine weeks.

It is difficult to determine in what manner Ernie expressed his POW experiences to LaRue since very few of his letters to her and to the many other individuals he wrote were kept. It is apparent from his diary entries that he often exhibited signs of frustration and near depression over his deteriorating health, his constant hunger, and his living conditions. These concerns are not evident in his letter written on December 24, 1944, after being a POW for nearly 22 months. In it he remains upbeat and describes a positive experience to LaRue:

> Merry Christmas, Honey. My heart-thoughts are ever with you. How I long for your nearness-love. I am thinking Dear of our last Christmas together as I can't be with you. Pray God yours was a beautiful one. A thing in common will be both eating turkey this year. Par R. C. Christmas Very Nice. Your volumes of love continue to arr [arrive]. ... In show again with band. Only wish I could send you a picture Dearest but impossible. About the only way I have changed is loss of one back tooth—weight. You still have plenty to love. Hope I didn't shock you asking for cigarettes. ... Best wishes.
> Your Dearest Lover. Always loads of kisses, Ernie

In this letter not only did he wish LaRue a merry Christmas but emphasized that they both would be eating turkey this year since the special Christmas RCP contained canned turkey. He finally responded to LaRue's repeated requests for a picture saying that it was impossible to have one taken and then sent out of the camp in the mail. Ernie spoke of how he has lost a lot of weight and a back tooth, but she will still have plenty to love. He goes on to list the names of 10 other prisoners and say that they are all doing well. In a later letter LaRue comments that Ernie's 33-inch waistline is too thin for him, and he is to remember that she fell in love with a much bigger man.

The theater was the social gathering place for the camp. In it the POWs conducted 52 different shows. These included complete musicals, cantatas, band and orchestra concerts, glee club concerts, variety and comedy shows, movies, and various lectures by fellow POWs. Once again, Ernie provides a complete listing of these in his diaries as he is detailing his daily activities. The performances included: "*Nocturne*," "*Show Boat*," "Christmas Cantatas," "Beat the Band," "*Gay Nineties*," "Kay Kyser," "Rhapsody & Rhythm," and "Oratorio." The chapel and theater also served as classrooms. The 10th camp show on October 13, 1943,

92 • GUEST OF ADOLF

consisted of performances by the glee club and band plus comical acts. Ernie comments: "Really good. Alot o [A lot of] enjoyment but depressing because I still miss your presence with me Honey on such occasions." The German stalag leadership obviously bragged to their superiors about the excellent theater and revolving stage since on the night of a performance Axis Sally arrived to record it. However, the POWs refused to perform until the recording equipment was removed from the theater. Ernie enjoyed and eagerly anticipated all these performances whether he was a patron or a participant. After attending another performance, he wrote, "Again my heart went back to the many times we attended plays, show together Honey, It is never right without Yo—u, Sweet Heart at my side." Although participating in the glee club concerts and attending the various camp shows assisted in passing the time and provided some enjoyment, Ernie believed that "the worst part of entertainment is the sad awakening after it is over, barbed wire fence—P. O. W. Like a slap on the face." For Christmas 1944, the band and glee club joined up to present a special program. The many songs performed included the "Hallelujah Chorus," "Jingle Bells," "We Three Kings of Orient Are," "Good King Wenceslas," "Why Do I Love You," and many other Christmas carols. Afterwards the glee club "went Carol singing 4 in each end billets from 11 to 20 B-ends then A-ends."

The clandestine camp photographer, Sergeant Angelo Spinelli, captured the glee club in a group photograph wearing their robes in late October 1943. Another photograph was taken before one of the Glee Club Oratorio performances a few days before Christmas 1943. The glee club was photographed on a few other occasions including one in March 1944. Ernie's artifact collection contains three prints from this photographic session. In the photograph of the glee club taken in front of the stage, Ernie is clearly visible in the middle of the front row. In addition to the regular glee club rehearsals, he often participated in impromptu jam sessions occurring in various barracks. The POWs created their own educational academy offering a variety of self-improvement courses and lectures on a variety of topics. Some of the lectures Ernie attended were about art appreciation, fundamentals of drawing, music in our lives, architecture, and purchasing a radio. He enrolled in a music theory course and an algebra course. Throughout his diary he provides details on the topics covered in these courses and his struggles with mastering the materials. He participated in the algebra class for three months, May to August 1944. After the first week of instruction, he already voiced his displeasure with the subject material: "Went to work again on Algebra. In fact, really taxing my gray matter." He repeated this discontent with the algebra course every few days until it ended in August. Although he enjoyed the music course, he repeatedly expressed having difficulty in mastering the material. During the months of May and June 1944 these are a few of his comments: "Studied music till dinner. Barley soup with milk. Worked out music composition phrases for new class. What a job. Don't believe I will make a good composer." "Worked out music les [lesson] for Sat, scales, harmonizing. About ten when finished, tired ready for bed." "Harmony music class. Russ gave us a heck of an assignment for homework. Makes my head swim." "Started on music lesson. I am mighty easily discouraged. Might be trying to do to [sic] much."

Athletics was a large part of prison life. During the first few months at Stalag IIIB Ernie served as the player-manager of one of the camp's baseball teams, the Screwballs. He recorded the 15-man team roster and player positions in his diary (Table F). Nine members of the team were from his company, including two members of his gun crew. These nine soldiers were all captured with him in North Africa. Two more—Francis Harper Jr. and Thomas J. Wright—were from the battalion, and the remaining four—Hensen, Meade, Seker, and Webster—were from a different outfit. Since May 31, 1943, was "Opening Day of baseball season AM-Ntl [American-National] League," the team managers drew lots to see which two teams were going to play the first game of the season. The Screwballs lost their first two games—to the Scrubs 27–1 on June 1 and to the Magnets 13–6 on June 4—before winning the next two against the Reds 4–0 on June 4 then against AC 21–5 on June 8. Initially, the POWs made their own playing equipment. The bats were fashioned from branches brought back by a member of the wood-clearing detail. The balls were also made from materials found in the camp. In early 1944 this changed when "the YMCA furnished the baseball uniforms, bats, gloves, balls, and things of that nature." Playing

94 • GUEST OF ADOLF

baseball was a popular activity for the POWs. Ernie recorded the scores of numerous baseball and softball games in his diaries. There was even a championship series won by Barracks 18B. "Everybody was invited to get into the thing, just to go out and have a good time and we got some good crowds. Fellows came out and the Germans, they would come out and stand around with their dogs and watch the game."

Table F: Team Roster for Screwballs Baseball Team, June 29, 1943

Ernie Focht—Manager	Norm Houck—Captain	Hensen—Catcher
Meade—Pitcher	Cunningham—First Base	Seker—Second Base
Gordon—Third Base	Harper—Third Base	Banfield—Shortstop
Webster—Left Field	Hornberger—Center Field	Ringler—Right Field
Slaybaugh—Right Field	Red Wright—Roving Field	Moore—Roving Field

As the camp population increased and Ernie began to have some minor health concerns, he stopped being the team manager and only enjoyed watching the baseball, softball, and volleyball games. He limited his physical activities to playing catch with two or three other POWs—"tossed football around finished up by playing sev [several] games volleyball till dark"—taking daily strolls around the compound, and performing calisthenics. On many days he would walk around the compound at three different times a day simply to occupy himself. On one such occasion he "walked up around Russian compound. Purchased halts [wood] over the fence for a couple of cigarettes." Then later that day: "The corn husker Joens and I took eve [evening] walk. Another time a German guard near Russian camp accidently fired rifle endeavoring to reach cigarette between fences with rifle given to him by a Yank." He recorded all these strolls, indicating how many half-mile laps he made each time he went out to walk the compound. During the winter months he mentioned that it took four laps until his feet began to get warm. The most he walked in one day was 14 laps or seven miles. The laps around the compound became monotonous by mid-January 1944 when he commented, "Went walking this afternoon but that already has become very monotonous. The same old thing, sand–barbwire, no new scenery. The traffic on the Oder Canal was more than usual on each lap around another line of barges. Am under par not sick but badly disgusted with this life."

Ernie was fastidious about his appearance and health. He waited patiently, sometimes for hours, to obtain hot water for bathing, washing clothes, and for cooking. The showers in the barracks were very rudimentary, where only cold water flowed down upon you from a small pipe into a basin. In this manner you were to somehow wash your entire body. The camp did have a building with proper showers outside of the main gate, but these were not available to Ernie on a regular schedule. When it was announced that the showers were available to the American POWs Ernie would hurry to stand in the shower line. Many times, his wait ended in disappointment, as he was not lucky enough to be permitted to get a shower. A typical comment when he was successful in getting a hot shower was "Terrible time getting though. Oh! To be able to take as many and as often as I wished." Sometimes he was able to secure a hot shower on consecutive days. However, during the first six months of his time at Stalag IIIB he usually was able to get a hot shower once a week. The period between hot showers gradually increased to where he was fortunate to secure a hot shower once every two weeks and then to once a month. In between, he would wash a part of his body using cold water or water heated in his canteen in what he referred to as birdbaths. Since the showers were outside of the main gate, he frequently was searched on his way out. On several occasions the guards took a food item or packages of cigarettes from him. "Went for hot shower. Got shook down at gate. 1 pk [package] butts taken."

The washing of clothes was a twice-weekly activity as he would only wash a few things each time and set them outside to dry. This task was one that he despised, and he mentioned frequently his dislike for it, calling washing clothes a boring or dreadful job on numerous occasions. In early September 1943 he commented: "Washed new things before wearing as well as dirty. … Again was at it to [sic] long, nerves bad." Although he disliked washing clothes, he did it so frequently based upon the amount of hot water he could secure on any given day and if the weather conditions were suitable for air-drying the clothes. His typical comments on doing his laundry were: "Heated water for wash,

96 • GUEST OF ADOLF

Becoming a task," "All cleaned up and no place to go, so I washed my field jacket. As usual it rained before finished," and "Did wkly [weekly] wash, Oh! What a job. Mighty tired of it." These negative comments did not stop him from ensuring his clothes and body were as clean as possible under the circumstances.

Ernie was fortunate in that he was able to maintain a large quantity of clothes throughout his captivity. He never missed an opportunity to secure additional clothing, scarves, hats, gloves, boots, personal hygiene items, cups, and cooking gear. He would often wait in the clothing department line for hours to try to secure a specific item, but he gladly accepted any item. "Sweat out Canteen line for over an hr only to get coat hanger, talc powder." Ernie describes his haul of September 25, 1944: "Had Glee Club but skipped to go for O'coat, but didn't get. Rec [received] shoe brush, polish, soap case, tooth powder, clothes, sewing kit." On this occasion, since he didn't receive the overcoat he desired, he went back later in the day and waited again but again experienced disappointment. There were a few times he provided some of his friends who were commandos additional articles of clothing (combat jacket, overcoat, etc.) before they left Stalag IIIB and returned to their work locations. "Tom, Roy, Joe, Price, Harper, others had to go out on Commando again. Gave Roy combat jacket. Seemed funny without." In the middle of November 1944, Ernie writes of a clothing collection being done for the boys who were soon to depart for one of the commando camps: "Took up donation excess clothes for the boys (buddies) other camp." There was one occasion in December 1944 when a German guard demanded Ernie give up some of his much-needed clothing. When he refused, he "was threatened at gun point for failing to give up much needed clothing."[6] It appears that he was able to keep whatever clothing the guard was demanding. Table G from his diary records the articles of clothing that were in his possession on November 10, 1943. It is interesting to compare the amount of clothing in his possession when he was captured in North Africa with this listing. The increase in the type and quantities of clothing are dramatic. Ernie never missed an opportunity to visit the clothing issue hut or trade some of his hoard of cigarettes for additional clothing. There are additional lists of clothing and personal items in Appendix 2.

Table G: Clothing and Personal Articles in Ernie's Possession on November 10, 1943

2 pr O.D. Pants	2 O. D. Shirts	1 Field Jacket
1 Combat Jacket	1 Coveralls	1 British O'coat
3 prs Wool Socks	3 prs Cotton Socks	1 pr British Socks
2 pr Drawers, G.I.	2 Sweat Shirts, G.I.	1 Drawer, Jockey
1 Sweat Shirt [sic]	2 Shorts—Shirts	4 Blue Handerchiefs [sic]
4 White Issued, Home	1 G.I. Jockey Hat Wool	4 Towels, Issue, Home
2 Wash Cloths	1 Wool Scarf, G.I.	1 pr O.D. Shoes, Brown
1 pr Barricks [sic] Slippers	1 Bowling Shoes	1 Wooden Clogs
1 Belt French 7-A	1 Bible—1 Testament	3 Sewing Kits

As his time in the POW camp increased, he began to record his health issues. He repeatedly wrote about his loss of weight ("put on a pair of my new jockeys which are four sizes to [sic] big which was easily remedied"), an aching back and legs, numerous head colds, inability to sleep, and sore throats. Beginning in early January 1944 his sore throat became a weekly issue. The usual treatment was to gargle with salt water. This remedy worked for a couple of months until April 20, when his symptoms grew worse. Over the next 12 days his diary entries bore out the seriousness of this illness: "Went to bed right after dinner, fever rising, mighty tough. Hot choc for sup. Jim nurse maid. By 8:30 fever started to break. Slept half decent. Excused roll call. Mighty weak, Gripp or Flu." The next day: "Throat-Glands are sore. Still in bed. Just coffee for dinner. Some better except throat. Looks like tonsils broled [broiled] as well throat." Finally, he took himself to the infirmary, where the first doctor admitted him for a persistent high fever, sore throat, and enflamed tonsils. "Given pills—aspirin—seemed to upset system. … The pills they give me makes everything red I pass. Don't sleep so good. Also make me half sick."

A few days later a second doctor listed his illness as diphtheria. During his stay his bunkmate, Jim, brought down new clothes and toiletry articles. A couple of days into his stay he received two invalid parcels containing "chicken noodle soup, honey, milk, ovaltine, toast, cheese, biscuits, and salt water for gargling." He was slow to recover to the point where he could return to his barracks. On May 1 "Dr. Hughes said I could return to Billet. Ovaltine-toast-bis-finished up lemon curd. Waited for rations. Arr billet about 3 P.M. still weak, throat tender but coming along OK." This hospitalization period lasted 12 days and stayed with him the remainder of his time as a POW. He never fully recovered from this illness to the level of fitness he exhibited prior to the onset of the illness as evidenced by a comment made a couple of months later: "Since in Reviere [sic, infirmary], April, my resistance has been low. Have to fight to keep going. Hasent [hasn't] gotten me down, but I don't give a hoot if things get done or not. Patience not what used to be."

Including his hospitalization Ernie recorded going on sick call 39 times while at Stalag IIIB and three times at Luckenwalde. Many of these incidents were after April 1944. The most frequent reasons were for head colds, pimples, and sores on his rear, cut fingers, sore throats, enlarged tonsils, ear infections, chest X-rays for his lungs, and athlete's foot. He also visited a Russian dentist on multiple occasions. On a visit to the dentist on November 14, 1944, he recorded: "Went to Dentist noon had lower right back tooth pulled as usual abessed [sic]. Novocane [sic] took little effect. Hurt. Toast-mashed spuds-cab. Jaw aching." The usual treatment for any ailment was to take an aspirin or apply a salve to the sore area. From his time in the infirmary, Ernie learned that a visit to sick call might result in his receiving an invalid RCP. Since he was a first-rate scrounger, this gave him another avenue to secure additional foodstuffs for his small mess group. In addition to the two he received during his hospitalization he received two other invalid parcels during his time at Stalag IIIB. These many sick call visits were the foundation of his health concerns that lasted the remainder of his life.

LaRue continually included snapshots of herself in her letters to Ernie. He cherished these, securing one of her above his head on the bottom of the bunk above his and a second one inside the third volume of his diary. Ernie also carried another of these photographs in his wallet along with photos of his siblings, children, and grandchildren for the remainder of his life. She wanted to see a picture of him so badly that she instructed him to stick his nose in one sometime. She often mentioned that whenever a picture of Stalag IIIB appeared in the *Red Cross Bulletin* she studied it to see if he was in the photograph. In an October 1944 letter she said, "Darling, I wish you could send me a picture. I've looked at a lot of pictures taken at your camp but never see anyone who looks like you."[7] She finally was rewarded when Ernie appeared in the September 1944 issue. LaRue wrote to Ernie: "[I had] quite a time convincing your people that there was any resemblance between you and the picture from the bulletin."[8] Eventually after studying the picture for a while Ernie's parents finally agreed with LaRue that the photo in fact included their son. The request for a picture of him continued all through his period of captivity.

In three of her November 1944 letters LaRue inquired, "Have you met Kenny Eschbach or Johnny Harmon or Joe Lingle from Harrisburg. Joe Lingle has been in Stalag IIIB for almost a year."[9] She did not offer an explanation as to her connection to them. Four months later LaRue wrote that he would not find Kenny since he was in Stalag Luft IV and Johnny is a POW in Stalag VIIA. Ernie never responded to these inquiries, most likely since he received the first of these letters the day before his forced march to Stalag IIIA began at the end of January 1945 and the November 19th letter in March 1945 while at Stalag IIIA in Luckenwalde, where writing any letter was very difficult. In fact, during the three months at Stalag IIIA he was only able to write four letters to LaRue and his parents.

Life in the barracks could be very boring with the repeated roll calls. Ernie especially hated the "by-POW-number" roll calls since they took hours to complete. One reason for these long roll calls was to locate specific prisoners. On multiple occasions soldiers who were assigned to a commando detail refused to report. This stopped all activity in the camp until they were located and forced to go on the commando assignment. Ernie only records one instance where a couple POWs escaped. Ernie may be referring to one of the two escapes made by Sergeant Ed Wisneski of the 47th Infantry Regiment of the 9th Infantry Division, who was also captured in North Africa. He was recaptured both times, and after his second escape the Germans used a rifle butt to smash and break the top of his right foot to deter further escape attempts.[10] During these prolonged roll calls often the barracks were being searched simultaneously.

100 • GUEST OF ADOLF

Ernie complained on numerous occasions that upon returning to the barracks all his possessions were scattered, some of his extra food items and part of his stash of cigarettes were stolen, and that some of the cans of food were punctured. He details one such experience that occurred on September 24, 1943: "Morning very quiet, Afternoon the Devil and all his angels came in camp. Jerries pulled a search. Very disgusting procedure. Entire afternoon belongings searched and scattered. Can punctured, some stolen—tobacco also. Sure be glad when this terrible nightmare ends and I get home to live as a civilian person should." Another instance occurred on March 2, 1944, when the POWs in his barracks "spent 8 A.M. to 5:30 P.M. outside in stormy weather during search. Jim—I fared well, lost cig—soap, but some lost to thefts, cigs, soap, blankets, cof, R.C. material, cof, razor, milk, butter, and other articles." At one point during this search the Germans removed all the articles from the building. This was just one example of losing items during the searches. In other searches he would lose a blanket, coffee, and many items in his stash of RCP foodstuffs to the guards.

In addition to the guards stealing items, other prisoners were stealing wire, wood, light bulbs, and food from their fellow POWs. Ernie expressed his displeasure towards both groups, but more towards his fellow POWs. After enduring an extra POW count conducted to locate a couple of missing French commandos, he commented, "During this count some so and so Posten [guard] stole our prem. I won't put here what I said but I did blow my top. Had to open res [reserve] can and dang lucky to have that."

More than anything he detested the times the camp was visited by high-ranking German officers, German civilian authorities, and by a representative of the Red Cross from Geneva, Switzerland. One of these meetings occurred on Wednesday July 7, 1943, with a "German Mjr [major] from Berlin, formerly from the States. Gave us great promises, which I only hope come true. As for going to another camp with better conditions & said we would be home soon." Ernie did not believe any of these promises or comments. Overall, these visits caused a disruption to his daily routine and to the camp's workings. He especially hated it when the visits were on the days RCPs were to be distributed since this activity was canceled. Ernie indicates that on these days the Germans orchestrated a display for the visitors, providing a very positive impression of the prisoners' daily life.

STALAG IIIB FÜRSTENBURG • 101

While in the barracks Ernie would often read a book from the prison library. He repeatedly comments on the books he was reading in his diaries. A few were *Kitty Foyle, Daphine, Phoebe of France, Loads of Love, Man of Manhattan, The Robe,* and *Unforbidden Fruit.*

After reading *Kindred of the Dust* by Peter B. Kyne, Ernie writes, "Very Good. Certain phases of it I compared our lives of heartache, etc. Oh! How I long for your Love Dear and to Hold you in my arms again. I pray our years will be of great happiness." He engaged in many discussions with his bunkmate, Tom, and another POW named Joens, typically right before he turned in for bed. Ernie would play dominoes to pass the time, particularly on days that the weather was bad and he was not able to get outside to walk around the compound. On a nice day he might say to his buddies, to get a laugh, "Let's go out and count barbed wire." An alternate activity to walking around the compound was to go stand near the fence and watch life on the outside. There are several comments in his diary regarding observing the people walking past the camp. He had duties within the barracks to perform on a rotating schedule such as fireguard and cleanup tasks. Another facet of camp life was contending with the multitude of rumors continually circulating. One such rumor circulating in August 1943 was that the war was to end in 40 days and the citizens of Hamburg were rioting.

The amount of food available for consumption daily was a major concern voiced consistently in Ernie's writings. The Germans provided only meager rations daily or weekly. A typical ration distribution consisted of small amounts of coffee, a couple slices of bread, a watery soup that might have a few shreds of vegetables and meat in it, and potatoes. An International Red Cross delegate reported on May 22, 1943, that these weekly rations consisted of 5 pounds of bread, 10 ounces of meat, 5 pounds of vegetables, 5 ounces of salt, 8 ounces of margarine, 11 pounds of potatoes, 6 ounces of marmalade, 2 ounces of cheese, and 6 ounces of sugar. This variety of foodstuffs decreased as the war progressed into its final year.[11]

Two months after his arrival to Stalag IIIB, Ernie made this comment on the food given to him: "Just had dinner, 90% water, 5% spuds, 5% some green food. Place sure looks like a tramp camp when we get cooking on home made stoves. Have one stove about 3 ft long 1½ ft

102 • GUEST OF ADOLF

wide for 300 men to cook on otherwise." The food the Germans provided was distributed from the stalag's kitchen to a member of an eating group. Ernie's group typically had four members, but later the same quantity of rations was to feed six men. His meals for September 29, 1943 consisted of "coffee and toast for breakfast, barley soup with milk for dinner, for supper toast, spuds, L. [liver] paste, coffee." The men in the mess group shared the responsibilities of securing the German-provided rations, contributing foodstuffs from their RCP stashes, and preparing both the supper and dinner meals. Typical diary entries read: "Jim had toast, fried L. paste-cof ready … Joens—Jim got sup ready C. Willie, spuds, veg noodle soup, salt, pepper, butter," "Came back to billet Joens—Jim were preparing supper mashed spuds with fried prem mixed in, toast-tea," and "Joens stewed prunes while I prepared Stalag puddin rasins [sic] -biscuits-butter-choc-bread-milk." A loaf or a couple slices of bread was a staple for most supper and dinner meals. It was of a different consistency than what Ernie ate at his mother's table. "We used to call it sawdust bread, because it came in and seemed as though it had a lot of real fine, it looked like sawdust in it. It was sort of loose, like, you could almost rub it off."

Potatoes issued by the Germans were one of the ingredients for two of his daily meals. Initially, they were distributed from the kitchen a couple of times a week to each food group. This pattern changed in late May 1944 when Ernie complained: "Get very few spuds about once a week, and them half spoiled." In August 1944 the Germans cut the food rations by one-third due to a perceived waste of food by the prisoners. In actuality, the wasted food was rotten or inedible. His food intake for August 22, 1944, was "coffee and prunes, coffee and L. paste, and for supper mashed steamed c. willie above spuds, L. paste, gravy, coffee." The amount of food issued by the Germans continued to decline as the war progressed into 1945. In late January Ernie ate "toast, toast biscuit, barley soup, coffee-toast-L. paste-choc-bread puddin" for his three meals. On another occasion, combining a few of the items from an RCP, he "mixed up a mixture of orange-milk-sugar, called it ice cream. Put it out in the snow to freeze." As the quantity of food provided by the Germans decreased the soldiers relied heavily upon RCPs for most of their food. Ernie expressed his feelings concerning the importance of these parcels: "If not for R.C.P would sure be hurting. Rec [receive] little otherwise." A month later this was reaffirmed with "1,488 R.C.P. arr [arrived] also 400 invalid. Thank the dear Lord for parcels were getting low." The liver paste, corn willie, biscuits, sugar, chocolate, and bread pudding mentioned in these quotes from his diary came from the contents of RCPs.

The American Red Cross shipped millions of food, medical, and first aid safety kit relief packages to American POWs in both the European and Pacific Theaters. The International Red Cross Committee in Geneva, Switzerland, assisted with the transfer of these relief packages to German authorities. POWs in the Pacific Theater did not typically receive any of these relief packages due to the lack of cooperation from the Japanese. The food relief package was intended to supplement the daily German-issued food ration of one prisoner. However, this was rarely the case: as Ernie recorded in his diaries, he often shared a parcel with between two and 10 others at various times while a POW. He records the contents of four of the seven different parcels received during his captivity. There was a special parcel for those who were convalescing in what passed as the prison hospital and a Christmas parcel. The American Red Cross began to assemble a special Christmas parcel for POWs in the summer of 1943. In addition to the normal contents these included additional items to remind the soldiers of home and Christmastime. It included fruitcake, fruit bar, candied fruits, nuts, hard candy, chocolate, assorted preserves, Christmas candles, handkerchiefs, and a game or puzzle.[12] Ernie mentions receiving this type of parcel on December 24, 1943. It was the contents of these parcels that kept Ernie and the other POWs from starving.

Red Cross Parcel A-1

1.	Milk Powder	1
2.	Cheese	8 oz
3.	Liver paste	6 oz
4.	Corned Beef	12 oz
5.	Pork Meat (prem, Treet)	16 oz
6.	Rasins [sic]	12 oz
7.	Sugar	8 oz

8. Lemon Powder	12 oz
9. Cocoa	8 oz
10. Coffee	8 oz
11. Chocolate (D–Bar)	4 oz
12. Candy (Hard)	6 oz
13. Cigarettes	40
14. Tobacco, G.W.	2¼ oz
15. Lunch Biscuits	7 oz
16. Matches	2 boxes

Red Cross Parcel A-9

1. Milk Powder	1 lb
2. Cheese	8 oz
3. Liver paste	6 oz
4. Corned Beef	12 oz
5. Pork Meat (prem, Treet)	12 oz
6. Raisins	16 oz
7. Sugar	8 oz
8. Orange Juice Concentrated	4 oz
9. Butter	1 lb
10. Coffee	4 oz
11. Chocolate	2--2 oz bars
12. Salmon	12 oz
13. Cigarettes	60
14. Sardines	2 oz
15. Lunch Biscuits	7 oz
16. Matches	2 bxs
17. Salt	2 oz
18. Soap	1 Bar

The RCPs were initially distributed a couple times during the week on a one-for-two-men basis. Typically, Ernie and his fellow POWs received American parcels, but occasionally the parcels were from England, Norway, Argentina, and other countries. Ernie does comment that the meat products tasted different from those in the American RCPs. "Argentine C. willie tasted different than what rec in our country." The distribution frequency changed in September 1944 as the German

STALAG IIIB FÜRSTENBURG • 105

transportation, road, and rail network became more unreliable due to the Allied bombing of these facilities. The POWs did not receive any RCP parcels between October 5 and November 5, 1944, as a result of these logistical difficulties. On November 5 Ernie commented: "Finally rec [received] R.C.P. 2,040." The next day when the Germans distributed these the normal ratio of one parcel for two men was changed to one parcel for six men. This 1:6 ratio would remain standard practice until the end of January 1945. Ten days later another consignment of "Fin [Finnish] 2,940 RCP arr [arrived]. Thank Dear Lord."

On numerous occasions the parcels were opened, and the Germans took items for their own consumption. Other times the tins of meat (spam, salmon, corned beef) were punctured so the food would spoil if it was not eaten immediately. The occurrence of missing and punctured items increased beginning in late September 1944. On one such occasion he commented, "Was issued R.C.P. No. 10, 1–2 without cans-containers, short cigs-D-bars-cof." Ernie and his pals cooked their own rations using homemade stoves, frying pans, and cups to heat their food and homemade utensils to stir and eat their meals, as the Germans did not provide any of these items. "We would try to take a piece of wood and shape up a form like a ladle for a spoon." Not having a table knife posed a major problem for cutting the loaves of bread to divide it among a group of men. "We managed to get one for a pack of cigarettes or so many cigarettes." Eventually, all these items were made using the metal from RCP cans. They tapped into the barracks wiring or created a fire using compressed coal, twigs, or bed slats for fuel. Frequently, the Germans withheld RCPs and personal parcels, showers, and writing paper as a form of punishment for various camp incidents.

Throughout his time at Stalag IIIB Ernie writes of the times when a commando group returned for a few days. He enjoyed catching up with the members of Company A, 805th TD Battalion, who were on these details. They would often share meals, take strolls around the compound, or simply talk. A group that returned in August 1944 brought sad news with them. A POW in their group, Lloyd Shaffer who was in A Company, died the previous November 1943 from appendicitis and pneumonia and was buried at Stalag Luft III in Sagan, Germany (now Zagan, Poland). Somehow, Ernie acquired photographs of the funeral and brought them

106 • GUEST OF ADOLF

home after the war. They are in his artifact collection. On one other occasion, December 30, 1944, he records attending the funeral service of Long and Thompson, two fellow POWs, in the stalag's chapel.

There are numerous occasions where Ernie writes about his trading with the guards, the Russian prisoners, and other POWs. He describes the conditions of the Russian camp as deplorable, something that reminded him of a pigsty. The Germans provided the Russians even less food and access to fresh water than they did prisoners of other nationalities. Cigarettes were the primary medium of currency in the camp. The source for these was the RCPs. Each parcel contained 80 cigarettes, 16 per pack, in five packages. Another source of cigarettes was through the American cigarette manufacturers. These companies provided the families of POWs with order forms they could use to purchase five or six cartons of cigarettes for 60 cents a carton every three months. The company would then process the order and mail the cigarettes to the POWs at the address provided by the family.

In an early letter to his parents, Ernie requested that they order cigarettes for him through this process. Since he was not a smoker, he easily accumulated a large stash of stalag currency. Ernie traded cigarettes with the Russians on numerous occasions for wood to cook his food and to heat the barracks. There were times in late 1943 and early 1944 when Ernie "would give them food etc. and return wood would come over the fence." He also traded cigarettes for extra bread (two packs for a loaf), potatoes, onions (four for a package), a watch (45 packages, 720 cigarettes), clothing repair ("deniums [denims] repaired by Russians cost of two cigarettes"), and watch repair (seven packages). Other purchases made with his cigarettes include the book used for the third volume of his diary (two packages), a haircut (two cigarettes), and an overseas cap, also known as a garrison cap (one package) in November 1943. He purchased two coffee cups from a guard on December 30, 1943, for two packages of cigarettes. Ernie purchased items not only for himself and his meal buddies but also for some of his other prison pals, particularly those going out to work in one of the commando camps.

On July 29, 1944, Ernie purchased a ring inscribed with his initials, date, and IIIB. During the 1943 Christmas season the American POWs took up a collection of food items to give to the Russian POWs. As a New Year's gift from the Germans, the American POWs were "going to get the Argentine Parcel containing more meats fruit cocktail, etc., but due to the fact of our generosity of contributing 250 cans salmon to the Russians of which was found by the Ger [Germans] and confiscated German Stalag leadership would not permit it." As punishment for their generosity the Americans were denied the Argentine parcels, and the Russians received additional punishments.

Ernie was extremely faithful throughout his period of captivity in recording in his diaries his daily activities, the weather, and menus for his meals. His entry for February 2, 1944, illustrates this practice: "Wed—Still cloudy—not so cold. Cof-bread-jam. Grp on clean up #6. After which had morning Dev and finished book (Daphine). Then dinner Cof-L. paste (sand) Dev. Finally got hot shower, after 5 weeks, how good it felt, filed nails. Cof-c. willie (sand). Went walking till prayer time, 7:20, and then walked a while. Afterwards it was bedtime." Besides recording his daily activities, he copied more than 50 poems and jokes written by fellow POWs. He listed the contents of a typical day's ration provided by the Germans in 1943 and an outline of his regimented day. Examples of other items included are the members of his gun crew, the members of the baseball team he managed in the first summer in Stalag IIIB, and the eating utensils in his possession upon arriving at Fürstenburg. These were a "R.C. Pan, R.C. Spoon, Butter Can for Drinking Cup, and a German Chow pan." Ernie kept a record of almost everything he possessed and received during his period of captivity. This encompassed the contents of any personal parcels he received; the contents of the various RCPs; the clothing, equipment, and shaving gear he possessed; and recipes. The recipe for fudge was "sugar 23 squares, D-bar, milk, & butter. Saved for about a week to get enough sugar." A sampling of these lists, poems, and parcel contents is in Appendix 2.

Allied aircraft bombing near Frankfurt an der Oder, Fürstenberg, and Guben frequently disturbed Ernie's evenings. He referred to these times as being visited by termites and routinely commented on these visits in his diary. On August 23, 1943, he wrote: "Termites over again midnight for two hrs in a fierce raid." Then, on October 20: "Termites visit for couple of hrs raid West-Northwest of Camp. In fact sounds-rumbles feld

108 • GUEST OF ADOLF

[felt] in camp." A month later he says, "Went to bed about 9 P.M. and the termites visited again." The bombings on December 2, 1943, really made an impression: "Termites and what a show of fireworks and rumble. It was a beautiful ful [*sic*] new moon lit night with a mackerel sky and stars." One of his best descriptions of the bombings reads: "Termites, and what a sight at high altitude, vapor streams, largest yet formation. First planes seen for almost a year, moral [morale] builder." Often the bombing interrupted his glee club or performance rehearsals, supper, and most regularly his bedtime routine and sleep.

The incidence and intensity of the bombings increased in late 1944 and in January 1945. This led to a decrease in the number of RCPs available for distribution to the POWs. Furthermore, the Russian offensive was moving through Poland and approaching the Oder River that formed the German–Polish border. Ernie mentions that on January 20, 1945, the Germans repatriated seven POWs through the Red Cross due to their medical condition and on the next day "Repats [repatriated] Medics left sp [special] R.C. train this A.M. for Home." In addition, a couple of American medics were permitted to accompany these soldiers on the Red Cross train out of Germany. On January 31, 1945, the Germans distributed an RCP, one for every two men, and notified the prisoners that they were being moved and were to prepare to leave Stalag IIIB later that day. After discarding some extra articles, Ernie gathered up all his remaining belongings, placed them on a sled, and waited for the order to march out the main gate.

CHAPTER 7

Stalag IIIA Luckenwalde

On July 19, 1944, Adolf Hitler issued an order that all prisoner camps along the eastern front should prepare to evacuate their internees. This order included the POWs from all nations and all others held in the multitude of concentration camps. However, for the POWs in Stalag Luft VI at Heydekrug, East Prussia, the order arrived six days too late. The camp commandant began the evacuation of his camp on July 13, 1944, as the Russian army was moving through Lithuania and was also near the Southern border of East Prussia. This was the first of what was to become a mass western migration of Allied POWs that continued to the end of the war. The American National Red Cross in the March 1945 issue of their *Prisoners of War Bulletin* reported 53 percent of all American POWs began moving westward beginning in January 1945. They estimate that more than three hundred thousand POWs of all nationalities were evacuated from camps in Poland and Eastern Germany.[1] Many of these evacuations occurred during the winter months of December, January, and February 1944–45. This winter was known for its extreme cold temperatures, snow, and harsh winds. POWs were given only a few hours' notice of the evacuation, which made it difficult for them to create rucksacks in which to carry their belongings and food reserves. Since the evacuations were conducted by nationalities as each group departed, they tossed supplies and clothing into one of the remaining compounds. The last group to depart then destroyed whatever supplies and food items they were unable to carry with them.

These soldiers and airmen suffered immensely during the migrations with some being forced to move multiple times. They were marched in long columns to other prisoner of war camps; as many as seventy

110 • GUEST OF ADOLF

were stuffed into forty-and-eight railcars or crammed into the holds of freighters traversing the Baltic Sea. They suffered horrendously during these exoduses, receiving little food or medicine and almost no shelter along the way. Their main source of food and protection from the weather was what they were able to take with them as they left their camp. Once stuffed into the railcars the POWs remained inside for days until reaching their destination. They endured repeated Allied bombing raids while in the rail yards and strafing by other aircraft while in transit. As they marched on the roads and through fields, aircraft from both sides attacked the long, snaking columns, wounding and killing some of the POWs.

As the columns of ragged and weak POWs marched through towns and cities devastated by the repeated Allied bombing raids, they were subjected to multiple forms of physical abuse and harassment from their guards and the towns' inhabitants. Upon nearing the new prison camp, the guards had one more act of vindictiveness waiting for the POWs. A corridor of soldiers and civilians lined the road leading into the camp. The prisoners were forced to run between these lines while being physically abused with clubs, fists, and bayonets. All the deprivations and acts of cruelty were designed to antagonize the POWs into some type of reaction. Those who tried to fight back or break away from the columns or who dropped out of the columns were executed. Once inside the gates of their new home, the POWs were still in danger from the guards. The existing group of POWs did not necessarily welcome the new arrivals as they swelled the number of individuals in the camps. This only made the already deplorable conditions even worse as the camps were greatly overcrowded with the existing facilities being unable to provide proper care and shelter.

There is no logical explanation for why the prisoners had to endure the hardships of the evacuations. Their lives were endangered by marching through the winter along open roads and being stuffed into railcars and left in the marshaling yards to endure repeated bombings. These evacuations were definitely "not to protect the prisoners from being in danger, but to use them as human shields or hostages at the end of the war. The plain fact is that their lives were deliberately and unnecessarily put at risk, and those who died on the marches were victims of cruel and inhuman treatment."[2]

The prisoners of Stalag IIIB unknowingly became part of Hitler's mass migration on the evening of January 31, 1945 (Map 10). In preparation for the march, Ernie ate a good meal of bread, salmon, and liver paste from his food stash. At 7 p.m. his nearly 637 days or 21 months of imprisonment at Stalag IIIB ended as he and the other 2,800 American POWs marched out the main gate heading west. The journey started out on a cold night with snow and freezing rain. Like the other evacuations this ouster was to move the prisoners further west away from the advancing Russians to another stalag. They walked all through the night of January 31 through freezing rain and ice. At one of the brief rest stops, Ernie wrote: "Still on road. Endurance low. Trusting God, Hungry."

The column finally stopped around 5 p.m. after walking for 22 hours. Ernie found refuge in a barn in the vicinity of the current German town of Krugersdorf for the night. The march continued at 11 a.m. on February 2, covering 25 kilometers with the "men standing it fair" before stopping for the night. During this day's march, Ernie received the first food—coffee and a sandwich—provided by the Germans since leaving Stalag IIIB on January 31. On this night Ernie slept "in dairy barn. Soft, warm, comfortable. In fair condition yet. Restless night." The next day he awoke to another cold morning and received a ration of bread for breakfast. His thighs and shinbones were sore, but he overcame the soreness during the day's march of 15 to 20 kilometers. The column of POWs stopped for the day around 3 p.m. He was ushered into a horse barn in the town of Leibsch, where he spent the night. He was "tired sore. But spirits up. God helping along. Cof [coffee]-sandwiches. Legs ache."

The next morning, Ernie was served coffee, beans, and some bread for breakfast before starting out on the road at 8 a.m. It was another cold day, but it was not snowing or raining, which made it a better day to be on the road. His right leg continued to bother him, but he kept going with the help of some friends. This day, the fifth day, they stopped by 11:30 a.m. in the town of Halbe and were lodged in a church. At noon he dipped into his food supply for some milk and made a corn willie sandwich. Monday, February 5, was a rainy day, and he received some coffee and bread with cheese for breakfast. He walked approximately 20 kilometers through the rain under constant harassment from the German guards before stopping near the current German town of Neuhof where he was given some soup for dinner. The routine was the same for the next day except when Ernie was slow in adjusting his pack after a rest stop, he was threatened at gunpoint by one of the German guards.[3] In the late afternoon the column stopped at a German military garrison for the night. Needless to say, the prisoners were very uneasy spending the night surrounded by so many more German soldiers. Wednesday, February 7, turned out to be the last day of his forced march. Around 2 p.m. Ernie and the other American POWs from Stalag IIIB walked through the main gate of Stalag IIIA at Luckenwalde. In all he walked and pulled his sled of belongings about 76 miles to his new POW camp, Stalag IIIA. He was tired, sore, and hungry, having had only some coffee and a piece of bread to eat this day. As his day ended, he wrote, "Journeys end. Leg bothering some. How I slept. Tired, dirty. Slept on straw."

Map 10: POW Camps in Germany, April 14, 1943 to May 6, 1945. 1. Moosburg an der Isar—Stalag VIIA; 2. Berlin; 3. Frankfurt an der Oder; 4. Fürstenberg—Stalag IIIB; 5. Guben; 6. Neuzelle; 7. Halbe; 8 Luckenwalde—Stalag IIIA; 9. Trattendorf. (Timothy M. Swartz. World Hillshade copyright © Esri)

The planning for Stalag IIIA began prior to the German invasion of Poland in 1939. It was constructed to house up to ten thousand men and was the largest camp in Wehrkreis III, the military district headquartered in Berlin. This district included the entire German state of Brandenburg, and within its boundaries were four POW camps for enlisted soldiers (Stalag IIIA, IIIB, IIIC, and IIID) and three camps for officers (Offizerslager (Oflag) IIIA, IIIB, and IIIC). Stalag IIIA and Oflag IIIA were collocated approximately 3.6 kilometers southwest of the town of Luckenwalde. In mid-September 1939 the first POWs arrived from Poland. They were initially housed in large tents until they completed the construction of barracks buildings. Upon completion of this work, they were moved to another location being replaced by Belgian and Dutch prisoners. By mid-1940 they in turn were replaced by more than forty-three thousand French prisoners. As the war progressed, Russian, British, British Commonwealth, Italian, Romanian, Yugoslavian, and American POWs joined the French. Separate compounds were created within the camp for the differing nationalities.

Stalag IIIA developed a reputation for the mistreatment of its prisoners. The guards often beat the POWs for no obvious reason and repeatedly withheld food, mail, and RCPs. The Germans maintained that the POWs were treated in accordance with the guidelines of the Geneva and Hague Conventions. The two most mistreated groups were the Italians and the Russians. The Italians were mistreated because of their September 1943 capitulation to the Allies. Since Russia was not a signatory to the Geneva Convention, the Germans believed they had no obligation to treat their POWs according to these guidelines. Consequently, they were the most mistreated and starved group in the camp.

The typical daily ration for the non-Russian POW consisted of one kilogram of rye bread to be shared among 15 POWs, a pea and horsemeat soup at noon, and a bucket of potatoes for 25 POWs at dinnertime.[4] The POWs' main source of food was the RCPs that were sporadically distributed by the Germans. During the nearly six and half years of its existence more than two hundred thousand prisoners were processed through the gates of Stalag IIIA. However, typically there were no more than eight thousand POWs living within its compounds.

114 • GUEST OF ADOLF

The remainder were distributed to more than one thousand commando camps throughout the state of Brandenburg. It is estimated that nearly five thousand prisoners died while in captivity at Stalag IIIA. The non-Soviet prisoners were buried with military honors in individual graves at the camp.

The camp was already overcrowded and very unhygienic when the American prisoners from Stalag IIIB arrived the afternoon of February 7, 1945. This stop was originally planned to be just for the night before the group continued moving further west the next morning. However, because of the deteriorating military situation on both the eastern and western fronts and the constant day and night bombings with their destruction of the roads, bridges, and rail networks, Stalag IIIA became their new home. Ernie's group then joined the five thousand American and four thousand British POWs already interned at the camp. Some of the British prisoners had been in the camp since 1940, while others had only recently been captured during the Battle of the Bulge in December 1944. The camp's existing facilities were already overextended, so the Germans had little to offer these new arrivals in the way of shelter, food, and activities. A barrier separated the officer and enlisted areas of the two POW camps, Stalag IIIA and Oflag IIIA. Unless a POW received permission from the Germans, there was no mingling between the two groups and the sharing of food or clothing was forbidden.

The Germans erected seven large tents to house Ernie's group of 2,800 men. Each tent held approximately four hundred prisoners. Initially, he slept on the ground in tent #4 until bunks were provided for the tents. For bedding he used straw or simply slept on the hard wood. The tents were not heated, so he wore most of the clothing (long johns, multiple shirts, a sweater, and overcoats) he had in his possession attempting to keep warm. Even wearing all these clothes, he repeatedly complained that he was cold: "All clothes on, still cold." His stash of clothing is greatly reduced from that which was in his possession 17 months earlier in Stalag IIIB. Although his movement between the two areas was restricted, he still managed to locate and talk with two officers from the 805th TD Battalion who also were captured in North Africa. They were 2LT John Glendinning, who was an officer in Ernie's company, and Captain Carl Hunsinger from the battalion headquarters staff.

Table H: Sergeant Focht's Clothing and Possessions on April 4, 1945

Coat O [overcoat]	Sweaters	2 O.D. shirts
Pants	2 long john-shirts	5 U-wear-shirts
Gloves	Scarf	Sweater cap
Socks	5 H-chiefs	Wash cloths
2 O.D. blankets	1 German blanket	All shaving equipment
2 towels	Field Bag	Stomach drops
2 belts, French	4 G.I. toothbrushes	Powder
Pen	Pencils	O/seas cap

Daily, the war moved closer to the POWs in this camp. While at Stalag IIIB, Ernie used the word "termites" to indicate Allied bombings. In this camp he changed to calling the bombings "air shows." These shows were more frequent than in the previous camp as the Allies were closing in on Luckenwalde from both the east and west. There was a constant theme of nervousness that the camp might be accidently bombed or strafed by Allied planes or fired upon by various artillery units. This did occur on several occasions, the last being around 11 p.m. the day the German guards left the compound. Fortunately, no one was injured during these times.

Ernie was constantly hungry and wrote often about the lack of food. Typically, a day's rations were even less than he received while at Stalag IIIB. His food for February 11 consisted of "tea-bread. ... Pea soup-spuds-s (slice) bread-butter-sugar. Praying for deliverance of bondage, for food." Five days later his comments regarding the food situation were "Tea-1 bread. Dear Lord give us food. Life here miserable. Can't endure much longer! (Dang long wait for soup 4:30 P.M). Barley soup-spud-butter. (7½ men on loaf bread). My God Why Hast Thou Forsaken Me, My Faith just isn't. Desperate. Heartsick. 2 yrs ago in same position."

He subsisted on tea, a slice of bread, potatoes, and a pea-barley or grass soup for many of his days while in Stalag IIIA. He complained about the amount of time he had to wait in line to get even this small amount of food. As February came to an end, he wrote: "4 wks (weeks) left IIIB. Waist 30 in. 4 wks misery, starvation. No R.C.P. Lightheaded. Dear Lord, Give us Peace-Food." The next day he received a portion of

116 • GUEST OF ADOLF

a French R.C.P., and then a couple of days later he was "sweating out par [parcel] till 5 P.M. R.C.P. #10 1–4." This was the first parcel he received in 33 days. A few days later the fortunes of all the POWs changed when "R.C.P. cars 18 arr. God's Blessings over 120,000 R.C.P."

Their arrival began a six-week period during which the parcels were distributed on a 1-to-1 basis weekly. However, Ernie still expressed his displeasure in not having enough to eat repeatedly saying, "Hard time getting enough to eat. Plenty weak." Or: "Another nerve aching hungry day. Should be happy but (NOT)." This constant state of hunger persisted during his entire 88 days of confinement in IIIA. His attempts to trade cigarettes for food were unsuccessful, as evidenced by his April 14 comment: "Outdoors all afternoon trying to trade cigs for food. No Success." The reason he was unable to effect a trade was that no one had any food to share. Ernie did find a way to gain extra food by visiting the unclaimed parcel area where he was able to receive multiple parcels every couple of days. On one such visit he was "issued 3 pkgs butts, 1 cigar. Tub food, unc (unclaimed) per par." He continued this practice through the end of his stay at Stalag IIIA.

He continued to care for himself, his clothing, and his health as best he could under these circumstances. The first hot shower he was able to take was not until March 28, 56 days after his arrival at the camp. In the meantime, he did take what he called birdbaths at least three times a week. He visited sick call on numerous occasions, but the most they could provide was either an aspirin for his aches or a salve for his sores. Regarding his overall health he chronicled it in these comments: "Slowly going down. Have to force myself to move," "Wt [weight] was down, 30 in waist. Light headed at time," "Hips-Legs suffering rheumatics [rheumatism]" and "Physically my body near wreck. Proper shelter-food lacking so long. Joints ache-teeth OK as far as known."

Despite the awful conditions, Ernie continued to place his trust in God and attend church on Sundays. A typical prayer of his was: "Dear Lord please hear my pray [prayer], comfort—sustain me. End this all and let me go home, Amen." On one Sunday, an English chaplain conducted the service. Ernie recognized the chaplain as the one who conducted services while he was at the POW camp in Capua, Italy, in early April 1943. There were no activities besides walking the perimeter of their portion of the camp compound. Losing the ability to participate in activities such as glee club, theater shows, and sports contributed to Ernie's growing sense of helplessness. Three days after arriving at Stalag IIIA he wrote: "Oh! To be Home. Endurance-Faith very low!! Might this grow." A month later he lamented: "Miserable Life, no brighter outlook." Finally, at the end of March, he summarized: "This rotten life causes man more heartaches."

Ernie's main concerns were keeping warm, rereading letters from LaRue and home, and attempting to secure enough food. He partially accomplished staying warm by staying in his bunk fully dressed and under his blankets for most of the day. As for the food, there was never enough to satisfy his hunger. His overall impression of Stalag IIIA was that it was a miserable, cold, wet, and overcrowded camp. There was "nothing to do but sit and think" and wait in lines for hot water or food. He received seven letters during his stay at Luckenwalde. The first of these arrived in early March nearly six weeks after leaving Stalag IIIB. The frequent arrival of letters from LaRue was a morale booster that greatly assisted his overall demeanor and contributed to his overall well-being throughout his period of captivity. The absence of these added to his sense of hopelessness, his sense of wasting his life, and further contributed to his overall mental and physical decline.

The rainy morning of April 21, 1945, began with "things in uproar. Spirits rising. Guards preparing to leave. To me a sad affair in spite. 12 noon last guard left. Excitement high. White flags waving alaround [all around]. Wholes [holes] in fence. Officers came down to take over, organization shaping up. Bought goat milk cheese. Sweating out relief troops. Staying in compound for safety. Glorious day to be free permantly [sic]." Once the last of guards departed, the camp was unsecured, with white flags flying from several locations.

For the remainder of the day everyone was unsure of what to do. Should they head west attempting to reach the Allies' lines or stay in the camp in case it was a trap? They decided to stay and see what happened the next morning. Since the camp really had no organization to it, Ernie wandered about the various compounds searching for and visiting with friends. He also used some of his cigarette hoard to purchase goat milk cheese, potatoes, and salmon. He combined these extra foodstuffs with some of his other rations to create a big meal for himself and some of his buddies. He ate until he was full, and when no troops had arrived by 7:25 p.m., he tried to sleep. However, he was up at 11 p.m. when a "plane came over straffing [strafing]. Boy did that arouse us. Hearts plopped sped up. Had suspicion of all planes after that." This sent everyone to the ground and searching for more secure shelter. Fortunately, it was only one plane, and it made only one pass over the camp, injuring no one. Ernie was eventually able to fall asleep.

In her letters, LaRue often discusses her work as a secretary at the Pennsylvania Department of Public Instruction and her boss. She relates how he interrupts her letter writing by asking her to take dictation or to do some other tasks. There were times when he kept her late or had her work part of a Saturday when she had plans to travel to Tyrone or go out with her friends. LaRue complained of having to work Christmas evening and the next day until 10 p.m. The senior secretary, Mrs. B., was frequently not at work due to an illness, and this caused LaRue to have more work. "Mrs. B was out sick yesterday and still out today. I hope she's better and in tomorrow because we have State Council of Education meeting."[5] LaRue regularly commented that she hoped Mrs. B. would return soon to relieve her of some of the workload and that she would not want her job of staying late and working weekends. Mrs. B. did return to work in early January 1945, but she resigned in mid-March 1945.

Another common thread in LaRue's letters was her daydreaming of looking up from her desk and finding Ernie standing there to surprise her upon his return. She was unsure what she would do if he did appear at the office unannounced, but she really wanted him to surprise her. She was also concerned about her appearance when she saw Ernie for the first time upon his return. This anxiety was expressed in one of her letters: "The other Saturday Fred Gutshall and I were sitting in our living room—I looked awful from giving the dog a bath and I said to Freddie 'Wouldn't be awful if I looked like this when Ernie came home' and he said 'Huh! I guess he wouldn't care what you looked like.'"[6] LaRue expressed her plans to take a leave of absence once he returned home even if she would lose her job. All she wanted to do was to get married and begin their life together.

Ernie's receipt of mail from his parents, his relatives, LaRue, and friends was sporadic at best. There were times that he did not receive mail for two or three weeks. On these occasions he would write that he longed to hear from home or from LaRue. Without the constant receipt of these morale-boosting letters his spirits would sink to the point of near despair. In July 1944 after another time going on sick call, he comments on the status of both his health and faith: "Resistance getting low as well as faith. At times I could scream. Pray God the end comes soon. Sweating out teeth also. Dang unhappy about all." This was simply one of the many times he expressed the feeling of being forgotten and abandoned by the U.S. Army and sometimes God. His faith was never shaken to the point of not attending church or prayer meetings. He was always praying to God for the end of the war and a return to his home and his darling fiancée. Additionally, he focused on what he would do once he was together with LaRue. "One thought if plans worked out when I get back to you Honey would be for us then married to take a big trip together. To where you visited me then to your relations on the coast and then back to Idaho. This plan seems perfect to me. But as long as you are with me is all that matters." LaRue persisted in writing to Ernie throughout his captivity. In many of these letters to Ernie she comments that his family does not understand why he does not respond to their letters as they write to him every week. LaRue likewise did not understand why he was not receiving more mail.

Every item mailed to him and by him was processed through a United States censor and then a German censor, or vice versa. Occasionally individuals would attempt to pass information to Ernie of a sensitive nature that they did not desire the censors to delete. In one letter his sister Vera wanted to inform Ernie that his brother Dean received a promotion in the Marine Corps. She accomplished this by stating that "he is now what you were when you had your picture taken."[7] This is a reference to the picture he had taken in February 1942 upon promotion to the grade of technician fifth class or corporal. Vera passed along Dean's location a few months later: "He was in the state you were in when Mama and others made the trip to visit you."[8] Vera was referring to the June 1941 visit her mother and others made to see Ernie at Fort Meade, Maryland. LaRue was not as adept as Vera in passing on sensitive information to Ernie.

A few of her surviving letters have whole sentences blacked out where one of the censors believed her words were inappropriate. The censors blacked out individual words, phrases, and entire lines from some of her letters.

The quality and tenor of LaRue's letters was primarily very heartening and uplifting. She encouraged him to look forward to the day he returned to her, and they could be together for the remainder of their lives. LaRue often discussed her preparations for their married life to include picking out and then buying stemware and China patterns: "Mother said she managed to get the dozen high stemmed goblets and I've had a dozen sherbet and cocktail goblets put back."[9] In other letters she described the style of house she would like to live in and even proposed a name for the son she was sure they would have together. Ernie commented on her encouragement in a January 7, 1945, postcard saying: "My Love, Your nearness pouring in Oct 18–25 letters." In the same postcard he included the fact that he was no longer a POW camp confidence man or a billet leader. Ernie then requested that she not judge him for how he looked in the *Red Cross Bulletin* photograph since he had lost a lot of weight. Her ever-present encouraging attitude was discarded in two of her December 1944 letters. In the first she wrote, "Some people have all the luck. Dean will be home for Christmas. Sometimes I feel so bad that we don't rate a little luck and happiness together. I get so sick of everyone saying, 'cheer up your time will come.' Golly, I've been telling myself that for so long I don't need anyone else to tell me."[10] In her letter of December 27 LaRue writes, "Things are probably pretty terrible for you right now, but try to hold out—we are all praying for you. It is so easy to say 'keep your chin up' but to do it is another thing. I know, I've tried hard to keep in good spirits, and so far I've succeeded pretty well."[11] Ironically, these downhearted messages were written in two of the last three letters Ernie received while a POW. Throughout the last couple of months of the war in Europe LaRue continued to express her concern for Ernie's safety in her letters. This distress stemmed from the information on the progress of the war she read in newspapers and heard on the radio. In all her writings this was the only time she ever wrote of worrying about his well-being.

The last two letters Ernie received from LaRue were dated December 5 and 9, 1944. He received these while at Stalag IIIA in Luckenwalde, Germany, on April 26, 1945. During the three months he was at Stalag IIIA Ernie was able to write four letters while he received seven. After his return to American lines at Hildesheim, Germany, through his stay at Camp Lucky Strike, France, Ernie wrote 11 letters to LaRue and his parents. His last letters to them were written on June 1, 1945. Many of the letters LaRue wrote after December 27, 1944, were returned to her as undeliverable. She received them between June 15 and July 15, 1945. Extrapolating the information in LaRue's letters indicating her writing frequency of at least five letters per week equates to her mailing at least five hundred letters between March 1943 and April 1945. His parents and siblings wrote at least 160, while friends contributed another 90 for a grand total of 750 letters and postcards mailed to Ernie during his period of captivity. In his diaries he records every piece of mail received and whom it was from. At the end of 1943, Ernie recorded that he received 47 letters from friends and family members. A year later he records receiving two hundred letters from LaRue and 66 from home. A review of his daily diary entries reveals that he recorded receiving only 32 pieces of mail during his final four months of captivity. Combining his 1945 total with his two diary entries indicates he received a total of 345 pieces of mail compared to the 750 pieces mailed, or only 46 percent of the items mailed to him. It is easily presumed that a similar percentage of his mail was received by his loved ones. This low percentage of letters mailed versus letters received assists in explaining why his family and LaRue constantly commented on his not responding to their letters.

The time a letter took to travel between the United States and Ernie's POW camp in Germany was a contributing factor to the angst one reads in their correspondence. Any item mailed to Ernie navigated a time-consuming process before he received it. The process involved multiple steps and multiple transfers between the United States, the International Committee of the Red Cross (ICRC), and Germany. After finishing a letter to Ernie, LaRue would place it into any United States Postal Service receptacle. The local post office would sort it and forward it to the appropriate Army post office. In this instance it would be one of the Army post office locations near New York City. It was here that the letter was opened and read by a censor, who blacked out any material deemed sensitive to the war effort. After passing the censor station the letter was reclosed and sent overseas either by ship or by airplane to an overseas Army postal unit. Since the letter was for a POW, it was then turned over to the ICRC. They in turn handed it to a representative of the German government and it underwent another reading by German censors. Only then was the letter ready to be forwarded to the appropriate POW camp and then delivered to Ernie. However, as the war progressed, the Germans' ability to move anything around their county decreased due to the destruction of their railroads and bridges. So it was not surprising that Ernie's first letters to LaRue did not arrive for six months, given that from his couple surviving letters written from Stalag IIIB they were received three months after he mailed them. Conversely, letters written to Ernie in June and July 1943 were received three months later, but letters mailed after July 1943 were not received until four months later. The last surviving letter from LaRue to Ernie was written on April 11, 1945, and it was returned to her on June 20, 1945, five days after Ernie arrived home in Tyrone, Pennsylvania.

CHAPTER 8

Liberation: The Way Home

After the German guards departed, the thousands of POWs in both Stalag IIIA and Oflag IIIA were wary of exploring beyond the confines of the two camps. Was this a trap set by the Germans to lure the POWs out so they would be justified in executing them in an escape attempt, or were the Germans truly gone? A group of American POW officers from Oflag IIIA entered the enlisted compound to take control and commenced organizing the POWs since the latest rumor was that the Americans would be evacuated back to the American lines beginning at noon. Additionally, they let it be known that everyone was to remain inside the compound. However, the evacuation did not begin that day.

On the morning of April 22, 1945, Ernie stated that, since the camp was in an area where the fighting was still raging, he was "free but not liberated. Half sick in stomach." It was the first day in 26 months and five days that Ernie was not a German prisoner of war. He had eaten so much food the evening before that his stomach was upset, so he ate very little for breakfast. Around 5 a.m. the first Russian soldiers entered the camp in a scout car with the news that the main force of Marshal Ivan Konev's armored column would arrive by nightfall. The Russians encouraged everyone to remain inside the barbed-wire fence line of the POW camps for their own safety. However, as there were no guards at the gates, numerous POWs decided to head out on their own or in small groups searching for the Allied lines. In the early afternoon, Ernie attended a church service conducted by an English chaplain to give thanks for his coming through the POW experience. By 3 p.m.

124 • GUEST OF ADOLF

the Americans were already organized into squads and formations with the officers establishing accountability for everyone by name and Army service number. When the armored column arrived in the early afternoon, the tanks drove straight into the compound. They were considered liberated, but they were not free. The Russians assumed control of the camp and posted guards around the perimeter fencing. There was a twofold purpose for this action: they desired to keep any German soldiers dressed as civilians from slipping into the camp, and to ensure that the prisoners remained in the camp. When the Russian column moved on, most of the physically able Russian prisoners joined the column and went off to fight the Germans.

One of the first things Ernie noticed was that the water was shut off and that the food supply was worse than normal. Ernie was unsure what was going to happen to him and the other American and British POWs after the Russians took control of the camp. He wrote: "Ever longing for home-foods, to be miles from this camp. Inside barbe [barbed] wire yet so freedom none to [sic] great. 2 P.M. no soup issued and my stomach calling for nourishment." Naturally, he busied himself with trying to secure enough food to sustain himself and his buddies. Since there was no central food distribution point, each POW scrounged food from wherever he could find it. Ernie first attempted to locate food by walking up to the British and American officer compounds, where he procured a "Cup Potsum [Postum, a powdered roasted grain beverage popular as a coffee substitute]. Also meger [sic] soup ration. Macaroni if you could find them sort tomato flavoring." He next visited several of the barracks, where he hit the jackpot and "had first fresh meat, fried liver with onions, gravy-M. spuds-Cof-with Gabeir, Stiver. What a meal." During the next few days, he raided the building where the unclaimed parcels were stored, searching for food and clothing. He also located a few RCPs, which he quickly secured, and for the first couple of days he was able to purchase extra food using cigarettes and items found in the unclaimed parcels. This apparent abundance of foodstuffs led to overeating and an upset stomach on multiple days. He became upset at the Russians for preventing his departure. Almost daily he expressed his loathing at not being on his way home with such comments as

LIBERATION: THE WAY HOME • 125

"Seems worse, supposed to be free and us very much confined. Longing for home" and "No word to removal. Very distressing, Seems eternity." As the days wore on, he settled back into his daily routine of taking walks around the compounds, showering, cooking, scrounging for food, and cleaning his clothes.

Unbeknownst to the American and British POWs of Stalag IIIA and Oflag IIIA, they became pawns in a disagreement over the return of all POWs to their respective countries. The first indication to the POWs that something was holding up their departure was when, on April 29, the evacuation committee representing the American and British arrived for discussions with the Russians. The committee left that same day without any announcement regarding the POWs' removal from the camps. This led Ernie and others to begin worrying that they would not be returning to American control, but instead be transported east into Poland and possibly into Russia. Later Ernie learned that the sticking point was that the Russians insisted that all their POWs be returned to their authority regardless of their desire to remain under the control of the American, British, or French authorities.

During this period of uncertainty as the days passed, some of Ernie's buddies decided to leave the camp and strike out for the American lines. However, many of these men returned the next day. Those who returned expressed how unsafe the countryside was with small bands of Germans and Russians roaming the countryside engaging in firefights. Ernie did leave the camp on two occasions. On his first trip beyond the fence, he walked into the town of Luckenwalde. He described the area as being a mess with nothing but rubble: "While in town saw lot German P.O.W. marching through. Sad lot." His other excursion beyond the fence line was for a stroll in the nearby woods. Both outings were against the regulations established by the Russians and the senior American officer of the camp.

On May 3, his fears of being transported into Poland were heightened again: "Started registering for repatriation by Russians. Food rations low. No R.C.P.s Becoming hard to get along. Tension for leaving becoming more acute." However, the next day these fears were allayed: "U.S. troops arr [arrived] gave Inf [information] for our departure." He calmed down

126 • GUEST OF ADOLF

even more when, on May 5, a convoy of American two-and-a-half-ton trucks entered the camp fully loaded with K-rations and fresh bread along with several military ambulances. However, the only POWs permitted to leave as the relief convoy departed were the seriously ill. On the morning of May 6 he was visited by a lieutenant from the 805th who was captured with him: "Lt Glendening down for brfast [breakfast]. Brought in K-rations, Canadian parcels. Plenty brd [bread] now."

At 4:30 in the afternoon of May 6, 1945, he received "orders to move out. Walked to trucks on camp. At last, the thing we waited for. G.I trucks." He boarded a truck to begin his journey west to the American sector. This was 15.5 days after no longer being a German POW and 15.5 days after being a quasi–Russian POW. On this day he rode in the back of the truck with 26 others, taking along his well-guarded and used belongings. The convoy "passed through much ruins Russian side. Went through Wittenberg. Barby crossed over Elbe River by pontoon bridge. And then what seemed all Peace-Quiet AM [American] side of Elbe," bringing him to the safety of a reception camp in the American sector. Around 9 p.m. he received a cold bacon sandwich for dinner and then was taken to a tent where his best friend, Jim, and he shared a bunk bed.

The morning of May 7 was another hurry-up-and-wait experience for breakfast per this comment: "2 hr sweat for cof-whole bread-oatmeal-jam-grapefruit juice." Ernie was extremely pleased with the amount of food when finally served around 9 a.m., however. Since there was nothing else to do but hang around the mess hall area, Ernie managed to secure several servings of breakfast for himself. Around 1:30 p.m. he boarded a truck to continue his journey towards home. The convoy passed through the heavily bombed out city of Magdeburg (Map 11) as it made its way to its destination of the Hildesheim, Germany, airport by 5 p.m. Upon arrival he was dusted for delousing and in the late evening provided K-rations for supper. The airport had no beds, so he slept on the concrete floor using a blanket for warmth. The next day while meeting with a representative of the Red Cross, Ernie asked them to send a notice to his father that he was released and safe. This same day, May 8, 1945, LaRue received this wire from United States Army Chaplain Richard Lipsky that her beloved Ernie was released and doing fine.

LIBERATION: THE WAY HOME • 127

8 May 1945
Germany
Re: Sgt Ernest V. Focht

Dear Miss Cassidy,
Your friend was in my office today and I talked with him for a while. He asked
me to write that he is safe. He appears to be well and is in good spirits. He is
anxious that you hear from him so that you will not worry. He will write at
the first opportunity.[1]

Ernie and his fellow American POWs were fortunate that they were
evacuated first. The British had a tougher time returning to their lines.
On May 10 a convoy of American trucks and drivers arrived to transport
them across the Elbe River. However, the Russians refused to release them
for another 10 days when a convoy of American trucks with Russian
drivers arrived for this purpose. Finally, the disagreement over returning
POWs was resolved, and the British from Stalag IIIA/Oflag IIIA began
their homeward journey.

The subsequent leg of Ernie's journey would have to wait four days
until May 11, 1945. During his four-day layover at the Hildesheim
airport, he complained about the lack of food. On May 8 he wrote:
"Food not issued and I am plenty hungry. Thought hurting days over.
Dang such luck. Hope to leave here soon. Food. Food." The next day
while waiting to be evacuated he received the first hot meal: "Cof-w
brd-M. [mashed] spuds, carrots, spinach, 2 helpings." After eating multiple
servings of breakfast, he learned the next day that his food intake was
being restricted by Army doctors to two meals a day with only one
serving at each meal. "Of course I made sev [several] visits for more."
He simply went through the serving line multiple times without being
questioned as the German civilians serving the food simply placed it on
the trays. He also visited the Red Cross canteen for coffee and sweets.
In the evening he went to the movies as a distraction for his longing to
be home with his family and fiancée.

Around noon on May 11, he boarded a C-47 for the flight to Reims,
France, arriving around 2:25 p.m. He spent the night and the next
morning in a transient camp 25 miles outside of Reims in a tent with
12 other men. Around 1 p.m. on May 12, 1945, he was taken to the
Reims train station to board Army hospital train number 39 for the
journey to Motteville, France, which is near the coastal city of Le Havre.

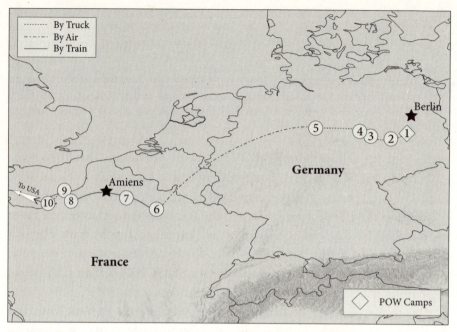

Map 11: Stalag IIIA to Le Havre, May 6 to June 2, 1945. 1. Stalag IIIA—Luckenwalde; 2. Wittenberg, 3. Barby; 4. Magdeburg; 5. Hildesheim; 6. Reims, France; 7. Tergnier; 8. Motteville; 9. Camp Lucky Strike (arrived May 13, 1945); 10. Le Havre, port of embarkation. (Timothy M. Swartz. World Hillshade copyright © Esri)

Ernie complained about the scarcity of food on the train—"Everybody treating us swell but food mighty scarce"—and the 17-hour trip to Motteville. He commented on how the train seemed to stop at every small village and town (Laon, La Feré and Tergnier) it passed. The train finally arrived at 8 a.m. the morning of May 13, 1945. He endured another three-hour delay before boarding a truck for the 20-mile ride to Camp Lucky Strike outside of the town of Saint-Sylvain, France.

The British captured the critical port city of Le Havre from the Germans in September 1944. Unfortunately, the city and its port facilities were almost totally destroyed during the struggle for the town. Afterwards, the U.S. Army assumed responsibility for reopening the harbor and the building of ramps for the transfer of men, supplies, and equipment. Once the port was operating, nine personnel staging areas for new soldiers arriving in the European Theater of Operations were created north and east of the city. All of the camps were named after popular cigarette brands: Old Gold, Pall Mall, Phillip Morris, Wings, Home Run, Chesterfield, Herbert Tareyton, Twenty Grand, and Lucky Strike. They were hastily built camps consisting of tents and a few wooden buildings all very primitive in nature with no comfort features. The soldiers carried their own wood for the small tent heaters, assembled their cots, hauled gravel to cover their dirt floors, and stood in long outdoor chow lines. As the war in Europe wound down, these camps became reception stations for returning servicemen to the United States.

Camp Lucky Strike was the largest of these camps, capable of administering close to sixty thousand soldiers simultaneously. It was in the town of Saint-Sylvain, five kilometers from Saint-Valery-en-Caux at the former site of a German airfield constructed in 1940. The airfield and its proximity—a mere 48 miles—to Le Havre made it the ideal location for being designated the primary camp used to repatriate liberated POWs. It continued to be called Camp Lucky Strike, but it officially was known as Recovered Allied Military Personnel Camp 1 (RAMP Camp 1). Once designated as RAMP Camp 1, the camp underwent a major renovation. It became a major city overnight, with new wooden buildings, tents with floors, mess halls, hospitals, a post office, movie theaters, barbershops, police stations, a jail, and Red Cross recreation facilities being constructed. The camp was subsequently subdivided into four sections—A, B, C, and D—each with 2,900 tents capable of handling 14,500 men.

The newly liberated POWs mainly arrived in a deuce-and-a-half truck from an assembly point near the town of Motteville, which had a train station, or by plane using the camp's runway if they had serious medical problems. The typical procedure for these newly arrived soldiers included being welcomed, completing a registration process, taking a shower, being deloused, and receiving an issue of new clothing and equipment. Their old worn and tattered clothing was immediately discarded and destroyed. They also underwent extensive medical exams and were given a variety of immunizations. Their diet was initially very bland and limited while they built up their tolerance for food again. This was due to the numerous gastrointestinal disorders almost every ex-POW displayed upon

130 • GUEST OF ADOLF

returning to military life where food was abundant and rich in content. Each returning POW underwent an administrative interview where he discussed the circumstances of his capture, the names of others captured with him, the prison camps he was held in, and the type of treatment he received as a POW. After completing these stations, all the POW had to do was to recover, lounge around, visit his friends, and relax until he was notified that his group would be traveling to Le Havre to board a ship for the United States.

Ernie arrived at Camp Lucky Strike around noon on May 13, 1945. He completed the required registration with the camp military command structure. After completing this task, he was assigned to a group of two hundred former POWs all of whom were from Pennsylvania, New York, New Jersey, or Delaware. This group completed the redeployment process together, moving through the myriad of required tasks as a group. At the time, Ernie viewed this process as another delay in his being able to get home to his family and fiancée. Ernie would spend the next 20 days at Camp Lucky Strike. He did not know at the time that this group would all end up at Fort Dix, New Jersey, before being granted a 30-day leave to go home. The rations here were the best he had had since leaving England in January 1943. They were the normal Army A-ration consisting of hot foods including eggs, bacon, oatmeal, fresh bread, fruit, roasted turkey, or chicken etc. Although the food quality was much improved, he still complained about the quantity in his writings. Initially he was not able to double back for seconds since his food intake was being monitored. He routinely supplemented his meals by visiting the Red Cross canteen multiple times daily for coffee, milkshakes, eggnog, and sweets. Finally, on May 24, he expressed his hunger being satisfied: "Right now cut down to one serving per meal. Getting satisfied. Carry piece bread to tent for snack."

Throughout Ernie's stay at Camp Lucky Strike, the Army closely monitored his recovery through multiple medical examinations, shots, and weight checks. He complained, however, that the medical exams were very routine and incomplete: "Walked through line Dr. looked at us. Just another med [medical] G.I. examination." He received multiple issues of clothing, equipment, and blankets. He completed what seemed like an endless stream of military forms and participated in a POW exit debriefing on May 26, 1945. He occupied himself by attending a variety of United Service Organizations (USO) shows, seeing movies, spending time with his buddies, and maintaining his regular attendance of Sunday church service. He also commented on meeting fellows from Tyrone and spending time talking about their experiences and what they knew of home. The fact that these fellows shipped out before him only made him more disgruntled with being stuck in the camp. Some of the other items he complained about included the enforcement of military discipline, wearing the uniform properly, and having most of his day free from any responsibilities or activities, which would bring him closer to departing Camp Lucky Strike. The frequent writing of letters to his parents, siblings, and his darling fiancée LaRue occupied some of his time each day.

While at Camp Lucky Strike, Ernie received a mess schedule, a post exchange slip for him to receive the weekly gratis items, and an exchange slip authorizing him to purchase two gifts and one bottle of perfume a week. He did use the weekly slip during his stay, but there is no evidence that he purchased any gifts or perfume. On a daily basis he expressed his displeasure with being held up from leaving Camp Lucky Strike and continuing his journey home with complaints such as "Sweating out home," "Longing for Home. Might make it by Christmas or may be sooner," and "No further word about going home." He believed his time at Camp Lucky Strike was a waste of his time, delaying his trip home. Finally, on the afternoon of June 1, there was progress: "Rec [received] word to leave here 6 A.M Sat. Very glad for food diminishing every meal. Still no salt. Have us on a diet." In the end 35.5 days elapsed between when the German guards abandoned their posts at Stalag IIIA and when Ernie was finally headed back to the United States. His group was up at 4 a.m. and ate breakfast at 5 a.m. before departing the camp at 7:45 a.m. on the morning of June 2, 1945, for the 48-mile ride to the port at Le Havre, France. Once there, they boarded a landing craft tank for the short ride out to the troopship, the SS *MorMacMoon*. He enjoyed two meals, the first at 1 p.m. and another at 5:00 p.m. before the ship set sail at 6 p.m. It was a "Beautiful Sat eve and Homeward bound. Thank Dear Lord." Ernie's time away from the United States was coming to an end after two years and 10 months of overseas duty.

132 • GUEST OF ADOLF

The transit time between Le Havre, France, and Newport News, Virginia, was nine days. The first day out it was stormy with choppy seas, which "tossed to [and] fro and of course I yoked 5 times but ate at all times if did have to calm down. Was sup [supposed] to conduct Church but to [sic] sick." During the time at sea, Ernie busied himself with walks around the ship, attending movies and shows, reading the daily ship newspaper, and rarely missing a meal. He continued the practice of recording what he ate and making comments. His comment for the fifth day at sea was: "For sup [supper] loads chicken-rice-beets-pickles-cookies-orange-ice cream-cheese. Serving on board, Bkfst [breakfast], Light Lunch, Supper, Midnight snack. More than one can eat. Felt good food going down good." Naturally his impatience to finally be home and in the arms of his fiancée manifested itself repeatedly during the voyage in these words: "Can hardly wait to get home," "Impatient about getting home," and "Pray Home this time next wk [week]." The night before the SS *MorMacMoon* was scheduled to dock in Newport News, Virginia, Ernie's comment was, "Don't seem possible almost home U.S.A." Ernie attended church services topside weather permitting, and on one occasion—June 10—he led the service.

The June 7, 1945, issue of the SS *MorMacMoon*'s daily newspaper, *The Port Hole News*, provided updates on the capture of the Chinen Peninsula on Okinawa and the attack of 450 Superfortress bombers on Osaka, Japan. There were additional updates on the finalization of the four occupation zones in Germany with the United States Army having to pull back to the Elbe River, turning over territory to the Russians. The movie for the day was *Andy Hardy's Blonde Trouble*, starring Mickey Rooney and Lewis Stone. Similarly, the June 10 issue of the newspaper continued to provide updates on the ground and air war in the Pacific and an update on a new discharge point score to be announced in July. In the world of sports, it announced that the Boston Braves beat the league-leading New York Giants by a four-to-nothing score. There was a note of thanks printed from the passengers to the ship's crew for excellent treatment during the voyage. The former POWs wrote: "After our enforced stay as 'guests' of Germany, this trip to the United States has seemed a veritable paradise compared with our former squalid existence. The companionship, entertainment, food, accommodations, and the hundreds of sundry small favors fostered upon us will not shortly be forgotten, and it can be safely said that not one returning person will ever lose from his memory the name *S. S. MorMacmoon*."[2] At 5 a.m. on the morning of Monday, June 11, 1945, the ship passed Old Point Comfort, Virginia, and anchored at the docks of Newport News by 9 a.m. Finally, Ernie and the other former POWs were back in the good old United States of America.

It would be another four days until he achieved his long, long desire to be home. Once off the troopship, the group boarded a Chesapeake and Ohio train for a 45-minute ride to Camp Patrick Henry. It was in Virginia's Warwick County, a short distance outside of Newport News, Virginia. Today Newport News/Williamsburg International Airport sits on the site of the camp.[3] After a welcome home ceremony, receiving his barracks assignment, eating lunch, receiving more clothing, and being paid, Ernie placed a telephone call to his "Darling Fiancée LaRue." This was followed by a call to his parents. The next 36 hours he spent making a few purchases at the canteen, organizing his belongings, shipping a duffel bag to Fort Dix, New Jersey, sunbathing, and "wasting time here doing nothing alday [all day]." Finally on June 13 at "1 P.M. fell out for formation to leave. Marched to train with Band accompanied. 2 P.M. boarded Norfolk Western" train for the 16-hour trip to Fort Dix, New Jersey (Map 12). The train stopped in Richmond and Washington, DC, before finally arriving at Fort Dix at 5 a.m. on June 14. During the day Ernie "drew more clothes, suntans, U-wear, socks, cigtob [cigarette/tobacco], ration card. Did nothing else but had to stay in area." The morning of June 15 he was up early: "On the go for it is the day of 'Days' Going HOME." This was to be the day when, after 1,097 days, he would be reunited with his beloved LaRue and his family. Ernie departed Fort Dix by bus for the Trenton train station, where he boarded the 4 p.m. train to Harrisburg. When the train pulled into the Harrisburg station, Ernie expected to be greeted by LaRue. However, she was not there. He quickly departed the train, hailed a cab, and went to her apartment on Graham Street. After a quick greeting they hastened back to the station and reboarded the train for Altoona. During the remainder of the trip Ernie commented on how much LaRue talked. At 10:45 p.m. they walked off the train in Altoona and were greeted by Ernie's parents and his older brother Mel. The group first stopped at LaRue's parents' home before continuing on to the Focht residence in Tyrone. Upon entering the house Ernie was greeted by many other family members. The happy reunion continued into the early morning hours when Ernie "took Honey home in the early A.Ms." Finally, "Home Sweet Home," the place he longed for throughout his POW ordeal.

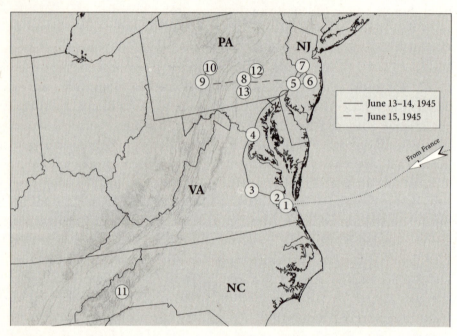

Map 12: Port of Debarkation to Army Discharge, June 11 to September 11, 1945. 1. Newport News, VA; 2. Camp Patrick Henry, VA; 3. Richmond, VA; 4. Washington, DC; 5. Philadelphia, PA; 6. Fort Dix, NJ; 7. Trenton, NJ; 8. Harrisburg, PA; 9. Altoona, PA; 10. Tyrone, PA; 11. Asheville, NC; 12. Indiantown Gap Military Reservation, PA; 13. Dillsburg, PA. (Timothy M. Swartz. World Hillshade copyright © Esri)

CHAPTER 9

Reunion and Asheville, North Carolina

This warm welcome home reception set the tone for the beginning of an approximately 30-day furlough from the Army. Ernie was not unlike most servicemen returning home in that he desired to move on with his life. He repeatedly recorded notes in his diaries of being home, having plenty to eat, and not wasting any more of his life. His foremost priority during this period was marrying his "Darling Fiancée LaRue." A reading of their letters to each other and Ernie's diary confirm how deeply in love they were and the firmness of their commitment to each other. In a letter to an uncle, LaRue expressed an anxiety that Ernie would be disappointed in her cooking skills. In a letter dated November 12, 1944, from "somewhere in France," her uncle Private Lee James wrote to her: "Don't worry any about your cooking as anything will taste good after the food he has been use to."[1] LaRue apparently heeded her uncle's advice, and the pair moved forward with their wedding plans.

During the next 22 days the arrangements for their long-awaited marriage were completed. Ernie purchased their rings for $47.50, wedding flowers for $31.50, a bracelet and ring as a wedding gift for $47.50, and the marriage license for $3.00. He also arranged for a room at the Hotel Lewisberger in Lewistown, Pennsylvania, for their wedding night. Now that he had completed the pre-wedding arrangements, all that remained was for the wedding day to arrive. On July 7, 1945, at 2:00 p.m. in Pleasant Valley United Brethren Church, Elizabeth LaRue Cassidy and SGT Ernest V. Focht were married by the Reverend James A. Woomer. Afterwards, the bride's family hosted a reception in their home before the happy couple departed for the Hotel Lewisburger in Lewisburg, Pennsylvania, for their first night as husband and wife. The next day they traveled to Pocono Pines, Pennsylvania, for their honeymoon trip.

After this trip, they had very little time together as Ernie had to immediately report back to the Army. When he departed Fort Dix, New Jersey, on June 15, 1945, he was issued two train ticket vouchers. The first voucher provided passage to Tyrone and then to Washington, DC, while the second was for his trip to his new duty station, the Army Ground and Service Forces (AG & SF) Redistribution Station, Asheville, North Carolina. Ernie was partially aware of what lay ahead for him at this duty station as he received a welcome booklet prior to departing Fort Dix, New Jersey. However, he had been a POW for so long that regular army life seemed foreign to him, and he was surely unhappy at leaving his bride behind in Harrisburg, Pennsylvania, for an undetermined length of time. All he wanted to do was to be discharged so he could get on with his life and put his army experience behind him as much as possible.

The redistribution station concept was a consequence of the March 1942 Army implementation of a significant reorganization of its command structure. The Army Chief of Staff, General George C. Marshall, desired to reduce the number of commands and officers who reported directly to him. This reorganization accomplished his objective. It provided for three autonomous components of the United States Army: the Army Ground Forces, the Army Air Forces, and the Army Service Forces. This third command, the Army Service Forces, brought together five pre-existing elements of the United States Army under the command of General Brehon B. Somervell, who reported to the Army Chief of Staff. These five Army elements were: the War Department staff, in particular the G-4 (logistics) division; the Office of the Undersecretary of War; eight administrative bureaus; the nine corps areas that were renamed service commands; and the seven supply arms and services (quartermaster, signal, medical, ordnance, engineer, chemical, and transportation), which became known as the technical services.[2] Soldiers returning from overseas duty without a specific assignment, soldiers being returned to duty after a period of hospitalization and recovery, or former prisoners

REUNION AND ASHEVILLE, NORTH CAROLINA • 137

of war returning to the United States were assigned to the Army Service Forces.

The pre-existing corps commands were redesignated service commands under the 1942 Army reorganization. Of these nine, it is the Fourth Service Command under the command of Major General Frederick E. Uhl that was an integral part of Sergeant Focht's last months of military service. This was a geographic command stretching over eight southern states (Alabama, Florida, Georgia, Louisiana, Mississippi, North Carolina, South Carolina, and Tennessee). The command was responsible for administration; all elements of supply and services; and the development, manufacturing, storage, distribution, and issue of equipment to the Army Ground Forces within its geographic area of responsibility. A component of its administrative responsibilities was handling soldiers returning from overseas duty and preparing them for reassignment to various Army or Army Air Force units. The accomplishment of this mission was facilitated through the establishment of two AG & SF redistribution stations, one located in Miami Beach, Florida, and the other in Asheville, North Carolina.

The AG & SF Redistribution Station in Asheville, North Carolina, was established on June 14, 1944, at Camp Butner, North Carolina (located 15 miles northeast of Durham). This installation served as the initial recruitment and training site for the Asheville station while facilities were being acquired and set up in Asheville. The soldiers assigned to the station were drawn from the Eastern Personnel Reassignment Center located at Camp Butner. Many of these soldiers had recently returned from overseas duty, recovered from wounds, or were former POWs. The Asheville station opened on September 5, 1944, under the command of LTC Ulric N. James when the first returnees reported for processing and reassignment. The station facilities included the Asheville-Biltmore Hotel, The George Vanderbilt Hotel, The Battery Park Hotel, and the Grove Park Hotel all for use as quarters for the returnees and their spouses. The permanent party personnel were housed in a building at the Asheville College. Additionally, Asheville Auditorium was used as the main in-processing building and for many of the offices for permanent party soldiers. Lastly, the Pearlman Building was home to a recreation center, game rooms, the main post exchange, a dental clinic, laboratories, chaplains, the Red Cross, and the Army's Personal Affairs Division and Information and Education Division. All these facilities were to support up to fifteen hundred returnees and spouses along with seven hundred permanent party personnel.

The station's primary purpose was to conduct a thorough medical examination of each soldier and to determine in what capacity he could contribute to the ongoing war effort. If this required a soldier to reclassify into a different military occupational specialty, arrangements were made for the soldier to attend the appropriate military schooling. Additionally, the Asheville station desired to provide a first-class recreation and relaxation center that returnees would always remember. The station's welcome booklet specified that all returnees were to participate in a mandatory organized program of in-processing during the first five days. This program's scheduled events were:

> Day 1—Registration, hotel room assignment, initial pay and allowance payment, and a personal interview to update and verify the soldier's military record.
>
> Day 2—Comprehensive medical and dental examination.
>
> Day 3—Classification and assignment interview during which time a soldier could request to take the Army General Classification Test.
>
> Day 4—Instruction on submitting a claim for personal property loss.
>
> Days 1–4—Participation in six organized discussions conducted by the Information and Education Division on these topics: the progress of the war, G. I. Bill of Rights, the home front, democracy and citizenship, America's postwar plans and problems, and "Sound Off" (a general gripe session).
>
> Day 5—Completion of any unfinished business.[3]

Upon completion of the five days of mandatory activities the remainder of the soldier's time at the AG & SF Redistribution Station was devoted to rest and relaxation activities. The returnees were not required to stand any military formations, perform any duties such as kitchen police or police calls, nor were there any reveille or retreat ceremonies. The Fourth Service Command arranged activities with a plethora of local and regional recreational facilities of which the soldier and his spouse could avail themselves. The station's Special Services Office published a bimonthly booklet titled "The Servicemen's Guide to 'The Land of the Sky.'" The booklet provided the soldier with all the various activities open to both him and his spouse. A sampling of the activities offered during the two-week period of August 20 to September 2, 1945, provides a glimpse into the relaxing atmosphere of the Asheville Redistribution Station. The recreational, athletic, and tourist activities advertised in this issue were provided free of charge and included:

1. **Movies:** These were available nightly at one of the three town theaters.
    a. *Along Came Jones*, with Gary Cooper and Loretta Young
    b. *Tarzan and the Amazons*, with Johnny Weissmuller, John Sheffield, and Brenda Joyce
    c. *30 Seconds Over Tokyo*, with Van Johnson and Phyllis Thaxter
    d. *Lost in a Harem*, with Bud Abbott and Lou Costello
    e. *Song of Nevada*, with Roy Rogers

2. **Athletic Activities**
    a. Golf was available at either the Municipal Country Club (enlisted) or the Asheville Country Club (officers). Fifty cents per ball deposit was required, which was refunded when the ball was returned; otherwise there was no fee to play or to borrow clubs
    b. Tennis and swimming at different locations for enlisted and officers
    c. Skeet shooting
    d. Baseball
    e. Horseback riding at the Grove Park Riding Academy
    f. YMCA offered handball, swimming, tennis, basketball, wrestling, softball, and volleyball

3. **Day Trips**
    a. Biltmore Estate
    b. Coco-Cola Plant
    c. Chimney Rock
    d. Gatlinburg
    e. Enka Rayon Plant

4. **Social Opportunities**
    a. YMCA USO Club
    b. Salvation Army canteen

140 • GUEST OF ADOLF

    c. Laurentine canteen

    d. Community Service Lounge

    e. Churches

    f. Stage shows[4]

In addition to the variety of activities listed above, a variety of entertainers and performers visited the Asheville station. These included: Kay Kyser and his "Kollege of Musical Knowledge," Lena Horne (singer), Eddie Bracken (screen star), John McCormack (opera singer), Robert St. John (NBC News), Blackstone (magician), Spud Chandler (New York Yankees pitcher), and the Spotlight Band. Besides these special entertainers, the 380th Army Service Forces Band was permanently assigned to the station in September 1944. During the week, elements of the band furnished music during lunch and dinner in each of the three dining facilities. It also played for the weekly enlisted dances and the twice-weekly officer dances. The full band performed concerts and provided martial music for the weekly retreat ceremony at the Asheville College for the permanent party and for civic parades and war bond rallies.

This sampling of leisure and entertaining activities provides a glimpse of the relaxing environment each soldier enjoyed during his stay at the AG & SF Redistribution Station. Almost all of these items were provided to the service member at no cost. However, if a spouse accompanied the soldier, there were nominal fees for the services. The cost of a hotel suite was $1.25 per night and for three meals a day was $1.05 for a total of $16.10 per week. In addition, there was a one-time fee of $2.00 paid by all returnees and spouses into a service fund. This fund provided fresh fruit, cookies, and drinks and supported the variety of activities available for the returnees' enjoyment.[5]

The Asheville Redistribution Station began its deactivation process in November 1945 and was completed by mid–December 1945. During its 14 months of operation 33,500 returnees were welcomed and processed. Including the six hundred permanent party personnel, thirty-four thousand one hundred individuals consumed more than two million meals during this time while the snack bar served more than three hundred thousand persons hamburgers, hot dogs, cookies, fruits, and drinks.[6] The returning servicemen were treated to an experience like no other the Army had provided them previously. They enjoyed all

REUNION AND ASHEVILLE, NORTH CAROLINA • 141

the comforts of home without any of the responsibility as many began the transition back to civilian life and many to a married life with their prewar sweethearts.

Ernie was required to report to the Asheville station no later than July 15, 1945. Therefore, Ernie and LaRue had very little time together before he shipped out again. In preparation for their arrival, the Army sent two welcome letters. The letter to LaRue discussed the activities available for the wives of the service members in and around Asheville. His welcome letter was from the Protestant chaplain with information on the various religious services available. Approximately one week after their wedding, Ernie said goodbye to his bride and reported to Asheville. LaRue returned to her apartment and job in Harrisburg. In Ernie's absence she used the time to find another apartment for the two of them and prepare for his return to her in mid-September 1945. She did make one trip to Asheville, arriving on August 24, 1945, staying with her husband in the Battery Park Hotel room 930 until September 7, 1945. While together in Asheville, they availed themselves of the many recreational activities and trips offered. These included trips to the Biltmore Estate; Chimney Rock State Park; Gatlinburg, Tennessee; the Great Smokey Mountains National Park; and Cherokee Village, North Carolina. They also enjoyed spending time with some of the other couples, walking around the town of Asheville, and sitting on the Battery Park Hotel veranda.

Ernie received instructions he was shipping out of Asheville to the Separation Center at Indiantown Gap Military Reservation in Pennsylvania on September 7, 1945. Unbeknownst to Ernie he was promoted to staff sergeant on September 5, 1945. He was honorably discharged from the United States Army on September 11, 1945, after four years, five months, and one day of service, spending two years, 10 months, and 11 days overseas of which two years, two months, and 20 days was as a German POW. Now he was once more a civilian and could finally get on with his life, as he dreamed of doing many a night during his captivity.

Ernie joined his bride, LaRue, at their apartment on 1916 Penn Street in Harrisburg, Pennsylvania. In addition to learning how to live as part of a married couple, Ernie learned the details of the wartime rationing

142 • GUEST OF ADOLF

program. As a former POW he was familiar with rationing his food and other possessions, but as a civilian this was a new experience. He needed to learn the differences between the four ration books, the number of ration coupons required for each item, and how frequently you could purchase an item.

It appears that he learned the system well, for when rationing ceased for most items at the end of 1945, both Ernie and LaRue had many coupons remaining in their books. Beginning in 1942 the United States Office of Price Administration produced war ration books. Shortages of essential war materials such as rubber, gasoline, and sugar were initially anticipated, but soon rationing grew to include food and fuel as well. Most commodities were removed from rationing by the end of 1945. Charts and tables were published showing the number and types of ration coupons that were necessary to buy an item. The purchase of four gallons of gasoline required seven coupons from Book A. A number 2 can of applesauce required 14 blue stamps, while a number 2 can of green beans required 14 blue stamps in addition to some cash.[7]

CHAPTER 10

Civilian Life

During his time in Asheville, Ernie applied for a civil service rating in the hopes of gaining employment in one of the government facilities near Harrisburg, Pennsylvania. Initially, he worked in a soda fountain while waiting for a civil service position. He received his rating of 77 to include a five-point veteran's preference on September 12, 1945.[1] He began his career as an employee of the naval supply depot in Mechanicsburg, Pennsylvania, five days later as a storekeeper in the repair parts section of the internal combustion diesel engine department. Early in March 1946 Ernie and LaRue moved to a new apartment at 1245 Mulberry Street, also in Harrisburg. While living at this address, they "wound up with an ice box so that was considered a luxury." Every couple of days the iceman would deliver and place a 50-, 75-, or 100-pound block of ice in the box. In this manner their food would remain cold. A few months later they purchased a dining room set from Buttorff & Company in New Cumberland for $310.

Although Ernie received his discharge from the Army in 1945, during the next couple of years he maintained a continual correspondence with various departments of the Army. In August 1946 he submitted a request for reimbursement for items taken from him by the Germans upon his being captured. He listed $50.00 worth of Algerian francs, over $24.00 dollars of British pounds, and a Swiss wristwatch. The Army reimbursed him a total of $82.00 for this claim a month later. During 1946, separate requests were initiated to correct his separation document to reflect his promotion to staff sergeant, to adjust his pay based upon his promotion for his last seven days of service, and to secure payment for his unused leave. In response to these requests his separation document was corrected, and he received additional pay. However, in October 1946 the Army's finance office forwarded a notice indicating that he owed the government $15.19 for an overpayment of pay as a staff sergeant. There is no record of his settlement of this claim among his papers.

Ernie's position at the naval supply depot was a war service appointment, meaning that it was temporary and could be ended at any time. He desired a permanent position, so he turned to using political influence for this in December 1947. He enlisted the assistance of Harry Glass, the president of the Tyrone school board. Ernie believed he was not properly credited for his supervisory position in the Army, which, if recognized, would result in a higher civil service rating. Mr. Glass wrote a letter of recommendation to Congressman James Van Zandt asking him to intercede on Ernie's behalf. In turn, the congressman wrote to Rear Admiral Charles W. Fox, officer in charge of the naval supply depot. When Ernie had not received a permanent position by March 1948, he wrote directly to the congressman asking him for further consideration. He did receive a response that indicated it was not advisable for him to make further contact with the admiral.[2] Ernie listened to this advice and did not request further action on the congressman's part. At some point, he did transition to a permanent position. In July 1950 he completed his initial supervisory training program. He received recognition for 20 years of federal service in April 1961 and again for 30 years of service in April 1971. In both instances his name and picture appeared in the naval depot's monthly newspaper, *The Mechnews*.

Sometime during 1975 he applied for disability retirement to the Civil Service Commission. In early January 1976, upon arriving home from work, he informed LaRue that his request for disability retirement was approved effective immediately. Ernie remained on extended sick leave through May 2, 1977, when he officially retired from the naval depot after slightly more than 36 years of federal service.

After obtaining his permanent position at the naval supply depot, Ernie's next challenge was getting the Veterans Administration to recognize his physical ailments as being service connected. He elicited and received supporting letters from two of his closest POW buddies, Robert "Lefty"

Gearinger and James Cunningham. Jim was his bunkmate at Stalags IIIB and IIIA, and Lefty was in his close circle of friends during his POW days. In their October 1948 letters they describe the unsanitary conditions under which they lived for over two years and Ernie's hospitalization period for diphtheria in April 1944. Also included are examples of Ernie displaying a nervous condition throughout his POW experience and being threatened by a German guard at gunpoint twice for failing to give up clothing and for taking too long to prepare to move out during the forced march from Fürstenberg to Luckenwalde in February 1945.[3] There were a few other letters and postcards from fellow POWs offering assistance to Ernie with his Veterans Administration (VA) claim. Ernie's claim was eventually recognized, and he frequently received care at the VA hospital in Lebanon, Pennsylvania, and later at the VA clinic in Camp Hill, Pennsylvania. Over time, his conditions worsened, and his VA disability rating increased to 100 percent. As a former POW with a 100-percent disability rating, he was granted commissary and post exchange privileges by the military. He made numerous trips to Carlisle Barracks to use these facilities. In October 1988, his son–in–law Major Michael Zang arranged for Ernie to receive his POW medal at an Army Reserve Brigade pass-in-review ceremony from Brigadier General Walter E. Katuzny, Deputy Commander of the 79th Army Reserve Command at Fort Indiantown Gap, Pennsylvania. This was a fitting location since it was from here that he departed the United States for overseas duty in August 1942 and here that he received his honorable discharge from the Army in September 1945.

While residing at the Mulberry Street address Ernie and LaRue welcomed their first child, their son Stephen, in July 1948. Ernie, LaRue, and Steve moved from the third-floor apartment in Harrisburg to Dillsburg into a new house at 315 Mountain Road in May 1950. There was one home beside theirs, owned by Lavere and Helen Kinter, and a huge farm located just behind the backyard. This farm would become Range End County Club several years later. Their daughter, Karen, was born into this household in October 1951. This completed their "Million Dollar Family." Several years later a garage was added to the Focht property. During the next few years, Ernie continued to work at his job at the naval depot while LaRue stayed home to raise their two children. In the early 1960s, LaRue would work at the Range End Country Club pool and snack bar during the summer months. A few years later she began working for Presbyterian Homes in Dillsburg, eventually becoming the executive assistant to the president before she retired.

After moving to Dillsburg, they immediately searched for a new church home, joining Calvary Evangelical United Brethren Church. Ernie and LaRue were very much involved in the life of the church. As Steve and Karen grew, they too were active in the church. The entire family participated in numerous church-sponsored activities, including family picnics, monthly family nights with great food and fellowship, and choir rehearsals for Ernie, LaRue, Steve, and Karen. In 1968, Evangelical United Brethren Church merged with the Methodist denomination and formed Calvary United Methodist Church in Dillsburg. This merger did not diminish the family's participation in the life of the church. However, in the 1970s LaRue stopped participating in the choir, instead choosing to play the piano at home. They made many lifelong friends and developed close relationships with members of the congregation. This included the Wileys, Davises, Fishers, Harts, Selders, and Smileys, to name a few. These friendships lasted well into the 1990s.

The Fochts consistently traveled to the Tyrone and Juniata-Altoona areas to visit their parents, Clayton and Rhoda Cassidy and Gerald and Mary Helen Focht. LaRue's parents lived in Juniata-Altoona and Ernie's parents in Tyrone. This happened with regularity on Thanksgiving, some Christmases, Easter, Mother's Day, and during the summer. Many summer vacations were spent in this area. The family stayed with the Cassidys, where there was swimming at the Juniata Pool, picnics at a local state park, or fun at Bland Amusement Park. This was a real treat as the park had a merry-go-round whose horses went up and down instead of remaining stationary. During the other downtimes they took the short 20-minute drive to Tyrone to have fun at Ernie's parents' house. Ernie's brother Dean and sister Madeline and their families lived nearby, so there were plenty of visits to their homes. Ernie's sister Vera lived with Gerald and Mary Helen and became their primary caregiver in their later lives.

These vacations typically lasted two weeks, with a Cassidy family reunion on one Saturday and a Focht reunion on the next Saturday. These were exciting events with almost all aunts, uncles, and cousins attending.

The main gate to Stalag VIIA at Moosburg an der Isar, Germany. Ernie was in this stalag from April 14, 1943, to May 4, 1943. (Sammlung Josef Schmid, Stadtarchiv Moosburg, Germany)

> ...gefangenenlager Datum: MAY 16-1943
>
> DArling Well + O.K. Hope you Are the sAme. Ever in My PrAyers & thoughts. Hope everything is going Along Fine Sure keeping the Chin up, the Lord being ALWAYS NEAR. Getting sun tANNed. Hello to Fotures & ALL. Love & kisses ALWAYS Ernie

Postcard Ernie sent to LaRue from Stalag IIIB, Fürstenberg, Germany, May 16, 1943. (Author's collection)

Ernie kept this photograph of LaRue in his prisoner of war diary for 27 months. (Author's collection)

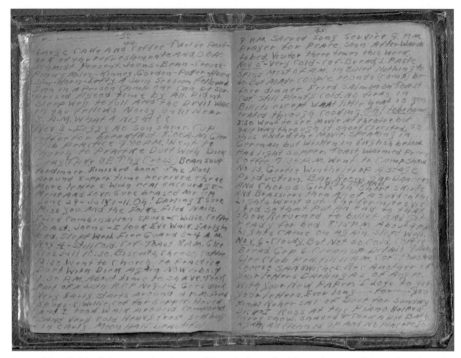

Pages 44 and 45 of the second volume of Ernie's diary for November 2 to November 6, 1943. (Author's collection)

Stalag IIIB prisoner of war pals. Standing: Clarence Potter, Robert Gordon, Robert Gearinger, Clair Kinney, and James Cunningham. In front: William McCormick, Norman Houck, John Fissel, and Ernie. (Author's collection)

Stalag IIIB glee club, March 7, 1944. Ernie is in the center of the front row. (Author's collection)

Stalag IIIB theater stage built by the prisoners of war with materials salvaged from Red Cross parcel crates, March 7, 1944. (Author's collection)

Playbill from *Showboat*, signed and dated August 18, 1944, by Ernie. This is one of the fifty-plus shows the prisoners of war staged at Stalag IIIB. Ernie sang in more than thirty of these shows. (Author's collection)

Jekyll-Hyde playbill, Stalag IIIB prisoner of war performance, November 20, 1944. Ernie participated in this performance. (Author's collection)

Funeral procession for American prisoner of war, Technician 5th Class Lloyd Shaffer, Stalag Luft III, Sagan, Germany, November 1944. Lloyd was a member of Ernie's unit and was captured with him in Tunisia, February 17, 1943. (Author's collection)

American prisoner of war, Technician 5th Class Lloyd Shaffer's graveside funeral service at Stalag Luft III, Sagan, Germany, November 1944. (Author's collection)

POWs behind a barbed-wire fence at Stalag IIIA, Luckenwalde, Germany. (Heimat Museum Luckenwalde, Germany)

American prisoners of war cooking their meager rations at Stalag IIIA, Luckenwalde, Germany. (Australian War Memorial, Public Domain)

Sergeant and Mrs. Ernest V. Focht leaving Pleasant Valley United Brethren Church on their wedding day, July 7, 1945. (Author's collection)

Ernie and LaRue Focht standing outside her parents' home in Juniata, Altoona, Pennsylvania, July 7, 1945. (Author's collection)

Ernie and LaRue relaxing on the veranda of the Battery Park Hotel, Asheville, North Carolina, September 1945. LaRue visited Ernie at this duty station while awaiting his discharge from the Army. (Author's collection)

Ernie and LaRue's house at 315 Mountain Road in Dillsburg, Pennsylvania, July 1950. They lived in this house for the remainder of their lives. (Author's collection)

Gerald and Mary Helen Focht pose with their children for their 50th wedding anniversary celebration, August 1962. Standing (L to R): Wayne, Mel, Madeline, and Ernie. Sitting (L to R): Mary Helen, Dean, Vera, and Gerald. (Author's collection)

Ernie Focht's family, December 1986. Back row (L to R): Michael, Patrick, Karen, Rhoda Cassidy, Ernie, LaRue, and Kathy. Front row (L to R): Kimberly, Andrew, Julia, Jeffrey, and Stephen. (Author's collection)

Ernie and LaRue Focht in the 1980s. (Author's collection)

Emblem on Staff Sergeant Ernest Focht's 805th Tank Destroyer Battalion reunion jacket. (Author's collection)

The 805th Tank Destroyer Battalion 1983 reunion photograph. Ernie is the eighth person from the left in the back row. (Author's collection)

Staff Sergeant Ernest V. Focht receiving his Prisoner of War Medal from Major General Walter E. Katuzny at the 1185th Transportation Terminal Unit Brigade Pass in Review, October 1989, Fort Indiantown Gap, Pennsylvania. (Author's collection)

Ernie surrounded by his grandchildren, December 1994. Back row (L to R): Andrew, Patrick, Ernie, and Kimberly. Front row (L to R): Jeffrey and Julia. (Author's collection)

Ernie and LaRue attended Calvary United Methodist Church in Dillsburg, Pennsylvania. (Author's collection)

SSG Ernest and LaRue C. Focht's headstone in Dillsburg Cemetery, Dillsburg, Pennsylvania. (Author's collection)

CIVILIAN LIFE • 147

Both reunions were held in Reservoir Park in Tyrone. Ernie served as the president for some of these reunions and was reelected to this position many times. A special reunion for LaRue was in 1968 when they returned to Tyrone for her 30th high school class reunion. Ernie remained very connected to his parents, his siblings, and their children. He performed the principle of Christian charity with this extended family through his unofficial role as the family banker. He regularly loaned money to family members in need while maintaining a record of the amount loaned, to whom it was loaned, and all repayments in a small black book.

Mary Helen passed away on March 25, 1971, and Gerald five years later on March 3, 1976. They are buried together in Eastlawn Cemetery in Tyrone, Pennsylvania, along with three of their seven children: Josephine, Dean, and Vera.

Ernie and LaRue always had many close friends scattered throughout Pennsylvania including Tyrone, Harrisburg, Mechanicsburg, and Dillsburg areas. Their Tyrone group included Bucky and Margie Baldridge, Les and Mardelle Fink, John and Sara Candy, and Ed and Ruth Gutshall. Ernie and LaRue stayed in close contact with them and often visited during trips home to Tyrone. While LaRue worked in Harrisburg during the war she met Sib Mays, Elizabeth Getz, Alice Drayer, and Anna May Oris. When Ernie and LaRue married, they moved to Harrisburg, where LaRue continued to work in the Department of Education. Ernie found a short-term job working in a soda fountain from his cousin Bud Focht until he started working at the naval supply depot in Mechanicsburg. The fountain job taught him how to make tasty root beer floats that everyone enjoyed. They quickly developed friendships with the spouses—Clarence Mays, Stanley Getz, Clarence Drayer, and Wayne Oris. These friendships lasted until everyone became incapacitated or passed away. Along the way Ernie and LaRue made many friends in the Harrisburg area through their church—including Janet and Loy Green, Ruth and Bob Diehl, and Myrtle and Bill Miller. Even after Steve and Karen were born, visits with all these folks happened often, usually on the weekend. The Drayers had a round swimming pool that the Fochts always enjoyed during their summer visits. The Mayses had a trained parakeet that could do several tricks for Clarence. Karen and Steve loved this when they were young. Ernie and LaRue often vacationed with

148 • GUEST OF ADOLF

the Drayer and the Oris families at Ship Bottom, New Jersey, during the summer. This continued even after Ernie and LaRue and the Orises had children. They always rented the same large house located on the beach. It was the only beachfront property they ever stayed in.

Several years after returning home, Ernie and his POW pals began having reunions. Most of the group was from his friends who formed the nucleus of the original Company A of the 805th Tank Destroyer Battalion. Many of these men hailed from Tyrone and Bloomsburg, Pennsylvania. Ernie related that they all connected during the various training exercises before departing the United States for England. The reunions were normally held in the Bloomsburg area, although in the 1980s some were conducted in Lancaster, Pennsylvania. The wives were invited to these events, so LaRue became familiar with many of the men and their wives. On several occasions Steve and Karen went to the reunions and enjoyed themselves. They especially enjoyed staying at the Candlelight Motel and eating breakfast at the Magee Hotel on these trips. Steve recalled that many of these former POWs were real characters, and their stories were most interesting and sometimes extremely funny. His favorite was the man who told of his walking out the main gate of the prison camp four times by bribing the guards with chocolate or cigarettes from the Red Cross parcels. This former POW possessed a great sense of humor, but he was caught all four times and returned to camp. Ernie said his downfall was that American men were raised to respect women, but the German men were not raised in this manner. Unfortunately, when he practiced this trait after leaving the camp the authorities took notice resulting in his being captured and returned to Stalag IIIB. Ernie also attended several of the 805th Tank Destroyer Battalion reunions. In the 1980s and early '90s he frequently attended the annual National POW/MIA Recognition Day observances conducted at one of central Pennsylvania's five military installations: Fort Indiantown Gap, New Cumberland Army Depot, Mechanicsburg Naval Supply Depot, Carlisle Barracks, or the Veterans Administration Hospital in Lebanon, Pennsylvania.

One of Ernie's favorite television shows was *Hogan's Heroes*. He professed there was a similarity between some aspects of the show and his experiences in Stalag IIIB. He noted specifically how the men in his barracks dug and maintained a hidden room below the barracks floor to hide a clandestine radio. They used the radio to track the progress of the war by listening to the British Broadcasting Corporation daily programs. After the Germans discovered this room and confiscated the radio, another one was secured. This time instead of hiding it in one location, the prisoners moved the radio between barracks. Sergeant Shultz from *Hogan's Heroes* reminded Ernie of the large German guard who often came into the barracks. Whenever this guard entered, someone would shout "Timber" to alert everyone that he was present and to hide the radio. Ernie also related that occasionally some of the POWs went out on work details to dig ditches or holes for concrete forms. While working they would often throw their tools into the holes when the Germans were not watching.

Dillsburg offered the family many small-town activities to participate in and enjoy. The third weekend in October was the annual Farmers Fair. This event was probably the family's favorite as it included displays of many farmers' goods and wares. This included awarding ribbons for the best apple pie, largest beet, or the largest pumpkin, to name a few examples. The main street closed for the weekend to permit numerous food vendors and school groups to set up booths selling a variety of food items and souvenirs. Additionally, the fair included an antique car display and two parades. On Friday night there was the children's parade in which both Steve and Karen participated dressed in their Halloween costumes. The Saturday night parade included numerous bands, floats, farmers' equipment, clowns, and other marching units. This was probably the children's favorite Dillsburg event. Even after Steve and Karen went to college and moved away from Dillsburg, they would often return for Farmers Fair. Other favorites included the Memorial Day parade and the ice cream treat afterwards, Northern High School band concerts, a day outing at Williams Grove Amusement Park, and local summer festivals that were always a great time for food and fellowship. Ernie and LaRue were active in Freemasonry, Ernie as a member of the Eureka-West Shore Masonic Lodge and LaRue as a member of the Order of Eastern Star for many years.

Growing up Ernie had enjoyed riding the rails with his father's railroad employee pass. Gerald "GrandPap" Focht was a railroad engineer who made trips between Altoona and Harrisburg. Many times, he overnighted in Harrisburg, staying in the railroader's bunkhouse that was just north of Harrisburg. Ernie often took Karen and Steve to the bunkhouse to visit with GrandPap when he was in town. Whenever possible, GrandPap would take Karen and Steve for a ride in the diesel engine that he operated on passenger trains on round trips from Harrisburg to Altoona. They boarded near the bunkhouse in the rail yard where the train engines were parked and took about a 15-minute ride to the edge of the station, where Ernie picked up the kids and GrandPap continued into the station to hook on to the train cars.

LaRue created wonderful meals, so going out for a meal didn't happen often. When the family did venture out for a meal, the favorite restaurant was Ditmer's. The restaurant is still operating today, but now it is Baker's Restaurant. The family enjoyed walking, sledding, and skating on the golf course. Almost every winter weekend, with snow on the ground or ice frozen on the golf course pond, Ernie or LaRue or both were out with Steve and Karen and the other neighborhood kids sledding or skating for hours, even after dark with a fire at the pond. Ernie enjoyed putting chains on the winter treads of the family's 1956 Chevrolet station wagon and taking the family for rides through the snow drifts that accumulated on or along Mountain Road in Dillsburg. The family relished watching the snow fly. Deep snows were a regular event in the 1950s and '60s. Of course, there would be the occasional shoveling party on the "gravel" driveway so they could get the car out.

Going on a family vacation was always a fun time. Some of their first trips were to Mount Olive Township in northern New Jersey to spend time with two of Ernie's siblings, Wayne and Vera, who were working in the area. Vera lived on a small lake that afforded the family with lots of swimming, picnics, and great food. Wayne was ministering to a church in the area, and one member, Ky Van Orden, resided in a fantastic home on Budd Lake. Ky invited the family to join him on the seven-mile-long lake for water activities. The children's favorite was going for a ride in his speedboat. One year the family went on a memorable one-week driving trip with LaRue's parents, Clayton and Rhoda Cassidy, to Niagara Falls, Toronto, and the Thousand Islands. In the early 1960s the family along with Clayton and Rhoda vacationed for a week in Wildwood, New Jersey. Ernie and LaRue were avid swimmers, as was Clayton, so it was only natural that most of the week was spent in the ocean. The group enjoyed the boardwalk on several evenings during this trip as well.

While the kids were in elementary school LaRue served as a den mother when Steve was in Cub Scouts and a leader for Karen's Brownie group. Ernie and LaRue were very supportive of all the school events that Karen and Steve participated in. Ernie especially enjoyed football, basketball, and wrestling events. Both kids were involved with the Northern High School marching band. Steve was in the band, and Karen was in the band front, so there were many band events to attend.

During the college years for Steve (Millersville University) and Karen (Indiana University of Pennsylvania), there were few vacations other than the Juniata-Tyrone trips. During the summers LaRue was still working part-time managing the snack bar at Range End swimming pool so the family could swim free. So, for most weekends, time was spent at the pool. These were wonderful times for family fellowship.

After Steve and Kathy married in 1970, Ernie and LaRue started vacationing in Stone Harbor, New Jersey. This became an annual event that continued for close to 30 years. During the first several years they rented two-bedroom apartments with an additional sofa bed so that Karen and her good friend Deb or Steve and Kathy could join the fun for several days. After Karen and Michael were married in 1973, the apartments became cottages so that Karen and Mike and Steve and Kathy could join for a week of family fun. As Steve and Karen started families, the grandchildren, Jeff and Kim, came along on these vacations. To say that they were overjoyed when grandchildren started to arrive is an understatement. Between 1977 and 1986 three grandsons and two granddaughters were born. These were wonderful times for Ernie and LaRue as it gave them a week of undivided time with their grandchildren. As the families grew, Karen and Michael added Andy and Pat, while Steve and Kathy added Julia. Ernie and LaRue started two-week vacations. One week was devoted to Karen's family and the second week was with Steve's family, with a fun overlapping Saturday in the middle. The last cottage, rented for over 15 years, was on Pennsylvania Avenue and only half a block from the beach. Not only did everyone enjoy the beach, biking, and shuffleboard, but also the grandchildren especially enjoyed the cottage's balcony and the deer head hanging over the fireplace. LaRue cooked tasty meals, and Ernie enjoyed putting the American flag up and down daily, as he was very patriotic to the end. Stone Harbor vacations were probably the best that Ernie and LaRue ever had. Ernie continued to vacation in Stone Harbor with Karen and Steve and their families until the summer the cottage was sold.

Ernie and LaRue enjoyed traveling to visit family and friends throughout the United States, and then internationally after he retired from the naval depot. They traveled to Bermuda, Portugal, Canary Islands, Morocco, Acapulco, Hawaii, and Germany to visit the places Ernie was during the war. Julia was the beneficiary of their travels as they brought back a doll for her collection from every place they visited. LaRue once commented that she was so glad that they had traveled while they both had their health. Unfortunately, her health started to decline in 1985, limiting their travel. LaRue died in October 1987 and is buried in Dillsburg Cemetery.

The grandchildren eagerly anticipated a visit to Pappy's house in Dillsburg, Pennsylvania, since it meant eating dinner out and spending time alone with their grandfather. His grandson Andy recalls the many Friday nights and Saturdays spent with him. While in elementary school Andy would frequently call Pappy after school and ask if he could spend the night. Almost always the answer was yes, and with that the inescapable trip to Paul's Pancake Barn for dinner Friday night. Afterward, back at Pappy's place Andy completed a little weekend schoolwork before the two of them tossed a tennis ball in the basement until it was time to watch Friday night television titled "Thank Goodness It's Friday." All this meant staying up until after 10 p.m. Friday night. In the morning, Andy would quietly turn on the television to start watching cartoons until Pappy awoke. Breakfast then ensued while watching cartoons and while Pappy busied himself doing various things around the house. When there were no good cartoons on, they would go back to the basement to throw a ball or sometimes Andy would just throw the ball at the wall with a pretend strike zone on the blocks. After lunch, usually a frozen pizza, Andy would head home. Granddaughter Kimberly also recalled the many special meals with Pappy at Paul's Pancake Barn and the mandatory watching of *The Lawrence Welk Show* Friday evenings with her grandfather as he sang along.

CIVILIAN LIFE • 153

Ernie loved his sweets and had a collection of candy jars on a small glass cart in the dining room. On the cart was a collection of glass decanters each filled with a different variety of candy. He always made sure they were full (and if they weren't, refill bags were close at hand). Ernie used his oven to store his cookies, cakes, pies, and an assortment of his favorite Little Debbie treats. After asking permission, the grandchildren would indulge themselves. Andy recalls that the candy jars were never empty and that he never left Pappy's without eating way more candy than he should have: candy corn, spearmint leaves, and multi-colored after-dinner mints. Andy stated that it's amazing he did not end up with cavities as a child after eating all this candy. Ernie also carried a small baggy full of candy in his pocket that he routinely offered to the grandchildren when seeing them at sporting events or stopping by their house on the way to or from shopping or an appointment.

All the grandchildren looked forward to the annual summer beach trips to Stone Harbor, New Jersey. Typically, it was the last week in June or the first week in July that they would spend a week at the beach with Pappy and Grammy. Ernie and LaRue never traveled lightly and often would bring their own kitchen appliances with them. Their grandson Jeff especially enjoyed the automatic toaster and how Pappy would entertain them with it. The toaster had sensors that would recognize a slice of bread in one of the slots and automatically slowly lower the bread and slowly raise it once it was toasted. The beach house was only a half block from the beach. Right after lunch the grandchildren led the procession to the beach with the adults trailing behind them. After setting up an area with chairs, umbrellas, and beach toys the grandchildren enjoyed digging large holes in the sand, burying their fathers in the sand, and playing in the ocean. Jeff and Julia especially enjoyed swimming with Pappy as he demonstrated his water survival training including bobbing and floating. Ernie was a master at floating. He would float on top of the water with his eyes closed for what seemed like hours. During this time, he would float into the breakers and be tossed around, which worried the grandchildren. Afterwards, he simply walked further out in the ocean and resumed his floating and teasing the grandchildren. The time at the shore also included bike rides and mini golf in the morning, and the park and sometimes shuffleboard in the evening. Julia remembers the annual

154 • GUEST OF ADOLF

evening walk into town with Pappy for the purpose of purchasing a big bucket of caramel popcorn that they would enjoy for the remainder of the week. She also enjoyed watching the fireworks with Grammy and Pappy on the Fourth of July.

The grandchildren, when they were small, enjoyed having their pictures taken with the mounted deer head while staring across the room at a swordfish. This was a week that they looked forward to every year and had a lot of fun with Grammy and Pappy.

One year, Kim, Andy, and Pat thought Pappy needed some daily company. So, for his birthday they presented Pappy with a guinea pig that they named Bert. The grandchildren thought it was hilarious that together the guinea pig and Pappy would be known as Bert and Ernie. Bert, as it turned out, was a very spoiled guinea pig. Pappy placed his cage on the kitchen table near the refrigerator. Every time someone opened the refrigerator door, Bert would squeal for food. Pappy kept a jar containing small cut carrots in water just for these occasions, and Bert quickly learned that the sound of opening the refrigerator door meant a carrot. Bert was a rather overindulged guinea pig.

Kimberly recalls how from a very early age Pappy would talk to her about his time in the Army. He shared stories of his training at Fort Meade, the Carolina Maneuvers, his journey to England and North Africa, and his POW experiences. Ernie never spoke of these times in a sad or angry tone; he gave the facts of what he experienced. She recalls how he spoke fondly of his fellow soldiers and even, at times, his German captors. Pappy often told the grandchildren that he was treated well in the POW camp. He especially was thrilled that he was able to keep his Bible, the POWs were able to hold "church" services, and that they were even able to put on short plays and musicals among the prisoners. While Kimberly was confident his length of time as a POW was not pleasant, Pappy's comments about it reflected that he was never bitter and used that time as a learning experience that would carry him throughout the remainder of his life. Julia recalls that practically every time she saw Pappy, he shared his life experiences and stories with her. She called him her walking history book and appreciated the wealth of knowledge he offered to her. These lessons of strong faith, devotion to family, seeking the positive, being prepared, and having mercy for even

CIVILIAN LIFE • 155

those who wrong you, he passed on to his children and subsequently to his grandchildren.

Pappy loved to tell stories, and he was never without them. It is impossible to recall how many times the grandchildren heard the same stories. His stories usually involved trains, the Carolina Maneuvers of 1941, his time in North Africa during World War II, and his extensive POW experiences. Pappy would relate these stories to anyone and everyone with an ear. Over time it became a waiting game until someone asked THE question to get the whole ball rolling and the story would or could continue for quite a long time. THE question focused on the very distinctive Stalag IIIB ring he wore all the time. There were instances when the grandchildren could tell the stories were about to happen, and it became mission-critical to slip away quickly before they began and then they were stuck listening again. On these occasions, some of the grandchildren would comment, "Look Pappy's got another one!"

Jeff remembers and appreciates hearing Pappy's firsthand accounts from World War II, as did his friends. During Jeff's high school years, Pappy was a guest speaker in his history class, sharing his stories of fighting in North Africa, getting captured by the "Desert Fox," marching through the frigid German winter, and spending years in a German POW camp. Jeff also had the privilege of attending one of Pappy's World War II reunions. Jeff met many former members of the 805th TD Battalion and some of Pappy's POW buddies. He listened attentively as the old soldiers relived and shared their harrowing tales of evading death and hiding from German infantrymen. A few years before he passed, Andy recalls a high school American history class project where he was required to interview an older person; Andy chose to interview his grandfather even though he was positive he already knew the answers to his questions. The interview only needed to be about 30 minutes in length and tape-recorded. Andy asked only a handful of questions, and Pappy proceeded to talk for at least an hour on tape and then nearly two more off tape. At times Pappy would say, "Turn that thing off, I have more to say." Ernie was a frequent speaker to the grandchildren's classes concerning his World War II experiences. He enjoyed sharing these with school groups and continued this practice through 2001.

Every Memorial Day Pappy, his children, and grandchildren would converge on his hometown of Tyrone, Pennsylvania, to attend a reunion of Gerald and Mary Helen Focht's descendants. Upon arriving in Tyrone, Pappy's first stop was always at Eastlawn Cemetery to visit and clean up the gravesites of his parents. The grandchildren would listen, as Pappy would tell stories of his parents, his extended family, and his time as a youngster growing up in Tyrone. Afterwards, everyone drove the short distance to Tipton Baptist Church for the gathering of his brothers, sisters, and their families.

Jeff remembers that his grandfather remained kind and cheerful, always wearing a smile in his later years. He also recalls the sights and smells of the house on Mountain Road in Dillsburg, that Pappy constantly had candy in his pocket and smelled of peppermint. As the years passed, Ernie's various health issues resulted in his being moved from his beloved Dillsburg home to a nursing home in Lewisberry, Pennsylvania. He died there on February 23, 2003. He was buried with full military honors next to "His Darling Fiancée" LaRue in Dillsburg Cemetery.

APPENDIX I

105th/805th Tank Destroyer
Battalion History

The 805th Tank Destroyer (TD) Battalion has its beginnings in the Army's anti-tank discussions of the early 1930s. These talks and the belief that tanks were a formidable force that could not be stopped with the existing military force structure resulted in the development of the Army's initial anti-tank doctrine in 1936. Under this concept each division was to be assigned an AT battalion and each regiment an AT company. The next logical step was the testing of this concept under simulated field conditions, which the 2nd Infantry Division successfully conducted in 1937. Two years later in 1939, General George C. Marshall, Army Chief of Staff, implemented the recommendation for the creation of an AT battalion as a division asset. His decision led to the authorization of eight provisional infantry battalions, anti-tank on January 1, 1940. Three of these units (93rd, 94th, and 99th) were formed from deactivating existing active-duty units while the remaining five (101st, 102nd 103rd, 104th, and 105th) were formed from existing Army National Guard units in New Mexico, New York (2), Pennsylvania, and Washington over the next nine months.

The 105th Infantry Battalion (Anti-Tank) was created on September 22, 1940, with an authorized strength of 20 officers and 284 enlisted soldiers. It was established from several existing Pennsylvania Army National Guard units within the 28th Infantry Division (ID). The units and their locations, which formed the 105th Infantry Battalion (AT), are illustrated in Chapter 3, Table C.

In October 1940 the newly formed 105th Infantry Battalion (AT) began its reorganization and training during its monthly drill periods for

158 • GUEST OF ADOLF

a mission that was still being defined by the Army. Compounding their problem was the lack of approved anti-tank doctrine and an anti-tank weapon. Regardless of the turmoil and lack of specific guidance from the Army, the 105th Infantry Battalion (AT) began to train its soldiers for their new mission. Around this time, the Army's Ordnance Department made a unilateral decision on an anti-tank weapon. It adopted a weapon very similar to the German 37-mm AT gun and rushed it into production. It was not until the beginning of 1942 that any of these AT guns were available for the unit to conduct training.

Germany's invasion of Poland in 1939 stunned the world, leading President Franklin Roosevelt to declare a state of limited national emergency. General George Marshall remembering the Army's lack of preparedness when it entered World War I was determined that history would not repeat itself. He began to restructure the Army's fighting formations, strengthening its readiness and updating its doctrine. As the fighting in Europe continued to spread President Roosevelt implemented the Protective Mobilization Plan in September 1940 and Congress approved the Selective Service Act. Under the mobilization plan National Guard divisions were to be mobilized for a one-year period with the first divisions beginning this period of service in late 1940.[1] The 28th ID of the Pennsylvania National Guard reported for mobilization training on February 1, 1941. As an organic unit to the 28th ID, the 105th Infantry Battalion (AT) simultaneously reported for duty at their respective armories. The initial rosters for the battalion, dated February 3, 1941, confirm that 26 officers and 274 enlisted soldiers reported for duty. The battalion's leadership was composed of LTC Charles L. Supplee, battalion commander; CPT Lewis W. Anderson, headquarters company commander; CPT Carl J. Hunsinger, Company A commander; CPT Edward C. Houser, Company B commander; CPT Robert R. Stormer, Company C commander; CPT Howard C. Thompson, medical detachment commander; and 1LT Hugh J. Mattia, adjutant. The senior enlisted soldier was MSG Charles W. Nevius.[2] This was an excess of six officers and an understrength of 10 enlisted soldiers when compared to the unit's authorized strength figures. A few days later the unit moved to its mobilization station at Fort Meade, Maryland, to embark on a period of extensive individual-, platoon-, and company-level training exercises.

105TH/805TH TANK DESTROYER BATTALION HISTORY • 159

These exercises continued until August 1941, when the battalion departed Fort Meade and traveled to Camp A. P. Hill, Virginia, for training in preparation for participating in an Army-wide exercise beginning in September, commonly referred to as the Carolina Maneuvers. This exercise occurred in southern North Carolina and northern South Carolina during October and November 1941 involving the forces of First Army and IV Corps (Reinforced). The battalion's assembly area was in the southern pines area of North Carolina near the town of Hoffman, approximately 50 miles west of Fort Bragg, North Carolina. It arrived in this area in late September 1941, and, while awaiting the formal start of the exercise, it conducted a series of training exercises. As an asset of the 28th ID the 105th was a member of First Army (Blue Forces) until the maneuvers concluded on November 29, 1941.

While the soldiers of the 105th prepared to return to Fort Meade, Maryland, at the conclusion of the Carolina Maneuvers the Army published two orders that significantly impacted the unit. A War Department letter of November 27, 1941, officially ordered the activation on or about December 1, 1941, of a Tank Destroyer Tactical and Firing Center at Fort Meade.[3] This letter established a specific command element to oversee the formulation, development, and training of the Army's anti-tank forces. Then, on December 15, 1941, the 105th Infantry Battalion (AT), along with the other seven provisional AT battalions, was redesignated the 805th Tank Destroyer Battalion and was reassigned from the 28th Infantry Division to the Army General Headquarters (GHQ). The directive also created an additional 44 tank destroyer battalions from other existing Army assets. This new Table of Organization (T/O 18–25) dated December 24, 1941, resulted in a substantial change to the battalion's personnel and equipment. Now the authorized strength was 35 officers and 807 enlisted soldiers for a total of 842 personnel. This was an increase of 12 officers and 523 enlisted men, an increase of more than 2.7 times the previous unit authorization for personnel. Table I at the end of this appendix illustrates the battalion's personnel authorizations for each table of organization update.

In early February 1942 the unit received its new individual equipment, new vehicles, and new AT weapons. The biggest difference was instead of towing all their artillery pieces using wheeled trucks each company was

160 • GUEST OF ADOLF

issued a few of the new M3 Gun Motor Carriage (75-mm) half-tracks. This led to an alteration of the battalion's training program. The new program had its basis in the training notes, procedures, and experiences of the 93rd/893rd TD Battalion during both the Louisiana and the Carolina GHQ maneuvers. The unit spent a considerable amount of time in the woods conducting field problems consisting of establishing a defensive position and then moving to the offensive. These drills were based on the pre-publication of FM 18–5, *Tank Destroyer Field Manual* in early March 1942 and continued through the middle of May 1942. The last week of May the unit departed Fort Meade, Maryland, for Camp Hood, Texas, to continue their training at Tank Destroyer Forces School. The first week of June the unit underwent its third change to its personnel and equipment authorizations since September 1940. This change increased the officer ranks by three to 38 and the enlisted to 860 with an overall strength of 898 soldiers, up from 842. The only significant changes to the equipment were the loss of the 18 self-propelled anti-aircraft vehicles and an increase in the number of 30- and 50-caliber machine guns. Table J at the end of this appendix illustrates the battalion's equipment authorizations for each T/O update.

Upon arriving at Camp Hood, the unit established its bivouac site in an area outside of Copperas Cove, Texas. This was necessary because there were no barracks, support, or training facilities in existence at Camp Hood as the construction of these facilities were recently started. From this austere environment the soldiers focused on the prescribed training program. There were two phases to the program, each lasting approximately four weeks. During the first phase, individual tactical and technical training was the focus, while the second phase emphasized squad-, platoon-, and company-level tactical proficiency. However, with the proposed invasion of North Africa approaching, the first group of TD battalions' training was ended early to facilitate their deployment. On July 30, 1942, the 805th TD Battalion departed Camp Hood with all its equipment and personnel by rail for Indiantown Gap Military Reservation (IGMR), outside of Annville, Pennsylvania, arriving there on August 2, 1942. The following two days were a flurry of activity as all personnel made final preparations for deployment to England. During this time Lieutenant Colonel Supplee was found to be gravely ill and

105TH/805TH TANK DESTROYER BATTALION HISTORY • 161

was hospitalized at Walter Reed in Washington, DC, thus ending his assignment to the battalion. The unit then departed IGMR and began its journey to Brooklyn, New York, where all the soldiers boarded troop transport ships that departed New York Harbor on August 6, 1942. The unit embarked upon its transport at approximately 72 percent of its personnel strength with only 650 soldiers out of the 898 authorized.

The ship departed Brooklyn, New York, and made course for Halifax, Nova Scotia, arriving off the coast on Saturday, August 8, 1942, to await the arrival of additional vessels. Once all the ships assembled, Convoy AT-18—the largest troop convoy yet assembled, consisting of 12 merchant/troopships and 19 escort cruisers and destroyers—departed for England.[4] While crossing the North Atlantic Ocean, Axis Sally reported a German submarine had sunk the 805th's troopship. However, they arrived safely at Firth of Clyde, Scotland, on August 17, 1942. While in England the unit was initially stationed at Tidworth Barracks before moving to Shrivenham in early October. During the time at Tidworth Barracks, LTC Allen H. Foreman was assigned as the new battalion commander. Throughout the unit's time in England, it continued to train and prepare for combat operations. When the unit's equipment arrived in early September, they were disappointed to learn that the Ordnance Department had issued some of their equipment and vehicles to a TD battalion having an earlier North African deployment date.[5] However, they quickly adapted to this setback and continued to prepare for a North African deployment.

On January 5, 1943, the unit departed their assembly area in Shrivenham, England, moving toward the coast of Scotland where the entire battalion boarded the vessel *Monarch of Bermuda* along with 3,354 other soldiers. The ship hoisted anchor on January 9, 1943, to join 18 other vessels comprising Convoy KMF.7 for the eight-day trip to Algeria. At first the convoy of 12 merchant/troopships and seven escort vessels headed further into the North Atlantic to avoid the German U-boats before changing its course towards Gibraltar and the Mediterranean Sea. The *Monarch of Bermuda* docked in Algiers, Algeria, on January 17, 1943, and the battalion immediately moved into staging areas in the vicinity of El Bair and El Achour, which are approximately four miles west of Algiers.

162 • GUEST OF ADOLF

The armored and tracked vehicles were loaded on railcars for the journey to the front lines by January 24, 1943.[6] The next day the train departed for El Khroub, 252 miles east of Algiers, with many of the unit's personnel riding with the equipment. As the battalion began its final preparations and initiated its movement into Tunisia, it did so at 69 percent of its authorized strength as illustrated in Table D in Chapter 4. On February 1 the advance party departed for Tebessa, Algeria, for the purpose of preparing the battalion's next bivouac site. The equipment train reached its destination this same day and proceeded to begin its 147-mile road march to Bou Chebka, arriving February 6. Finally, on February 7, the remainder of the battalion received orders to report for duty with II Corps at Tebessa, Algeria. However, this same day, 236 enlisted soldiers reported for duty as replacements. These new men brought the unit up to almost its authorized strength of 898 personnel. The entire battalion was settled into their bivouac site near Bou Chebka by early evening on February 9. Within four hours Company B and a platoon of the reconnaissance company were ordered to report to Colonel Frederic Butler, commanding officer of Allied Task Force Gafsa, Tunisia. The company assumed responsibility for protecting the Zannouch Station, located approximately 20 miles east of Gafsa.

On February 10 the remainder of the battalion moved to the vicinity of Fériana and was attached to the 26th Regimental Combat Team (RCT) of the 1st Infantry Division (ID) Division under Colonel Alexander N. Stark Jr. For the next three days elements of the 805th TD Battalion conducted numerous reconnaissance patrols along the Fériana–Gafsa and Gafsa–Sidi Bou Zid roads.[7] Three days later the Germans launched attacks towards Gafsa, Sidi Bou Zid, and Sbeitla. In response the battalion was ordered to attach Company A and one platoon from the reconnaissance company to the 1st Armored Division's Combat Command A (CCA) at Sbeitla under the command of Brigadier General Raymond McQuillin. Upon arriving the company received orders to immediately deploy platoons to Djebel Hamra (Hill 673) with the 1st Battalion 6th Infantry at what came to be known as "Kerns Crossroads" on the Sbeitla–Faid road. A second platoon reported to Colonel Drake, commander of 168th Infantry Regiment (-) at Djebel Ksaira (Hill 560) and Djebel Hadid (Hill 620), six miles south of the town of Faid. This placed this platoon on

105TH/805TH TANK DESTROYER BATTALION HISTORY • 163

the extreme southern portion of the American front lines. During the next two days these platoons engaged German tanks as they executed a pincer movement surrounding their position.

While Company A was engaged around Sidi Bou Zid, B Company reverted to battalion control near Fériana. The company assumed responsibility for conducting patrols in the area bounded by the Fériana–Gafsa and the Fériana–Sidi Bou Zid roads for the next two days. Company C was employed setting up defensive positions in the pass leading into the town of Fériana. When the order to withdraw came, Company C failed to receive it, resulting in the company being isolated and nearly surrounded. The company attempted to fight its way back to Kasserine, but during this action it ceased to be an effective fighting force, losing 75 soldiers and all 12 of its anti-tank guns. By nightfall on February 18 the battalion was collecting the remaining soldiers of A and C Companies along with B Company into its assigned area west of Kasserine Pass astride the south fork of the road entering the pass. The battalion held its ground for the next two days until ordered to report to the commander of the 26th Armored Brigade at Thala. During its withdrawal it suffered the loss of additional personnel, guns, and equipment. After the German advance ended what was left of the 805th TD Battalion was removed from the line and sent to the rear at Aïn Beïda, Algeria, for reorganization and rehabilitation.

Over the course of the next 22 days its personnel and equipment shortages were addressed, and Major Camden W. McConnell assumed command from LTC Foreman on March 1, 1943. The battalion returned to action on March 17, moving first to Fériana, then on to Sbeitla, Gafsa, and El Guettar. During this time, it primarily provided static defense for various headquarters, established roadblocks, and conducted mine removal operations. These types of assignments continued for the remainder of the North African campaign with the battalion moving between Sened Station, Gafsa, Sbeitla, Bou Chebka, Sidi Bou Zid, and finally five miles south of Faid. Beginning on April 12, 1943, the battalion moved back to Bou Chebka and then moved an additional three times before ending up in the vicinity of Bizerte on May 29,1943. During this two-and-a-half-month period the battalion reported to eight different senior headquarters—1st TD Group, 894th TD Bn, Commanding General (CG),

164 • GUEST OF ADOLF

II Corps Artillery, 1st Armored Division, Force Commander II Corps, Commander 1st Ranger Battalion, and CG CCA 1st Armored Division—before being assigned to the 34th Infantry Division on May 18, 1943.

The month of June and the majority of July were devoted to welcoming replacements and training on basic soldier skills: physical training, radio communication, care and use of equipment, and small arms firing. At the end of July, the battalion moved to the Tank Destroyer Training Center at Sebdou, Algeria, to receive training on indirect fire with a towed 3-inch gun. In early August it was reassigned to the 1st Tank Destroyer Group while continuing its training program through the end of September. During this time Major McConnell was promoted to lieutenant colonel. The battalion received its alert for overseas movement on October 2, 1943. Between October 6 and October 24 all battalion elements were loaded upon various transports in the Oran, Algeria, harbor for Naples, Italy (Map 13). The last elements disembarked on November 10 after a 19-day sea voyage. Upon arrival in Italy, the battalion was assigned to Fifth Army with an attachment to VI Corps. Its mission was to protect the left flank of the corps. After conducting a live fire exercise with its 3-inch guns the battalion conducted an all-day motor march moving to Pratella on November 19. The march was impeded by several of the Volturno River bridges being washed out by flooding. After the arduous motor march, the battalion established its bivouac site on the west bank of the Volturno River near the intersection of Highways 6 and 85. During the next 13 days it performed primarily an artillery-supporting role to these II Corps units: 645th TD Bn, 45th Division Artillery, 71st Field Artillery Brigade, 18th Field Artillery Brigade, and the British X Corps. On December 14 it reverted to control of VI Corps and was instructed to support the 2d Moroccan Infantry Division, which it did beginning on December 18 with elements of the battalion moving into positions near Colli a Volturno, Rocchetta a Volturno, and Scapoli.

During 1943 the battalion celebrated its second anniversary of being activated under the Protective Mobilization Plan and its first combat operations against German and Italian forces. These operations occurred around Faid, Sidi Bou Zid, and Sbeitla before participating in the defense of Kasserine Pass. These engagements so battered the battalion that it was

105TH/805TH TANK DESTROYER BATTALION HISTORY • 165

no longer a functioning unit having lost most of its equipment and nearly 40 percent of its personnel, the majority of whom were captured during the engagements between February 17 and 19. After a short period of rehabilitation, the battalion returned to action and participated in the final stages of the Tunisian campaign. This was followed by five months of total reorganization under a revised table of organization in which the battalion trained on the 3-inch gun as their anti-tank weapon. It returned to action in the vicinity of Naples, Italy, in November. During the year, the battalion was attached to II and VI Corps, the 1st Infantry Division, 1st Armored Division, 34th Infantry Division, 1st Tank Destroyer Group, and the 2d Moroccan Infantry Division. While attached to these elements it was further attached to the 26th Regimental Combat Team, 19th Engineer Regiment, 26th Armor Brigade, 1st Ranger Battalion, 18th Field Artillery Brigade, and II Corps Artillery. It spent a total of 133 days in combat, with 89 of these in support of the Tunisian campaign and 44 in Italy as part of the Naples–Foggia campaign.

The year 1944, opened with the battalion in the same positions and continuing its support of the 2d Moroccan Infantry Division. This support ended in the middle of the month with the battalion being assigned to II Corps and attached to the 34th Infantry Division. A few days later it moved to the vicinity of Cervaro, Italy, to support an attack of the 36th Infantry Division towards Cassino. The support of the attack on the town of Cassino and the Monte Cassino Abbey continued through February 15, 1944. It then responded to a request to reposition its gun to support a New Zealand Corps attack on the abbey. After completing this mission on February 20, the battalion moved into a rest area near Alife. The next day, they were treated to a one-hour private USO show before beginning a 13-day period of rest, relaxation, equipment maintenance, and training. On March 10 orders were received to proceed to Naples, Italy, for embarkation to the Anzio beachhead.

Upon arriving at Anzio, the battalion was attached to the First Special Service Forces (FSSF) with C Company attached to the 601st TD Battalion. They were assigned to a position in the vicinity of the Mussolini Canal on the right flank of the elongated U that formed the beachhead. From here the battalion provided harassing and supporting

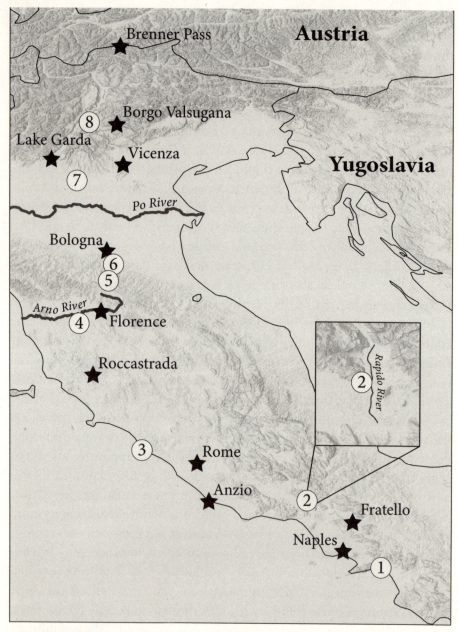

Map 13: 805th TD Battalion in the Italian Campaign, November 1, 1943 to May 27, 1945. 1. Salerno; 2. Cassino (also insert); 3. Civitavecchia; 4. Castelfiorentino; 5. Firenzuola; 6. Indice River Valley; 7. Verona; 8. Trento. (Timothy M. Swartz. World Hillshade copyright © Esri)

fires on observed enemy positions near Littoria and Sessano. It also continued to fire on targets of opportunity within its assigned sectors. In early April, the battalion commander received news that the 805th was being considered for conversion to the new M18 self-propelled AT gun. The middle of April saw the battalion supporting successful raids by the 1st FSSF on Strada, Littoreana [coastal road], and Cerreto Alto. These raids resulted in the battalion shifting its orientation to a more northerly one but still on the right flank. As the area of the beachhead continued to expand the battalion's position continued to move more in the direction of Velletri. On May 27, immediately prior to the initiation of the offensive resulting in the breakout, two companies were attached to the 36th Infantry Division and one to the 3rd Division. This offensive culminated with the reconnaissance platoon entering Rome at 0330 hours on June 4; the remainder arrived later that day.

On June 7 the battalion received orders to depart Rome and moved into an assembly area between Civitavecchia and Tarquinia, Italy, at which time it was released from all attachments. While in this area, it reorganized under an updated table of organization dated March 1944 (Tables I and J). The most significant change was with their AT weapon system. They turned in the 3-inch guns and received the new M18 self-propelled 76-mm AT guns, thus becoming the first TD battalion in possession of this weapon system. The next five weeks were devoted to reorganization activities and training with the new M18. On July 14, the battalion was attached to the 85th Division and moved with it to the town of Roccastrada, which is approximately 128 miles north of Rome. This attachment was short-lived, as on July 25 it was assigned to Task Force Ramo. It assumed the mission of the 91st Division and continued to push northward towards Pisa. The next day, Company B was detached and attached to a different task force with the 45th Infantry Brigade and 2nd Armored Group. For the subsequent 30 days, the battalion primarily acted as both field artillery and in an infantry role, with its companies and their platoons being attached and then detached from numerous units. These included the 6th Armored Infantry Battalion, 11th Armored Infantry Battalion, 930th Field Artillery Battalion, 894th TD Battalion, 148th Field Artillery Group, and the British 39th Light Anti-Aircraft Regiment.

On August 21, Lieutenant Colonel McConnell, battalion commander, was ordered to report to II Corps Headquarters. He was informed that for the previous month the battalion was still officially assigned to II Corps and attached to the 91st Division but under the operational control of VI Corps. His new instructions included being released from VI Corps and being attached to the 34th Infantry Division effective August 24, on which date the battalion was to move inland 50 miles to a position six miles southwest of the Castle of Santa Florentina and 12 miles south of the Arno River. After moving inland to their assigned assembly area, the battalion spent 11 days attending to maintenance and reconnaissance activities in preparation for returning to the front lines. This they did on September 6 in support of the Gothic Line Offensive.

The month of October found the battalion in the vicinity of Firenzuola, which is north of Florence, and attached to the 752nd Tank Battalion in the 85th Division Sector. One company from both the tank battalion and from the 805th was assigned to support one of the 85th Division's three infantry regiments (337th, 338th and 339th) in their upcoming offensive. After the first week of the attack, heavy rains prevented further advances by the infantry regiments. It also prevented the resupply of 105-mm artillery rounds, so the battalion assumed an indirect fire role in support of the 85th Division and the 752nd Tank Battalion. This continued until the end of the month when the battalion was released from its attachment to the tank battalion and attached to the division artillery.

As November opened the battalion (minus Company A) remained attached to the 85th Division, with A Company attached to the 88th Division. Fifth Army halted offensive operations and assumed defensive positions. Four divisions—34th, 85th, 88th, and 91st—formed a pronounced salient pointed at Highway 9 slightly east of Bologna. The 85th Division sector is generally organized along a sector north of Baccanello and Monterenzio, with the 88th Division to its right and the 34th Division on its left. The various elements of the battalion were in positions in the vicinity of Monte Calderaro, Monte Grande, San Clemente Road, Monterenzio Bassano Ridge, Castelvecchio, La Torre, and Osteria.

All these positions are accidental as the heavy rains immobilized all elements. This situation remained stable throughout the month. Additionally, the battalion did not fire any missions, as there were strict ammunition restrictions on the use of its 76-mm guns for artillery support. Before the month ended, the 85th and 88th sectors were realigned, resulting in the battalion now being attached to the 88th Division and the 752nd Tank Battalion.

The battalion remained relatively stationary in its existing sector throughout the month of December. A platoon from each company relocated to new positions with difficulty due to the terrain and weather. Company A's 2d Platoon moved into Savignano on December 14. The terrain made it difficult to move any equipment into new positions without engineer support to widen roads. German activity was intense at times throughout the month, resulting in seven casualties and a few pieces of equipment destroyed. The ammunition shortage continued, and fires were restricted to armored targets only on December 29. The M18s suffered from a lack of second echelon maintenance on their engines. Much of the required supplies and repair parts were too heavy for pack mules, which were being used to resupply the battalion. At this time, the battalion risked losing combat efficiency because of being in the line for 117 continuous days without proper vehicle maintenance being performed.

Throughout 1944 the battalion operated as part of four different Corps Headquarters: the II, IV, and VI U.S. Corps and the XX French Expeditionary Corps. It was attached to seven different infantry divisions: 3d, 34th, 36th, 85th, 88th, 91st, and the 2d Moroccan. In addition to these attachments, at various times through the year it was attached to the 18th Field Artillery Brigade, 45th Anti-Aircraft Artillery Brigade, 36th Engineer Brigade, the 752d Tank Battalion, Task Force Ramo, and the First Special Service Force. The battalion suffered 16 enlisted and five officers killed in action, 81 enlisted and 10 officers wounded in action. Its total losses for the year for any reason were 290 enlisted and 30 officers. The battalion spent a total of 299 days on the line with three breaks of between 13 and 35 days to attend to maintenance and to undergo a T/O reorganization when it received the new M18 self-propelled AT weapons system in June.

The battalion opened 1945 with its companies dispersed between Savignano, Castelvecchio, and Baccanello, attached to the 88th Infantry Division. The companies of the battalion provided supporting fires throughout the month to the 133rd, 135th, and 337th Infantry Regiments. On January 11, the battalion supplied three TD crews to operate equipment given to the British 1st Division in November at La Costa. The battalion was attached to the 34th Infantry Division after it relieved the 88th Division on January 14. The reconnaissance company was attached to the 91st Cavalry Reconnaissance Squadron on January 22. During this attachment they were employed as an infantry company. Throughout the month ammunition shortages limited the battalion to fire only on armored targets. The shortage was due to the poor road network and the fact that the European Theater of Operations had priority for supplies over the Mediterranean Theater. At different times during the month some of the M18s were immobile due to failing roads. Also, 19 of the unit's 36 tank destroyers were being resupplied by mules because of road, terrain, and weather conditions. These conditions were not conducive to the performance of required first and second echelon maintenance.

February 1945 found the battalion in the same relative positions in the Indice River Valley area it had occupied since October. Early in the month II Corps directed that battalion organic assets must accomplish all first and second echelon maintenance. Consequently, a plan was developed to rotate the vehicles to the rear area beginning the middle of the month. However, some of the M18s were immobile, and their maintenance was delayed. The new ammunition allocations enabled the battalion to engage enemy targets other than solely armor vehicles. Therefore, the companies began to provide harassing and supporting fires to the infantry regiments. Throughout the month the targets included enemy bunkers, command posts, observation posts, occupied houses, and known or suspected enemy positions. On the last day of the month the battalion was relieved of its attachment to the 34th Division and attached to the 91st Division.

The weather began to improve in early March, enabling the battalion to be more effective with their fires. The companies continued to provide direct support on targets identified by their observation posts. These targets included command posts, dugouts, shelters, outposts, firing positions, occupied buildings, and personnel. All companies could place effective fires on every target. During the third week, the Battalion finally received permission from the 91st Division to remove one company from the line for rest and maintenance. However, the other two Companies had to assume responsibility for their area. Through the rotations of vehicles to the rear for maintenance the overall condition of the battalion's vehicles improved significantly. Major Harry N. Carruthers assumed command of the battalion during the month.

April began with Company C being attached to the Italian Legnano Group while the remainder of the battalion prepared for the beginning of a new offensive campaign. During this process, the 34th Infantry Division assumed operational control of the battalion. Prior to the initiation of the campaign, both Company C and the reconnaissance company were returned to battalion control. In the early morning hours of April 21st Company A entered the city of Bologna with the remainder of the battalion entering by the end of the day. The next day the battalion was attached to the 88th Infantry Division, with Company A attached to 350th Infantry Regiment, Company B to 351st Infantry Regiment, and Company C to 349th Infantry Regiment. The enemy was in full retreat, and all elements were moving rapidly northward in pursuit. As the battalion reached the Po River on April 23, it assisted in the capture of more than nine thousand German soldiers. Over the course of the next few days, B Company crossed the Po River and assisted the 351st Infantry Regiment on its drive to Verona while C Company supported A Company of the 752nd Tank Battalion on its drive to Vicenza. The reminder of the battalion continued to seize objectives at river crossings, destroying numerous enemy vehicles, an enemy convoy of seven vehicles, and firing on an enemy column resulting in numerous casualties and prisoners to the enemy.

All elements of the battalion were north of the Po Valley driving towards Borgo Valsugana at the beginning of May. The companies were supporting various infantry regiments and engaging the enemy at every opportunity. At the close of the first day's action over 50 Germans were captured, and nine Americans recovered from friendly partisans. On May 2, the battalion continued it drive north throughout the day, knocking out enemy positions and capturing more than two hundred prisoners. The cessation of hostilities in Italy was announced at the end of the day. The next day the companies moved into these new positions: Company A at Arsiè, Company B at Trento, and Company C and one platoon of reconnaissance company moving towards the Brenner Pass. This placed one company at each end of Lago Di Caldonazzo. The disarming of German soldiers was the main activity being performed. From May 4 through 16, all elements of the battalion remained in position and continued to assist in the rounding up of German soldiers and equipment. On May 16, Company C moved to Merano to guard an enemy redistribution center, while the other elements continued with the mission of rounding up enemy soldiers. On May 27, the battalion moved to the Lake Garda area, awaiting movement orders to either an active theater or to the United States. There was another change of battalion commander during the month with Major Herbert B. Fowler assuming command.

The command structure for the battalion in 1945 was not as volatile as during the previous year. It remained assigned to II Corps for the year with attachments to the 34th, 88th, and 91st Divisions. There were times when elements of the battalion were attached to the 85th Division and the Italian Legnano Group. When the battalion moved to Lake Garda on May 27, it had performed front-line duty for 147 consecutive days—every single day of 1945. The battalion was not moved to another theater of war as the war in Europe ended on May 8 (with war in the Pacific ending with the formal surrender of Japan on September 2, 1945). As with all other units, individual soldiers began the redeployment process based upon the number of service points accumulated. On November 2, 1945, the 805th Tank Destroyer Battalion was officially inactivated at Camp Hood, Texas.

The battalion began its mobilization on February 1, 1941, and remained on active duty for four years, nine months, and two days until November 2, 1945. During this time, it performed overseas duty for approximately three years and two months since departing Brooklyn,

New York Harbor, on August 6, 1942. It was initiated into combat operations on February 9, 1943, and ended these operations on May 16, 1945. During these 728 days it was in direct contact with the enemy for 579 days. The battalion received credit for its participation in the Tunisian, Naples–Foggia, Anzio, Rome–Arno, North Apennines, and Po Valley campaigns. As of November 2023, Detachment 1, Company C, 1st Battalion, 109th Infantry Regiment of the Pennsylvania Army National Guard in Tamaqua, Pennsylvania, traces it lineage to Company B of the 805th Tank Destroyer Battalion. Thus, a portion of the 105th Infantry Battalion (AT)/805th TD Battalion lives on.

Table I: Personnel Authorizations by Table of Organization (1940–44)

	105th Bn	105th Bn	805th Bn	805th Bn	805th Bn	805th Bn	805th Bn
T/O Date	4/12/ 1940	11/1/ 1940	12/24/ 1941	6/8/ 1942	1/27/ 1943	5/7/ 1943	3/15/ 1944
T/O Number	PANG GO	7–115	18–25	18–25	18–25	18–35	18–25
Officers	20	30	35	38	36	32	35
Warrant Officers	0	0	0	0	1	2	2
Enlisted	284	680	807	860	636	763	634
Aggregate	304	710	842	898	673	797	671

This table illustrates the authorized strength figures of the 105th Infantry Bn (AT) and its successor, the 805th TD Bn, from April 1940 through March 1944. (Sources: 22nd Cavalry Division Disbanded, *The Pennsylvania Guardsman*, December 1940, Table of Organization 7–115 for the 105th and Table of Organization 18–25 for the 805th TD Bn) (Note: PANG GO stands for Pennsylvania Army National Guard General Order.)

174 • GUEST OF ADOLF

Table J: Equipment Authorizations by Table of Organization (1940–44)

	105th Bn	805th Bn	805th Bn	805th Bn	805th Bn	805th Bn
T/O Date	11/1/ 1940	12/24/ 1941	6/8/ 1942	1/27/ 1943	5/7/ 1943	3/15/ 44
T/O Number	7–115	18–25	18–25	18–25	18–35	18–25
.30 Carbine	340	504	633	42	360	293
M1 Rifle	51	0	177	534	117	283
.45 Pistol	325	314	62	78	3	79
50-caliber MG	0	36	60	54	25	44
30-caliber MG	0	15	32	35	50	30
Rocket Launcher	0	0	0	62	71	62
81-mm Mortar	0	0	0	0	0	3
37-mm AA	0	18	0	0	0	0
37-mm AT, SP	36 (towed)	12	12	36	0	0
3-inch AT Gun	0	24★	24★	0	25	0
76-mm SP, M18	0	0	0	0	0	36

★The 75-mm SP M3 gun was substituted for the 3-inch AT gun in the 1941 and 1942 T/Os. Table J illustrates the equipment authorization for the 105th Infantry Bn (AT) and its successor, the 805th TD Bn, from November 1940 through March 1944. (Sources: Table of Organization 7–115 for the 105th and Table of Organization 18–25 for the 805th TD Bn)

APPENDIX 2

Ernest Focht's Lists

Interspersed throughout SSG Ernest V. Focht's World War II diaries amongst the record of his meals, daily walks around the compound, books read, glee club practices and performances, and trips outside of the prison camps, he documented the names of more than one hundred fellow POWs, the contents of various types of Red Cross parcels and the personal parcels received, his hoard of clothing, the members of his gun crew, the baseball team he managed, and many poems and jokes written by his friends. In this appendix are some of these documented items not already incorporated into the text. They are presented here as supplementary materials to assist the reader in understanding an American soldier's life as a German POW. The spelling, grammar, and abbreviations are Ernie's own and in no circumstance has the author attempted to correct misspellings.

Prison Pals of Outfit

1. Merle Hornberger
2. Robert Gordon
3. Robert Gearinger
4. Joseph Slaybaugh
5. Paul Broadt
6. Charles Stiver
7. John Fissel
8. Harvey Conn
9. James Cunningham

176 • GUEST OF ADOLF

10. Norman Houck
11. Roland Eyer
12. [left blank]
13. Donald Moore
14. Lloyd Shaffer
15. Thomas Banfield
16. Walter Morris
17. Bill McCormick Jr.
18. Richard Hild
19. Lee Toy Wo
20. Rhudolph Price
21. Roy Ringler
22. Clair Kinney
23. Paul B. Gallo
24. Oscar Tayman
25. Charles A. Carroll
26. Leon Everett
27. Thomas J. Wright
28. Homer Howard
29. Francis Harper Jr.
30. Leslie G. Ott
31. Angelo Meffe
32. Charles Reichman Jr.
33. Joseph A. Boucher
34. Lawrence Thipoideau
35. William Corey
36. Carl. J. Hunsinger
37. John Clendinning
38. Paul J. Mizwa
39. Francis G. Lamb
40. Joseph E. Legarth
41. Clarence Potter
42. Jack Lewis

Other Prison Pals

1. Bill French
2. Robert I. Higley
3. S. Joe Nasralia
4. Fred C. Breckendorf
5. Otto T. Klein
6. George Everett
7. Edwin W. Jones
9. Arthur Warren*
10. George Jorgensen
11. Arthur F. Gage
12. James W. Powell
13. Dwayne L. Blackman
14. Elroy Vordenbbaum
15. Clyde Bowen
16. David E. Knott Jr.
17. Leonard V. Cofield
18. Charles L. Crouse
19. Edwin W. Pinky Miles
20. Frank Stebbling
21. Melvin Schultz—Bass
22. Halley Collins—Orch—Trombone
23. Harry Smith—Baritone
24. William B. Wilson
25. Harry Kaczorowski

*Ernie skipped the number 8.

Other Prison Pals

1. Otto Lehman
2. Franklin J. Cooley
3. Guadalupe T. Lopez
4. Freddie L. Wilson
5. Francis H. Gorgen
6. Charles B. Vandermark

178 • GUEST OF ADOLF

7. Frank Beneventano
8. Vincent F. Climaldi
9. Richard J. Ertel
10. John M. McMahan
11. John Stasio
12. Al Kosenski
13. George B. Coffman
14. Peter Salidla
15. James W. Smith
16. Leroy E. Hansen
17. Abe Thomas
18. Dale Boyd
19. James Sorber
20. Ross Boyce
21. Lester Haynie
22. Albert Meye
23. Arnold Labin
24. Jack E. Rose
25. Jack Helfridge
26. Donald R. Miller
27. Bruce Meals
28. Lewis V. Rowley
29. John W. Carson
30. Ansel C. Monghler
31. Neal Barnett
32. Charles Meyrowitz
33. Earl Beeth
34. William T. Lail
35. Pedro Carmond
36. Carn A. Godsey
37. Darrel Christensen
38. Everett E. Marion
39. Joseph V. Bilpush
40. Joseph G. Milo
41. Wm F. McGowan

42. Anthony J. Brianyk
43. Peter R. Peterson Jr.

German Food Issue

Breakfast—Black Coffee
Dinner—Soup (broth mostly)
Supper—⅓ to ¼ loaf of bread
      1 spoon syrup
      1 piece butter 1 to 1½
      ½ Cheese
      1 spoon sugar
      3 small potatoes
      Meat Occasionally
      Black barley coffee

Shaving Equipment, November 10, 1943

3 Razors
3 Brushes
3 Wms shaving soap
3 Large Combs
1 Pocket Glass
1 Hair Brush
40 Razor Blades
1 Zipper Kit from LaRue
4 Toothbrushes, New
1 Finger File
1 Tweezer
1 Cuticle Scissors
1 Stepic [styptic] Pencil
1 Bottle Drops, Stomach
1 Soap Tray, Issue
1 Blade Stone
2 Toothbrush cases
Tooth Powder
Tooth Paste

2 Mirrors, Metal
1 Mirror Glass
1 Fountain Pen

Contents of 1st Personal Parcel, September 7, 1943

Peanuts—Bag
Mixed Nuts—Box
Chewing Gum
Life Savers
Toothbrush powder
Razor Blades
Comb
Raisins
Socks
Jockey Shorts
Band [bandana]
Barricks slippers
Blue Towel
Soap, bath
Shaving
Oxydol
H. Chiefs
Stepic [styptic] pencil
Lead pencil
3 soups
Scrub brush
Emery boards

Contents of 2nd Personal Parcel. Received November 8, 1943, Damaged

1 Towel
1 Wash cloth
6 Beachnut [Beechnut gum]
4 Dentyne
1 Calox T.P.

ERNEST FOCHT'S LISTS • 181

1 Toothbrush
1 Sewing kit
1 Charms [candy]
4 Razor Blades
1 Pkg Egg Noodle Soup
2 Pkgs Tetley Soup Mix—6 complete
4 Drawers
1 Sweatshirt
1 Dish towel
1 Hard Candy
5 Prs shoe strings
4 Toilet Soap
1 Octagon Soap P.
1 Mirror
1 Shaving Soap
3 Candy Bars
1 Prunes
1 Rasins [*sic*]
1 Malted Milk Tab

Red Cross Parcel No. 9, July 15, 1943

1 corn willie
1 prem
1 cheese
1 liverpaste
1 sardines
1 D-ration bar
1 lb butter
1 rasins [*sic*]
1 biscuit
1 lb milk
1 orange drink
1 sugar square
1 coffee

1 soap face
3 cigarettes
3 matches
1 salt–pepper

American Invalid Parcel No. 1, June 12, 1944

Soups
3½ oz tins of meats
Milk
Butter
Sugar
Rasins [sic]
Cocoa
Coffee
9 pks cig

List of Poems

Ode to Independence
Three Men on a Box
It was the Tenth of May in 43
Sweethearts
Untitled
Mother
Pentacost [sic]
To My Darling
A Day in a Stalag
Forty-Eight Stars in the Sky Tonight
Ever in My Thoughts
A Lonesome Soldier's Thoughts
The Draft Dodger
Our House
To Mother and God in Heaven
Not If___But When
My Mother

Creed
The Lonely Night
To Mother & Father
Unforgettable Barbed Wire
Away
You____Bett
A Soldier's Prayer to Mother Sweetheart
My Honey
My Buddy
My Best Pal
Armistice
The Missing Stalag Gate
Chow Hound
The Sun Rose from Behind Faid Pass
Soldiers Temple
Blue Skies of Exile
Roads
Overnight Pass
Philosopher's Perch

Selected Poems

God's Minute

I have only just a minute
Only sixty seconds in it
Forced upon me, can't refuse it
Didn't seek it, Didn't choose it
But its up to me to use it
I must suffer if I lose it
Give account if I abuse it
Just a tiny little minute
But eternity is in it.

P.O.W. Author Unknown
Copied May 27, 1943
IIIB P.O.W. Camp

GUEST OF ADOLF

The Yanks

We are the Yanks who were captured first
We said a prayer as the shells around us burst
We are the Yanks who dug the holes
In the bullpen at Sfax like a bunch of moles
We are the Yanks who carried the stones
With lots of aches, grunts and groans
We stayed in the P.G with mud to our knees
We then moved to another to be bitten by the fleas
But now in spite of the past
We are all feeling better at last.

S/SGT Carl Davis
5–26–43
POW Camp IIIB 255

Little Did I Know

Little did I know as I scouted about
What was in stow at the end of my route?
Little did I know what America meant
As I and my friends in luxury went
Little did I think about my home
Until at last I started to roam
Little did I know of the far off lands
Until I landed on the shores of sand
Little did I know or ever think
Of what I ate or what I drank
Until at last I answered the call
I know that America means not little but all.

S/SGT Carl Davis
5–27–43
POW Camp IIIB 255

Ode to Independence—July 4, 1943

In this trying year of 43
The nations at war in misery

ERNEST FOCHT'S LISTS • 185

Lets pause—think—try to see
The real true meaning of liberty
We fought for it—some died
As their blood rushed forth, the silently sighed
For liberty, for freedom, were finished, we tried
Was it all in vain—Please God decide
We are in this war now—All the way
As prisoners of war to the end we'll stay
Here together on work—in play
For a speedy peace—Let's all kneel to pray.
It means so much to us here in camp
Independence—freedom—or our spirits so damp
I wonder if after we've passed Liberty's lamp
Will it mean the same, or shall we be easily vamped.
I solemnly vow—with all my heart
That I for one will never part
With the lesson I've learned—so bitter—so fast
We need independence, equality from the very start.

By Ed Murphy
IIIB
July 15, 1943

It was the Tenth of May in 43

In a prison camp in Germany
We rushed the gate for to see
Was Red Cross Parcels for you & me
Our moral [morale] was high as we filed by
The parcels were issued & up went the cry
Cigarettes for coffee & rasins [sic] besides
The price of canned meat went as high as the sky.
At supper that day the faces did smile
And laughter was heard for more than a mile
For eating and drinking was again in style
The result of which would have flooded the Nile.
All through the night we layed [sic] awake
Still buying & selling—per chance a bargain to make
One guy went to the stove with a puddin to make
Needless to say his belly did ache.
They're bombing poor Germany, especially the docks

186 • GUEST OF ADOLF

But we're safe in our Stalag, we're smart as a fox
We won't complain of our clothes, the holes in our socks
Just give us a week, our R.C. Box

IIIB, Furstenberg
June 16, 1943

A Soldier's Prayers to Mother and Sweetheart

Dear God watch over her for me
That she may safely guided be
Help her each lonely hour to bear
When I would Lord, if I were there
When she is sleeping, watch her then
That fear may not, her dreams offend
Be ever near her, through the day
Let none but goodness, come her way
Sweet faithful girl, that waits for me
Beyond a wide and spacious sea
Be merciful, Oh! God, I pray
Take care of her, while I'm away.

Lefty

APPENDIX 3

Ernest Virgil Focht's Chronology

November 1, 1914	Ernest Virgil Focht born in Tyrone, Pennsylvania
February 24, 1920	Elizabeth LaRue Cassidy born in Tyrone, Pennsylvania
summer 1921	Family trip to visit relatives in Goodling, Idaho
June 2, 1933	Graduated from Tyrone High School, commercial course
June 1933	Worked at a gas station and at a coffee packinghouse until mid-1936
mid-1936	Working for West Virginia Pulp and Paper Company in Tyrone, Pennsylvania, through April 11, 1941
October 4, 1936	Started dating Elizabeth LaRue Cassidy
June 2, 1938	LaRue graduated Tyrone High School, academic course
1940	LaRue graduated Zeth Business School of Altoona, Pennsylvania
December 1940	Received draft notice from Altoona Draft Board
February 19, 1941	Received postcard from Selective Service with instruction to appear for physical examination on February 26, 1941, at a doctor's office in Tyrone
February 26, 1941	Received notice from Selective Service Board of classification of 1-A with an order number of 571
April 5, 1941	Proposed to Elizabeth LaRue Cassidy
April 15, 1941	Inducted into the United States Army, Altoona, Pennsylvania

188 • GUEST OF ADOLF

April 15, 1941	Traveled to New Cumberland, Pennsylvania, for initial in-processing
April 19, 1941	Arrived Fort Meade, Maryland, for six weeks basic training and then seven weeks of training as a heavy truck driver. Assigned to Company A, 105th Infantry Battalion (Anti-Tank)
1941	LaRue employed by the Department of Public Education, Harrisburg, Pennsylvania
August 1941	Unit at Camp A. P. Hill, Virginia, for training
September 1941	Unit began its participation in the Carolina Maneuvers. Unit assembly area located outside of Hoffman, North Carolina
October 11, 1941	Attended North Carolina–Fordham football game at Kenan Stadium, Chapel Hill, North Carolina
October 18, 1941	Attended Duke–Colgate football game at Duke Stadium, Durham, North Carolina
October 1941	Advanced to private first class
December 7, 1941	Returned from Carolina Maneuvers with an overnight stop at Camp A. P. Hill, Virginia
December 8, 1941	Arrived Tank Destroyer Tactical and Firing Center, Fort Meade, Maryland
December 15, 1941	Unit redesignated 805th Tank Destroyer Battalion and was reassigned from the 28th Infantry Division to the Army General Headquarters. Ernie remained assigned to A Company
December 1941	Home for Christmas holiday for multiple days but returned to base before the end of December
February 1, 1942	Promoted to technician 5th class
April 27, 1942	Returned to Tyrone, Pennsylvania, on furlough from Camp A. P. Hill, Virginia
May 1942 to July 29, 1942	Unit trained at Camp Hood, Texas, as a tank destroyer battalion with the M3 75-mm gun half-track
July 25, 26, and 27	LaRue visited Camp Hood, Texas
July 30, 1942	Unit departed Camp Hood, Texas

ERNEST VIRGIL FOCHT'S CHRONOLOGY • 189

August 2, 1942	Unit arrived at Indiantown Gap Military Reservation (IGMR), Pennsylvania
August 5, 1942	Departed IGMR, Pennsylvania, for New York Harbor to board a troop transport ship. LaRue was present at IGMR to say goodbye
August 6, 1942	Departed New York Harbor for Halifax, Nova Scotia, as part of Convoy AT-18
August 17, 1942	Convoy AT-18 Merchant/Troopships arrived Firth of Clyde, Scotland
August 18, 1942	Arrived Tidworth Barracks, England
September 1942	Promoted to corporal
September 6, 1942	Moved to Shrivenham, England
January 5, 1943	Departed Shrivenham, England, for Liverpool, England
January 6, 1943	Departed Liverpool, England
January 7, 1943	Arrived at mouth of Clyde River, Scotland
January 9, 1943	Left Scotland on troopship *Monarch of Bermuda* as part of Convoy KMF.7
January 9–17, 1943	Atlantic Ocean, seasick
January 15, 1943	Promoted to sergeant while onboard ship
January 16, 1943	Passed Rock of Gibraltar at 9:20 p.m.
January 16, 1943	Sea burial of steward of *Monarch of Bermuda*
January 17, 1943	Landed at Algiers, Algeria, and saw first lemon and orange trees, stayed in abandoned brickyard, El Bair
January 23, 1943	Moved to El Achour
January 24, 1943	Left El Achour to move closer to front lines in Tunisia
February 7, 1943	Arrived woods in vicinity of Bou Chebka, 20 miles southeast from Tebessa
February 9, 1943	Left Bou Chebka for Fériana, Tunisia
February 14, 1943	Company A and one reconnaissance platoon, 805th TD Bn, ordered to report to Combat Command A at Sbeitla, Tunisia
February 15, 1943	Moved closer to front towards Faid Pass, replaced an element of 701st Tank Destroyer Battalion

190 • GUEST OF ADOLF

February 16, 1943	Position extreme front, ordered to abandon equipment
February 17, 1943	Captured by German troops at 7:00 a.m., transported toward Faid Pass, Tunisia
February 18, 1943	Marched through Faid Pass
February 19, 1943	Transported to Sfax, Tunisia, in a German military truck
February 20, 1943	Left for Tunis, Tunisia, by boxcar
February 21, 1943	Arrive Sousse, Tunisia, by boxcar
February 22, 1943	Arrived Tunis, Tunisia, walking to German camp
March 2, 1943	Walked to Tunis, Tunisia, airport; flew Mediterranean Sea in Ju 52; arrived Palermo, Sicily, Italian *prigioniero di guerra* (prisoner of war) camp, PG 98 San Giuseppe Jato
March 23, 1943	Left Palermo by train for Messina, Sicily
March 24, 1943	Boarded ferry and crossed Strait of Messina to Reggio di Calabria (St. John's), Italy
March 25, 1943	Boarded train to go farther up west coast of Italy passing Pompeii, Mt. Vesuvius, and Naples and continuing on for 30 kilometers to Capua, Italy
March 26, 1943	Left train and marched one mile to Italian camp PG 66 at Capua, Italy; received first Red Cross parcel
March 31, 1943	Received a Christmas 1942 booklet from a Catholic priest that became his first diary
April 2, 1943	Germans assumed control of Capua POW camp
April 11, 1943	Attended his last church service in Italy
April 12, 1943	Boarded a forty-and-eight rail boxcar for trip to Moosburg, Germany
April 13, 1943	Traveling through northern Italy
April 14, 1943	Passing Innsbruck, Austria, arrived Moosburg, Germany, marched the one mile to Stalag VIIA from the train station
April 17, 1943	Attended a concert in Munich, Germany
May 4, 1943	Left Moosburg, Germany, by train, passing Leipzig, Gaschwitz, and Reisa, en route to another POW camp

ERNEST VIRGIL FOCHT'S CHRONOLOGY • 191

May 6, 1943	Arrived Fürstenberg, Brandenburg, Germany, along the Polish border; marched two miles from the station to Stalag IIIB; the Oder Canal formed the rear boundary of the camp
May 9, 1943	Elected confidence man for Barracks 12-B
May 14, 1943	Moved to Barracks 10
May 22, 1943	Moved to Barracks 15
July 12, 1943	Elected billet leader
July 15, 1943	Trip outside of camp to railroad station
August 5, 1943	Approximately 1,400 American POWs in Stalag IIIB with 2,700 men in commando camps
August 20, 1943	Left camp for railroad station, boarded train for Frankfurt an der Oder to observe a trial of a commando who was convicted of a crime and given a nine-month sentence; visited the city and several churches
August 29, 1943	Went with glee club and orchestra to Fürstenberg commando camp
September 18, 1943	Relieved as billet leader
September 19, 1943	Glee club rode in a truck for one hundred kilometers for four hours to Trattendorf, Germany, to perform for commando camp
September 27, 1943	Ernie and LaRue's original wedding date
October 3, 1943	Glee club gathered for trip to Fürstenberg Commando Camp 5
October 8, 1943	Glee club walked to Neuzelle, Germany, about five kilometers southwest of Fürstenberg, Germany; visited cathedral, pictures taken by guard
April 20, 1944	Went to infirmary for illness
May 2, 1944	Returned from infirmary to Billet 18
Aug 18–19, 1944	Musical production *Showboat* performed in prison camp
January 22, 1945	Left camp on work detail to unload three railcars of Red Cross parcels at the town of Guben. It is located approximately 30 miles south of the POW camp

192 • GUEST OF ADOLF

January 31, 1945	4 p.m. received notice all American POWs were departing the Stalag; left Stalag IIIB at 7 p.m., walking through the night; pulled sled with all belongings
February 1, 1945	Halted 5 p.m. near the current German town of Krugersdorf, slept in barn
February 2, 1945	11 a.m. back on road walking, 25 kilometers, slept in a dairy barn
February 3, 1945	Stopped at Leibsch; slept in a horse barn
February 4, 1945	8 a.m. back on road; 1:30 p.m. stopped Halbe, 15–20 kilometers, and stayed in a church for lodging
February 5, 1945	Stopped near the current German town of Neuhof, 20 kilometers
February 6, 1945	Stopped at a German military garrison
February 7, 1945	Arrived Stalag IIIA, Luckenwalde; approximately seventy-six miles (one hundred twenty-three kilometers) from Stalag IIIB; lived in large tent #4
April 21, 1945	Camp guards depart
April 22, 1945	Liberated at 5 a.m. as Russian scout cars enter camp; 10 a.m. Russian tanks enter camp; Stalag IIIA is about 85 miles west of the town Magdeburg that is on the Elbe River, the stopping point for the American and British armies
April 28, 1945	Walked into town of Luckenwalde from Stalag IIIA
April 30, 1945	Left the camp area for a stroll in woods
May 6, 1945	4:40 p.m. boarded G.I. trucks and departed Stalag IIIA; traveled through Wittenberg; at Barby crossed the Elbe River by pontoon bridge; spent night at a POW reception camp
May 7, 1945	1:30 p.m. loaded trucks for Hildesheim, Germany, passing through ruins of Magdeburg, Germany; 5 p.m. arrived Hildesheim, South of Hanover
May 11, 1945	Departed Hildesheim, Germany, onboard a C-47 around 12:00 p.m.; arrived at a camp 25 miles outside of Reims, France, at 2:25 p.m.; in tent #D-14

ERNEST VIRGIL FOCHT'S CHRONOLOGY • 193

May 12, 1945	Departed camp at 1 p.m. for train station at Reims, France; departed station at 3 p.m. onboard U.S. Army hospital train #39; made stops at Laon, La Feré, and Tergnier
May 13, 1945	Train arrived 8 a.m. Montivilliers, France (northeast of Le Havre); 11 a.m. boarded truck for 25-mile drive to Camp Lucky Strike, located between Cany-Barville and Saint-Valery-en-Caux, France, near the port city of Le Havre, France
June 2, 1945	7:45 a.m. departed Camp Lucky Strike for Le Havre, France; 10 a.m. boarded landing craft tank for transport to troopship SS *MorMacMoon*; 6 p.m. troopship departed for return journey to the United States
June 11, 1945	9 a.m. ship arrived in Newport News, Virginia; 10 a.m. disembarked troopship and boarded a Chesapeake and Ohio train for 45-minute ride to Camp Patrick Henry; 12 noon attended welcome home speech in theater; 4:15 p.m. called LaRue
June 13, 1945	1 p.m. final formation at Camp Patrick Henry, Virginia; 2 p.m. boarded Norfolk Western train; 4 p.m. in train yard Richmond, Virginia; 10 p.m. in Washington, DC; 2 a.m. in Philadelphia, Pennsylvania; arrived Fort Dix, New Jersey, at 5 a.m.
June 15, 1945	1:30 p.m. departed Fort Dix by bus for Trenton, New Jersey, train station; boarded train for Harrisburg, Pennsylvania, at 4 p.m.; arrived Harrisburg, Pennsylvania, but LaRue was not at station; took taxi to her apartment at 514 Graham Street; both returned to train station and boarded train for Altoona, Pennsylvania, at 7:50 p.m.; 10:45 arrived Altoona, Pennsylvania, train station, was met by parents; went to meet Ma Cassidy, then to Tyrone home, where Mel, Madeline, Wayne, Vera, and Elda were waiting

194 • GUEST OF ADOLF

July 7, 1945	Married Elizabeth LaRue Cassidy at Altoona, Pennsylvania
July 7–12, 1945	Honeymoon trip to Pocono Pines, Pennsylvania
July 15, 1945	Reported to the Army Ground and Service Forces Redistribution Station, Asheville, North Carolina
August 24, 1945	LaRue joined Ernie in Asheville, North Carolina
September 6, 1945	Promoted to staff sergeant
September 7, 1945	Departed Asheville, North Carolina, for Indiantown Gap Military Reservation, Pennsylvania
September 11, 1945	Discharged from the United States Army at the rank of staff sergeant
September 17, 1945	Started employment at Mechanicsburg naval depot as a storekeeper
July 1948	Son Stephen Ernest Focht born in Harrisburg, Pennsylvania
May 1950	Purchased new house at 315 Mountain Road, Dillsburg, Pennsylvania
October 1951	Daughter Karen LaRue Focht born in Mechanicsburg, Pennsylvania
April 1961	Recognized for 20 years of federal service
July 13, 1963	Ernie and daughter Karen attended Focht family reunion, Tyrone, Pennsylvania
July 6, 1968	Ernie and LaRue attended LaRue's 30th high school reunion, Tyrone, Pennsylvania
August 1970	Son Stephen married Kathy Glenn in Shillington, Pennsylvania
April 1971	Recognized for 30 years of federal service
August 1973	Daughter Karen married Michael H. Zang in Dillsburg, Pennsylvania
February 24, 1976	Ernie's last day of work at the navy depot in Mechanicsburg, Pennsylvania
May 2, 1977	Official retirement date from the Navy Ships Parts Control Center, Mechanicsburg, Pennsylvania
August 1977	Grandson Jeffrey R. Focht born in Lancaster, Pennsylvania

ERNEST VIRGIL FOCHT'S CHRONOLOGY • 195

November 1977	Granddaughter Kimberly M. Zang born in Harrisburg, Pennsylvania
June 1981	Granddaughter Julia E. Focht born in Lancaster, Pennsylvania
July 1982	Grandson Andrew M. Zang born in Harrisburg, Pennsylvania
September 1986	Grandson Patrick M. Zang born in Harrisburg, Pennsylvania
October 8, 1987	LaRue died in Dillsburg, Pennsylvania
October 1988	Presented his Prisoner of War Medal by BG Walter E. Katuzny
February 25, 2003	Ernie died in Dillsburg, Pennsylvania

APPENDIX 4

Abbreviations and Acronyms

AA	anti-aircraft
AG & SF	Army Ground and Service Forces
AT	anti-tank
BBC	British Broadcasting Corporation
BG	brigadier general
Bn	battalion
Cav Div	cavalry division
CCA	Combat Command Alpha
CG	commanding general
CPT	captain
Co	company
COL	colonel
Commando	POW on a work party
Det	detachment
FM	field manual
FSSF	First Special Services Forces
G3	Operations, Plans, and Training
GHQ	general headquarters
HQ	headquarters
ICRC	International Committee of the Red Cross
ID	infantry division
IGMR	Indiantown Gap Military Reservation, PA
LT	lieutenant
LTC	lieutenant colonel

198 • GUEST OF ADOLF

Med	medical
NCO	non-commissioned officer
Oflag	officer POW camp
OD	olive drab
PANG	Pennsylvania Army National Guard
PG	*prigioniero di guerra* (prisoner of war)
POW	prisoner of war
Prem	canned meat similar to Spam
PRR	Pennsylvania Railroad
QM	quartermaster
RAMP	recovered allied military personnel
RCP	Red Cross parcel
RCN	reconnaissance
RCT	regimental combat team
SGT	sergeant
SSG	staff sergeant
SP	self-propelled
Sq	squadron
SS	steamship
Svc	service
SWL	shortwave listeners
TD	tank destroyer
T/O	table of organization
Unteroffizer	corporal
USO	United Service Organization
USS	United States ship
VA	Veterans Administration

Endnotes

Chapter 1

1   Mr. Edward Oswald, clerk of the Circuit Court for Washington County, issued the marriage license.
2   "Martin G. Buranovsky Obituary," *The Progress*, May 16, 1948; "Mrs. Mary S. (Wasilko) Buranovsky Obituary," *The Progress*, August 31, 1951.
3   Gerald Roy Focht and Mary H. Bernosky, Application for Marriage License, Marriage License, and Marriage Certificate, August 19, 1912.
4   Ancestry Library, "Hanns Dieterich Vogtens/Vogt Family Tree," accessed November 5, 2022, https://www.ancestrylibrary.com/family-tree/person/tree/60414433/person/132414630894/facts.
5   Rev. Ira M. Wallace, "The Focht-Henlein-Wallace-Garner Family Connection Sketch," Jersey Shore, PA, December 29, 1936, 1.
6   J. George Focht, Revolutionary War Pension Application Statement, October 31, 1832, Court of Common Pleas for the County of Schuylkill, Pennsylvania.
7   Wallace, The Focht-Henlein-Wallace-Garner Family Connection Sketch, 4; Ancestry Library, "John George Focht Family Tree," accessed February 23, 2022, https://www.ancestrylibrary.com/family-tree/person/tree/60414433/person/130116512485/facts?_phsrc=dMu10&_phstart=successSource.
8   In August 1861 George John's wife, Margaret, passed, and a year later, on July 7, 1862, George John passed. They are buried in St. John's Lutheran Church Cemetery in Clover Creek, Blair County, Pennsylvania. Ancestry Library, "George John Focht Family Tree," accessed February 24, 2022, https://www.ancestrylibrary.com/family-tree/person/tree/159711335/person/172090244251/facts.
9   Three of their daughters—Catharine, Margaret, and Emma—never married and died before their parents. Charlotte passed on February 23, 1891, and Adam on July 22, 1895. They and four of the children—Catherine, Margaret, Martin Luther, and Emma—and their son George's first wife, Emma Crawford Focht, are buried in Shaffersville Cemetery, Morris Township, in Huntingdon County, Pennsylvania, not far from the family farm. Their son, George Melanchthan Focht, and his second wife, Annie White Focht, are buried in the Williamsburg Lutheran Cemetery, Williamsburg, Blair County, Pennsylvania. Interestingly, this cemetery is only a few miles from his grandfather George John's Clover Creek farm. Ancestry Library, "Adam Focht Family Tree," accessed February 24, 2022, https://www.ancestrylibrary.com/family-tree/person/tree/159711335/person/172090243562/facts?_phsrc=dMu9&_phstart=successSource.

200 • GUEST OF ADOLF

10 "Focht-Bernosky Wedding," *The Tyrone Daily Herald*, August 29, 1912; Ancestry Library, "Martin Luther Focht Family Tree," accessed February 23, 2022, https://www.ancestrylibrary.com/family-tree/person/tree/159538592/person/282333513065/facts?_phsrc=dMu9&_phstart=successSource.

11 "Focht-Bernosky Wedding," *The Tyrone Daily Herald*, August 29, 1912.

12 It maintained reduced operations for another 30 years until being shuttered by its owner, MeadWestvo.

13 Ernest V. Focht, oral history, 1990, 16.

14 "Class of 115 to Complete School," *Altoona Mirror*, May 16, 1933.

Chapter 2

1 "Induction Procedure and Training of Selectees," *The Pennsylvania Guardsman*, December 1940, 3.

2 Christopher R. Gabel, *Seek, Strike, Destroy: U.S. Army Tank Destroyer Doctrine in World War II* (Fort Leavenworth, KS: Combat Studies Institute, U.S. Army Command and General Staff College, 1985), 5–8.

3 "Induction Procedure and Training of Selectees," *The Pennsylvania Guardsman*, December 1940, 4.

4 Gabel, *Seek, Strike, Destroy*, 18.

5 Gabel, *Seek, Strike, Destroy*, 64, 117, 128–129.

6 Lt. Col. Emory A. Dunham, *The Tank Destroyer History—Study No. 29* (Washington, DC: Historical Section of the Army Ground Forces, 1946), 4.

7 "805th Tank Destroyer Battalion (Heavy)," *The Pennsylvania Guardsman*, March 1942, 29–31.

8 "805th Tank Destroyer Battalion (Heavy)," *The Pennsylvania Guardsman*, May 1942, 25.

9 "805th Tank Destroyer Battalion (Heavy)," *The Pennsylvania Guardsman*, June 1942, 23.

10 Dunham, *The Tank Destroyer History*, 16–17.

11 "805th Tank Destroyer Battalion (Heavy)," *The Pennsylvania Guardsman*, August 1942, 24.

12 Wayne Von Stetten, *Distinguished Military Men, Word Portraits of Eight of Columbia's Finest* (Lancaster, PA: Minuteman Press, 2006), 146.

13 Arnold Hague, "Convoy AT.8," Arnold Hague Convoy Database, accessed July 18, 2021, http://www.convoyweb.org.uk/at/index.html.

14 "USS *Brooklyn* War Diary August 1–31, 1942," National Archives and Records Administration, World War II War Diaries, Other Operational Records and Histories, accessed December 3, 2022, https: www.fold3.com/image/267984528, 9–12.

15 Richard Lucas, "Axis Sally: The Americans Behind the Infamous Nazi Propaganda Broadcast," accessed May 9, 2021, https://www.historynet.com/axis-sally/?f.

ENDNOTES • 201

16 Patrick J. Chase, *Seek, Strike, Destroy: The History of the 894th Tank Destroyer Battalion in World War II* (Baltimore, MD: Gateway Press, 1995), 7.
17 Focht, oral history, 46.

Chapter 3

1 Gabel, *Seek, Strike, Destroy*, 21.
2 Gabel, *Seek, Strike, Destroy*, 11.
3 Gabel, *Seek, Strike, Destroy*, 14.
4 Gabel, *Seek, Strike, Destroy*, 17.
5 War Department, *Tank Destroyer Field Manual: Organization and Tactics of Tank Destroyer Units* (Washington, DC: United States Printing Office, 1942), 20.
6 Gabel, *Seek, Strike, Destroy*, 31.

Chapter 4

1 Volker Ullrich, *Hitler: Downfall 1939–1945* (New York: Vintage Books, 2020), 107.
2 John Keegan, *The Second World War* (New York: Penguin Group, 1989), 327.
3 Winston S. Churchill, *Memoirs of the Second World War, An Abridgement of the Six Volumes of The Second World War* (New York: Houghton Mifflin, 1959), 390.
4 Churchill, *Memoirs of the Second World War*, 393.
5 Keegan, *The Second World War*, 328–330.
6 Keegan, *The Second World War*, 328.
7 Keegan, *The Second World War*, 330.
8 Churchill, *Memoirs of the Second World War*, 542.
9 Keegan, *The Second World War*, 328–329.
10 Max Hastings, *Winston's War: Churchill 1940–1945* (New York: Vintage Books, 2009), 240.
11 Churchill, *Memoirs of the Second World War*, 614–615.
12 Keegan, *The Second World War*, 336–337.
13 Louis Morton, *Germany First: The Basic Concept of Allied Strategy in World War II* (Washington, DC: Center of Military History, United States Army, 1990), 35.
14 Rick Atkinson, *An Army at Dawn: The War in North Africa, 1942–1943* (New York: Picador, 2002), 16.
15 Atkinson, *An Army at Dawn*, 16.
16 Hague, "Convoy KMF.7."
17 Atkinson, *An Army at Dawn*, 308.
18 Charles E. Heller and William A. Stofft, eds., *America's First Battles 1776–1965* (Lawrence: University Press of Kansas, 1986), 247.
19 Headquarters, 805th Tank Destroyer Battalion, Battalion Diary, January 17, 1943 thru 29 May 1943 (1943, June 2), APO 302 United States Army, 1–2.
20 Heller and Stofft, *America's First Battles*, 248–250.

202 • GUEST OF ADOLF

21 Headquarters, 805th Tank Destroyer Battalion, Battalion Diary, January 17, 1943 to 29 May, 1943, Annex B, 11.

22 Ernest V. Focht, World War II personal diary, volume 1, 5.

23 Focht, oral history, 55–57; Focht's WWII diary, volume 1, 5; George F. Howe, *Northwest Africa: Seizing the Initiative in the West* (Washington, DC: Center of Military History, United States Army, 1993), 401–424.

24 Focht, oral history, 58.

25 Heller and Stofft, *America's First Battles*, 252.

26 Atkinson, *An Army at Dawn*, 343–344.

27 Heller and Stofft, *America's First Battles*, 241.

28 National Museum of the United States Air Force, "French 'Forty and Eight' Railroad Car," accessed June 3, 2022, https://www.nationalmuseum.af.mil/Visit/Museum-Exhibits/Fact-Sheets/Display/Article/196342/french-forty-and-eight-railroad-car/.

29 Headquarters, 805th Tank Destroyer Battalion, Battalion Diary, January 17, 1943 thru 29 May 1943, 8.

30 Heller and Stofft, *America's First Battles*, 254–257.

31 Heller and Stofft, *America's First Battles*, 260.

Chapter 5

1 Wikipedia, "List of Italian WW II prisoner-of-war camps in Italy," accessed July 13, 2021, https://en.wikipedia.org/wiki/List_of_World_War_II_prisoner-of-war_camps_in_Italy.

2 Mrs. H. B. Loomis, letter to Mr. and Mrs. Gerald Focht, April 25, 1943.

Chapter 6

1 Angelo M. Spinelli, *Life Behind Barbed Wire: The Secret World War II Photographs of Prisoner of War Angelo M. Spinelli* (New York: Fordham University Press, 2004), 17, 19.

2 "Between Two Stools. The History of Italian The Military Internees 1943–1945," NS Zwangsarbeit Dokumentationszentrum, http://www.ns-zwangsarbeit.de/en/italian-military-internees/.

3 "Commonwealth Prisoners of War 1939-1945," www.forces-war-records.co.uk/european-camps-british-commonwealth-prisoners-of-war-1939-45.

4 LaRue Cassidy, letter to SGT Ernest V. Focht, January 2, 1945.

5 LaRue Cassidy, letter to SGT Ernest V. Focht, August 18, 1944.

6 Robert Gearinger, letter to Veterans Administration, October 1948.

7 LaRue Cassidy, lettter to SGT Ernest V. Focht, October 4, 1944.

8 LaRue Cassidy, letter to SGT Ernest V. Focht, October 31, 1944.

9 LaRue Cassidy, letter to SGT Ernest V. Focht, November 9, 1944.

10 Edward Wisneski Jr., "SSG Edward 'Ski' Wisneski, The Wartime Memories Project—The Second World War," accessed March 27, 2022, https://wartime-memoriesproject.com/ww2/view.php?uid=248655.

ENDNOTES • 203

11 *Prisoners of War Bulletin*, Vol. 1, No. 5, October 1943, 4; *Prisoners of War Bulletin*, Vol. 2, No. 8, August 1944, 3.
12 *Prisoners of War Bulletin*, Vol. 1, No. 7, December 1943, 1.

Chapter 7

1 *Prisoners of War Bulletin*, Vol. 3, No. 3, March 1945, 4.
2 John Nichol and Tony Rennell, *The Last Escape, The Untold Story of Allied Prisoners of War in Europe 1944–45* (New York: Viking, 2003), 446.
3 James Cunningham, letter to Veterans Administration, October 1948.
4 Vernon M. White, "Liberation, 427th Lion Squadron Association," 427th Squadron Association, accessed April 27, 2022, https://www.427squadron.com/book_file/white/four_years_liberation.html.
5 LaRue Cassidy, letter to SGT Ernest V. Focht, November 30, 1944.
6 LaRue Cassidy, letter to SGT Ernest V. Focht, November 19, 1944.
7 LaRue Cassidy, letter to SGT Ernest V. Focht, August 25, 1944.
8 LaRue Cassidy, letter to SGT Ernest V. Focht, November 6, 1944.
9 LaRue Cassidy, letter to SGT Ernest V. Focht, March 2, 1944.
10 LaRue Cassidy, letter to SGT Ernest V. Focht, December 9, 1944.
11 LaRue Cassidy, letter to SGT Ernest V. Focht, December 27, 1944.

Chapter 8

1 Chaplain Lipsky, wire to Miss Cassidy, May 8, 1945.
2 "SS *MorMacMoon*," *The Port Hole News*, June 7, 1945.
3 Alison Skaggs, "A Look Inside Camp Patrick Henry. Camp The Mariners' Museum and Park," July 30, 2015, https://blog.marinersmuseum.org/2015/07/inside-look-at-camp-patrick-henry/.

Chapter 9

1 Lee James, letter to E. LaRue Cassidy, November 12, 1944.
2 John D. Millet, "United States Army in World War II, The Army Service Forces, The Organization and Role of the Army Service Forces," Center of Military History Online, accessed June 1, 2022, https://history.army.mil/books/wwii/ASF/index.htm#contents, 23–42, 312–416.
3 4th Service Command Asheville Redistribution Station Welcome Booklet (1945, May 25), Box 1/Folder 17, Marshall T. Wiggins Papers, WWII 267, WWII Papers, Military Collection, State Archives of North Carolina, Raleigh, NC, 7-8.
4 Servicemen's Guide to the "Land of the Sky" Asheville Booklet (1945, August–September), Box 1/Folder 18 Marshall T. Wiggins Papers, WWII 267, WWII Papers, Military Collection, State Archives of North Carolina, Raleigh, NC.
5 Welcome to the Army Ground and Service Forces Redistribution Station, Asheville, NC, Booklet, circa 1944–1945, Box 1/Folder 16, Marshall

204 • GUEST OF ADOLF

T. Wiggins Papers, WWII 267, WWII Papers, Military Collection, State Archives of North Carolina, Raleigh, NC.

6 Asheville Redistribution Station Typed Official History, [circa 1945], Box 1/Folder 15, Marshall T. Wiggins Papers, WWII 267, WWII Papers, Military Collection, State Archives of North Carolina, Raleigh, NC, 11.

7 Genealogy Today, "World War II War Ration Books," accessed May 27, 2020, http://www.genealogytoday.com/guide/war-ration-books.html.

Chapter 10

1 Notice of Veteran Preference (1945, September 12), United States Civil Service Commission, Third U.S. Civil Service Region.

2 Harry F. Glass, letter to Representative James E. Van Zandt, December 1, 1947; James E. Van Zandt, letter to Harry F. Glass, December 3, 1947; James E. Van Zandt, letter to Ernest V. Focht, March 8, 1948.

3 Gearinger and Cunningham.

Appendix 1

1 Gabel, *Seek, Strike, Destroy*, 5–8.

2 105th Anti-Tank Battalion, February 3, 1941, Record Group 19-BNGP-124, Records of Pennsylvania National Guardsmen Mustered into World War II 1940–1941, Pennsylvania State Archives, Harrisburg, PA.

3 Dunham, *The Tank Destroyer History*, 4.

4 Hague, "Convoy AT-18."

5 Focht, oral history, 46.

6 Focht, oral history, 53–54.

7 Headquarters, 805th Tank Destroyer Battalion, Battalion Diary.

Bibliography

Books

Atkinson, Rick. *An Army at Dawn: The War in North Africa, 1942–1943*. New York: Picador, 2002.

Charles, Roland W. *Troopships of World War II*. Washington, DC: The Army Transportation Association, 1947.

Chase, Patrick J. *Seek, Strike, Destroy: The History of the 894th Tank Destroyer Battalion in World War II*. Baltimore, MD: Gateway Press, 1995.

Churchill, Winston S. *Memoirs of the Second World War, An Abridgement of the Six Volumes of The Second World War*. New York: Houghton Mifflin, 1959.

Gabel, Christopher R. *Seek, Strike, Destroy: U.S. Army Tank Destroyer Doctrine in World War II*. Fort Leavenworth, KS: Combat Studies Institute, US Army Command and General Staff College, 1985.

Gabel, Christopher R. *The U.S. Army GHQ Maneuvers of 1941*. Washington, DC: Center for Military History, United States Army, 1991.

Gill, Lonnie. *Tank Destroyer Forces WWII*. Paducah, KY: Turner Publishing Company, 1992.

Hastings, Max. *Winston's War: Churchill 1940–1945*. New York: Vintage Books, 2009.

Heller, Charles E., and William A. Stofft, eds. *America's First Battles 1776–1965*. Lawrence: University Press of Kansas, 1986.

Howe, George F. *Northwest Africa: Seizing the Initiative in the West*. Washington, DC: Center of Military History, United States Army, 1993.

Keegan, John. *The Second World War*. New York: Penguin Group, 1989.

Kertzer, David I. *The Pope at War: The Secret History of Pius XII, Mussolini, and Hitler*. New York: Random House, 2022.

Morton, Louis. *Germany First: The Basic Concept of Allied Strategy in World War II*. Washington, DC: Center of Military History, United States Army, 1990.

Nichol, John, and Tony Rennell. *The Last Escape: The Untold Story of Allied Prisoners of War in Europe 1944–45*. New York: Viking, 2003.

Spinelli, Angelo M. *Life Behind Barbed Wire: The Secret World War II Photographs of Prisoner of War Angelo M. Spinelli*. New York: Fordham University Press, 2004.

Tyrone of Today: 1897–1976. Bicentennial Edition. Tyrone, PA: Tyrone Area Bicentennial Commission, 1976.

206 • GUEST OF ADOLF

Ullrich, Volker. *Hitler: Downfall 1939–1945*. New York: Vintage Books, 2020.

Von Stetten, Wayne. *Distinguished Military Men: Word Portraits of Eight of Columbia's Finest*. Lancaster, PA: Minuteman Press, 2006.

War Department. *Tank Destroyer Field Manual: Organization and Tactics of Tank Destroyer Units*. Washington, DC: United States Printing Office, 1942.

Wilson, Rev. W. H. *Tyrone of Today, The Gateway to the Alleghanies*. Pennsylvania: Press of the Herald, 1897.

Wolfgang, Ralph T. *A Short History of Tyrone Borough (1850–1950)*. Tyrone, PA: Tyrone Area Historical Society, 2017.

Documents

1st Armored Division, Combat Command Alpha. Narrative of Events, February 13, 1943 through February 19, 1943. APO 251 United States Army.

105th Anti-Tank Battalion, February 3, 1941, Record Group 19-BNGP-124, Records of Pennsylvania National Guardsmen Mustered into World War II 1940–1941. Pennsylvania State Archives, Harrisburg, PA.

4th Service Command Asheville Redistribution Station Welcome Booklet (1945, May 25). Box 1/Folder 17, Marshall T. Wiggins Papers, WWII 267, WWII Papers, Military Collection, State Archives of North Carolina, Raleigh, NC.

Asheville Redistribution Station Regulations Manual (1945). Box 1/Folder 13, Marshall T. Wiggins Papers, WWII 267, WWII Papers, Military Collection, State Archives of North Carolina, Raleigh, NC.

Asheville Redistribution Station Standing Operating Procedures Manual (1945). Box 1/Folder 14, Marshall T. Wiggins Papers, WWII 267, WWII Papers, Military Collection, State Archives of North Carolina, Raleigh, NC.

Asheville Redistribution Station Typed Official History. [circa 1945], Box 1/Folder 15, Marshall T. Wiggins Papers, WWII 267, WWII Papers, Military Collection, State Archives of North Carolina, Raleigh, NC.

Boonie, Brenda. "The Family of Gerald Roy and Mary Helen Focht." Unpublished manuscript, 1993.

Cassidy, LaRue. Letters to SGT Ernest V. Focht. March 31, 1943; August 12, 18, 24, 25, and 29, 1944; September 2 and 14, 1944; October 4, 18, 19, 27, and 31, 1944; November 6, 9, 14, 19, 22, 29, and 30, 1944; December 9, 24, and 27, 1944; January 2, 11, and 14, 1945; March 12, 16, 20 and 22, 1945; and April 11, 1945.

Cassidy, LaRue. Line-a-day diary. January 1, 1939 to December 7, 1943.

Cirillo, Roger, ed. Kasserine Pass Battles, 1st Armored Division, Readings, Volume 1, Part 1. Center of Military History, United States Army, 1992.

Cirillo, Roger, ed. Kasserine Pass Battles, Maps and Sketches Appendix. Center of Military History, United States Army, 1992.

Cunningham, James. Letter to Veterans Administration. October 1948.

Dunham, Lt. Col. Emory A. *The Tank Destroyer History—Study No. 29*. Washington, DC: Historical Section of the Army Ground Forces, 1946.

Focht, Ernest V. Oral history, 1990.

Focht, Ernest V. World War II personal diary. 3 vols. January 5, 1943 to June 15, 1945.

Focht, Gerald Roy, and Mary H. Bernosky. Application for Marriage License, Marriage License, and Marriage Certificate. Clerk of the Circuit Court for Washington County, Maryland, Edward Oswald Clerk (August 19, 1912).

Focht, J. George. Revolutionary War Pension Application Statement (1832, October 31). Court of Common Pleas for the County of Schuylkill, Pennsylvania.

Gearinger, Robert. Letter to Veterans Administration. October 1948.

Glass, Harry F. Letter to Representative James E. Van Zandt. December 1, 1947.

Headquarters, 1st Armored Division, Report of Operations 1st Armored Division, Sbeitla, Tunisia, 3 February 1943 to 18 February 1943 (1943, October 16). APO 251 United States Army.

Headquarters, 805th Tank Destroyer Battalion, Unit Personnel Roster (1942, February 1). APO 512 United States Army.

Headquarters, 805th Tank Destroyer Battalion, Battalion Diary, January 17, 1943 to 29 May 1943 (1943, June 2). APO 302 United States Army.

Headquarters, 805th Tank Destroyer Battalion, Report of Combat Activity, 16 March–11 April 1943, (1943, April 15). APO 304 United States Army.

Headquarters, 805th Tank Destroyer Battalion, Battalion History, 29 May–31 October 1943, 1 November–30 November 1943, 1 December–31 December 1943, 1 January–31 January 1944, 1 February–29 February 1944, 1 March–31 March 1944, 1 April–31 April 1944, 1 May–31 May 1944, 1 June–30 June 1944, 1 July–31 July 1944, 1 August–31 August 1944, 1 October–31 October 1944, 1 November–30 November 1944, 1 December–31 December 1944, 1 January–31 January 1945, 1 February–28 February 1945, 1 March–31 March 1945, and 1 April–30 April 1945. APO 464 United States Army.

Headquarters, 805th Tank Destroyer Battalion, Report of Operations, 1 March–31 March 1945 and 1 May–31 May 1945. APO 464 United States Army.

James, Lee. Letter to E. LaRue Cassidy. November 12, 1944.

Lipsky, Chaplain Richard. Wire to Miss Cassidy. May 8, 1945.

Loomis, Mrs. H. B. Letter to Mr. and Mrs. Gerald Focht. April 25, 1943.

Notice of Veteran Preference (1945, September 12). United States Civil Service Commission, Third U. S. Civil Service Region.

Servicemen's Guide to the "Land of the Sky" Asheville Booklet (1945, August–September). Box1/Folder 18 Marshall T. Wiggins Papers, WWII 267, WWII Papers, Military Collection, State Archives of North Carolina, Raleigh, N.C.

Table of Organization, T/O No. 7–115, Infantry Battalion, Anti-Tank (1940, November 1). War Department, Washington, DC.

Table of Organization, T/O No. 18–24, Tank Destroyer Battalion Heavy (1941, December 24). War Department, Washington, DC.

Table of Organization, T/O No. 18–25, Tank Destroyer Battalion (1942, June 8, 1943, January 27, 1943, May 7). War Department, Washington, DC.

Table of Organization, T/O No. 18–25, Tank Destroyer Battalion—Self Propelled (1944, March 15). War Department, Washington, DC.

208 • GUEST OF ADOLF

Van Zandt, James E. Letter to Ernest V. Focht. March 8, 1948.

Van Zandt, James E. Letter to Admiral G. E. Fox, commandant, Naval Supply Depot, Mechanicsburg, PA. December 3, 1947.

Van Zandt, James E. Letter to Harry F. Glass. December 3, 1947.

Wallace, Rev. Ira M. "The Focht-Henlein-Wallace-Garner Family Connection Sketch." Jersey Shore, PA, December 29, 1936.

Welcome to the Army Ground and Service Forces Redistribution Station, Asheville, NC, Booklet. Circa 1944–1945, Box 1/Folder 16, Marshall T. Wiggins Papers, WWII 267, WWII Papers, Military Collection, State Archives of North Carolina, Raleigh, NC.

Magazine articles

"22nd Cavalry Division Disbanded." *The Pennsylvania Guardsman*, October 1940.

"805th Tank Destroyer Battalion (Heavy)." *The Pennsylvania Guardsman*, March 1942.

"805th Tank Destroyer Battalion (Heavy)." *The Pennsylvania Guardsman*, April 1942.

"805th Tank Destroyer Battalion (Heavy)." *The Pennsylvania Guardsman*, May 1942.

"805th Tank Destroyer Battalion (Heavy)." *The Pennsylvania Guardsman*, June 1942.

"805th Tank Destroyer Battalion (Heavy)." *The Pennsylvania Guardsman*, July 1942.

"805th Tank Destroyer Battalion (Heavy)." *The Pennsylvania Guardsman*, August 1942.

"Induction Procedure and Training of Selectees." *The Pennsylvania Guardsman*, December 1940.

Newspaper articles

"Class of 115 to Complete School." *Altoona Mirror*, May 16, 1933.

"Focht-Bernosky Wedding." *The Tyrone Daily Herald*, August 29, 1912.

"Martin G. Buranovsky Obituary." *The Progress*, May 16, 1948.

"Martin L. Focht Passed Away Last Evening." *The Tyrone Daily Herald*, January 21, 1925.

Merryman, Richard. "In Every Season of Life, Tyrone Schools Offer Wisdom to Students." *TyNotes, A publication of Tyrone Area School District* 20, Issue 2 (Winter 2020–21).

Merryman, Richard. "Tyrone's Second High School … Memories Will Linger Still!" *TyNotes, A publication of Tyrone Area School District* 8, Issue 1 (November 2008).

"Mrs. Mary S. (Wasilko) Buranovsky Obituary." *The Progress*, August 31, 1951.

Prisoners of War Bulletin (Vol. 1, No. 5, October 1943; Vol. 1, No.7, December 1943; Vol. 2, No. 8, August 1944; Vol. 3, No. 3, March 1945). The American National Red Cross, Washington, DC.

"SS *MorMacMoon*." *The Port Hole News*, June 7, 1945.

"Twenty Men Are Passed for Year of Army Training." *Altoona Mirror*, 1941.

Websites

Ancestry.com

Belmont, Larry M. "Camp Lucky Strike." Skylighters The Web Site of the 225th AAA Searchlight Battalion. Accessed August 22, 2020. https://skylighters.org/special/cigcamps/cmplstrk.html.

Belmont, Larry M. "The Cigarette Camps, The U.S. Army Camps in the Le Havre Area." Skylighters The Web Site of the 225th AAA Searchlight Battalion. Accessed August 22, 2020. https://skylighters.org/special/cigcamps/cmplstrk.html.

"Between Two Stools. The History of Italian The Military Internees 1943–1945." NS Zwangsarbeit Dokumentationszentrum. http://www.ns-zwangsarbeit.de/en/italian-military-internees/.

The Borough of Tyrone, Pennsylvania. "Tyrone's History." Accessed December 18, 2021. https://www.tyroneboropa.com/history.

Engles, John. "Camp Lucky Strike." Accessed May 23, 2020. https://sites.google.com/site/97thfieldartillery/chronology-of-events/camp-lucky-strike.

Genealogy Today. "World War II War Ration Books." Accessed May 27, 2020. http://www.genealogytoday.com/guide/war-ration-books.html.

Hague, Arnold. "Convoy AT.8." Arnold Hague Convoy Database. Accessed July 18, 2021. http://www.convoyweb.org.uk/at/index.html.

Hague, Arnold. "Convoy KMF.7." Arnold Hague Convoy Database. Accessed July 18, 2021. http://www.convoyweb.org.uk/kmf/index.html?kmf.php?convoy=7!~kmfmain.

Lucas, Richard. "Axis Sally: The Americans Behind the Infamous Nazi Propaganda Broadcast." Accessed May 9, 2021. https://www.historynet.com/axis-sally/?f.

Millet, John D. "United States Army in World War II, The Army Service Forces, The Organization and Role of the Army Service Forces." Center of Military History Online. Accessed June 1, 2022. https://history.army.mil/books/wwii/ASF/index.htm#contents.

Moosburg Online. "Stalag VIIA—History 1939–1945." Accessed March 19, 2022. http://www.moosburg.org/info/stalag/st95eng.html.

National Museum of the United States Air Force. "French 'Forty and Eight' Railroad Car." Accessed June 3, 2022. https://www.nationalmuseum.af.mil/Visit/Museum-Exhibits/Fact-Sheets/Display/Article/196342/french-forty-and-eight-railroad-car/.

The National WW II Museum. "Camp Lucky Strike: RAMP Camp No. 1." June 26, 2020. https://www.nationalww2museum.org/war/articles/camp-lucky-strike.

Peek, Matthew M. "US Army Redistribution Stations in World War II: Asheville, North Carolina." Accessed May 21, 2020. https://www.ncpedia.org/us-army-redistribution-stations-Asheville.

Skaggs, Alison. "A Look Inside Camp Patrick Henry." July 30, 2015. https://blog.marinersmuseum.org/2015/07/inside-look-at-camp-patrick-henry/.

Spinelli, Angello. "Angelo Spinelli Papers." Archives at Yale. Accessed May 27, 2020. https://archives.yale.edu/repositories/12/resources/3451.

Stadt Luckenwalde. "Stalag IIIA Luckenwalde." Accessed August 12, 2022. https://www.luckenwalde.de/Stadt/Kultur/Museen/HeimatMuseum/STALAG-III-A-LUCKENWALDE/.

"USS *Brooklyn* War Diary August 1–31, 1942." National Archives and Records Administration, World War II War Diaries, Other Operational Records and Histories. Accessed December 3, 2022. https://www.fold3.com/image/267984528.

VintageMusicFm. "Fred Waring." Accessed May 23, 2020. https://www.vintagemusic.fm/artist/fred-waring/.

White, Vernon M. "Liberation, 427th Lion Squadron Association." 427 Lion Squadron Association. Accessed April 27, 2022. https://www.427squadron.com/book_file/white/four_years_liberation.html.

Wikipedia. "*Arbeitslager.*" Accessed May 23, 2020. https://en.wikipedia.org/wiki/Arbeitslager.

Wikipedia. "Army Service Forces." Accessed June 2, 2022. https://en.wikipedia.org/wiki/Army_Service_Forces.

Wikipedia. "Italian Military Internees." Accessed May 27, 2020. https://en.wikipedia.org/w/index.php?title=Italian_Military_Internees&oldid=1190579735.

Wikipedia. "List of Italian WW II prisoner-of-war camps in Italy." Accessed July 13, 2021. https://en.wikipedia.org/wiki/List_of_World_War_II_prisoner-of-war_camps_in_Italy.

Wikipedia. "M10 tank destroyer." Accessed April 18, 2020. https://en.wikipedia.org/w/index.php?title=M10_tank_destroyer&oldid=1184923283.

Wikipedia. "Red Cross parcel." Accessed December 24, 2021. https://en.wikipedia.org/wiki/Red_Cross_parcel.

Wikipedia. "Stalag III-A." Accessed November 2, 2022. https://en.wikipedia.org/wiki/Stalag_III-A.

Wisneski, Edward, Jr. "SSgt. Edward 'Ski' Wisneski." The Wartime Memories Project—The Second War. Accessed March 27, 2022. https://wartimememoriesproject.com/ww2/view.php?uid=248655.

WWII US Medical Research Centre. "Administrative Repatriation Procedures & Evacuation and Disposition of Recovered Allied Military Personnel." Accessed April 12, 2022. https://www.med-dept.com/articles/r-a-m-p/.

WWII US Medical Research Centre. "WWII American Prisoner of War Relief Packages." Accessed May 10, 2023. https://www.med-dept.com/articles/ww2-american-prisoner-of-war-relief-packages.

Photographs

Heimat Museum, Luckenwalde, Germany. n.d. *Stalag IIIA Camp Overview.*

Public Domain. n.d. *Stalag IIIA American POWs Cooking a Meal.* Accessed 2022. https://www.awm.gov.au/collection/C387621.

Sammlung Josef Schmid, Stadtarchiv Moosburg, Germany. n.d. *Stalag VIIA Main Gate.*